Innovative Engineering with AI Applications

Scrivener Publishing
100 Cummings Center, Suite 541J
Beverly, MA 01915-6106

Publishers at Scrivener
Martin Scrivener (martin@scrivenerpublishing.com)
Phillip Carmical (pcarmical@scrivenerpublishing.com)

Innovative Engineering with AI Applications

Edited by

Anamika Ahirwar
Piyush Kumar Shukla
Manish Shrivastava
Priti Maheshwary
and
Bhupesh Gour

Scrivener
Publishing

This edition first published 2023 by John Wiley & Sons, Inc., 111 River Street, Hoboken, NJ 07030, USA and Scrivener Publishing LLC, 100 Cummings Center, Suite 541J, Beverly, MA 01915, USA
© 2023 Scrivener Publishing LLC
For more information about Scrivener publications please visit www.scrivenerpublishing.com.

Wiley Global Headquarters
111 River Street, Hoboken, NJ 07030, USA

For details of our global editorial offices, customer services, and more information about Wiley products visit us at www.wiley.com.

Limit of Liability/Disclaimer of Warranty
While the publisher and authors have used their best efforts in preparing this work, they make no representations or warranties with respect to the accuracy or completeness of the contents of this work and specifically disclaim all warranties, including without limitation any implied warranties of merchantability or fitness for a particular purpose. No warranty may be created or extended by sales representatives, written sales materials, or promotional statements for this work. The fact that an organization, website, or product is referred to in this work as a citation and/or potential source of further information does not mean that the publisher and authors endorse the information or services the organization, website, or product may provide or recommendations it may make. This work is sold with the understanding that the publisher is not engaged in rendering professional services. The advice and strategies contained herein may not be suitable for your situation. You should consult with a specialist where appropriate. Neither the publisher nor authors shall be liable for any loss of profit or any other commercial damages, including but not limited to special, incidental, consequential, or other damages. Further, readers should be aware that websites listed in this work may have changed or disappeared between when this work was written and when it is read.

Library of Congress Cataloging-in-Publication Data

ISBN 978-1-119-79163-8

Cover image: Pixabay.Com
Cover design by Russell Richardson

Set in size of 11pt and Minion Pro by Manila Typesetting Company, Makati, Philippines

Printed in the USA

10 9 8 7 6 5 4 3 2 1

Contents

Preface

This book presents a study on current developments, trends, and the future usage of artificial intelligence. The impending research on AI applications—like improvements in agricultural systems, security systems, web services, etc.—has shown the usefulness of AI in engineering, as well as in deep learning tools and models.

Engineering advancements, along with innovative applications of AI, span the gap between the physical and virtual world. The result is a hyper-connected society in which smart devices are not only used to exchange data but also have increased capabilities. These devices are becoming more context-aware and smarter by the day.

This book thoroughly explores the immense scope of AI in the above areas for productivity and the betterment of society and all of humankind. Rather than looking at the field from only a theoretical or practical perspective, this book unifies both aspects to give a holistic understanding of the AI paradigm. It focuses on timely topics related to the field of AI applications and combines new and high-quality research works that promote critical advances. Readers will appreciate the overviews of the state-of-the-art developments in emerging AI research.

This book takes foundational steps toward analyzing stress among teaching professionals using deep learning algorithms. Various deep learning models are discussed, with a practical approach that employs the MNIST dataset. These models help to solve various complex problems in the domains of computer vision and natural language processing.

Also introduced are some emerging and interdisciplinary domains that are associated with deep learning and AI. The book touches upon the core concept of deep learning technology, which is fruitful for a beginner in this area. Furthermore, it compiles the various applications of AI in agriculture, such as irrigation, weeding, spraying with sensors, and other means that are facilitated by robots and drones. This book covers most of the popular and important deep-learning neural network models.

The advanced fields of AI, data analytics, deep learning algorithms, etc., can help in the fight against environmental pollution. Additionally, this book discusses how people with severe disabilities can use their laptops, personal computer, or smart phones to communicate with greater reach. Low-cost systems such as HOG or machine learning models will help disabled people to attain improved typing skills, or even perform coding.

Artificial agricultural intelligence not only lets farmers automate their agriculture, it provides them with accurate predictions for greater crop yield and results in better quality, all while using fewer resources. AI and ML techniques help farmers to analyze land, soil, health of crops, etc. This saves time and money, and allows farmers to grow the right crop per season, ensuring optimal yield.

AI has potential to be used for planning and resource allocation by health and social care services. It can be beneficial across all health care sectors due to its different technologies. As such, AI should be viewed as an exciting new addition to the healthcare sector, not as a threat to professionals.

The cross-disciplinary field of AI research attempts to understand, model, and replicate intelligence and cognitive processes by invoking computational, mathematical, logical, mechanical, and biological principles. AI plays a major role in many sectors. With continual enhancement, it will improve the quality of our lives.

The editors wish to thank Scrivener Publishing and their team for the opportunity to publish this volume.

The Editors
May 2023

Introduction of AI in Innovative Engineering

Anamika Ahirwar

Compucom Institute of Information Technology and Management, Jaipur, Rajasthan, India

Abstract

The widespread use of Artificial Intelligence [1] technology and its ongoing development have created new opportunities for creative engineering. Our daily lives have been completely taken over by the revolutionary realm of Artificial Intelligence (AI). It is the unique fusion of brains and therefore of machines. Artificial intelligence has been growing steadily over the last few years, establishing roots in most industries. There have been recent developments and technologies that support AI. The uses of AI don't seem to be limited to physical space; they can be found in everything from a secondary aspect to a novel development. A new society is being created by many technologies, devices, and even some brand-new inventions that have yet to be realized. Therefore, it offers a seamless route that leads to a promising future. This chapter intends to focus on an overview of innovative engineering in artificial intelligence and introduces the concepts of innovative engineering and artificial engineering with the aid of many innovation engineering guiding principles. This chapter covers the background, need for, and applications of artificial intelligence and also explains the various subfields of artificial intelligence [8]. This chapter covers the background, need for, and applications of artificial intelligence.

Keywords: Innovation Engineering, Artificial Intelligence (AI), Artificial Narrow Intelligence (ANI), Artificial General Intelligence (AGI), Artificial Super Intelligence (ASI)

E-mail: aanamika77@gmail.com

Anamika Ahirwar, Piyush Kumar Shukla, Manish Shrivastava, Priti Maheshwary and Bhupesh Gour (eds.) Innovative Engineering with AI Applications, (1–22) © 2023 Scrivener Publishing LLC

1.1   Introduction to Innovation Engineering

Innovation Engineering is defined as a method for solving technology and business problems for organizations who want to innovate, adapt, and/or enter new markets using expertise in emerging technologies (e.g. data, AI, system architecture, blockchain), technology business models, innovation culture, and high-performing networks.

When Dave Kelly specified the IDEO process for design in 1971, he changed the predictability of design projects around the world and made each design project more likely to serve its users well. In a similar way, this Innovation Engineering process is intended to make innovation projects in engineering more successful. The process builds upon many best practices in innovation, but it also brings them into a domain of more technically sophisticated areas.

The concept of Innovation Engineering also integrates many years of observing our students who have engineered novel technologies and companies. The goal is to specify an approach that anyone can use to better architect, design, and more effectively build things that are technically novel, useful, and valuable. And further, the goal is to be able to do this efficiently, on-time, and repeatable.

At its core, Innovation Engineering is the result of using the approaches, processes, behaviors, and mindsets of entrepreneurs/innovators with the context of engineering projects. This is illustrated in the Figure 1.1.

One thing that we have observed is that innovative technical leaders employ similar behavioral patterns as entrepreneurs even in areas of engineering architecture, design, and implementation. And further, these behaviors can be amplified within a process.

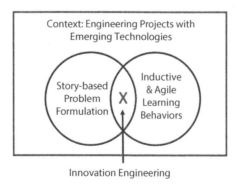

Innovation Engineering

Figure 1.1 Innovation engineering.

1.2   Flow for Innovation Engineering

A high-level process example is shown in Figure 1.2. It simply illustrates the concept of brainstorming a problem/solution, converting the problem/solution into a 'story' called a low-tech demo, and then using agile sprints to develop the project.

This simple process flow can be extended to include business and/or organizational context. Figure 1.2 shows a process flow for Innovation Engineering with greater detail and broader context. The flow illustrates that effective projects start always with a story or narrative. This narrative is generally based on background of the team and an observation of changes in the world (e.g. market, technical, societal, or regulatory changes). When a project does not start with a story narrative, it is typically too narrowly defined and generally goes off target in our experience. Note, the "Low Tech Demo" in the example maps to the Technical Story in the lower diagram which is used to kick-off an Agile project leading to an Implementation.

The story narrative is used to collect initial stakeholders, resources, and obtain initial validation for the project. In our experience, there is no better way to attract resources than by testing a story and/or initial prototype.

From here, the story narrative can be broken into two sub-narratives, one for the technical story and another for the broader context or business story. Each story is the starting point of a learning path, and specifically not an execution path. The technical path is an agile process that leads to an implementation starting first from the user's viewpoint. For example, in Data-X, we use the following components as part of the technical story which we call a "low tech demo".

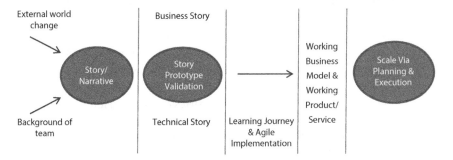

Figure 1.2 A process flow for innovation engineering.

Low tech demo outline, an example of a technical story:

1. What is it supposed to do – and ideally why
2. User's perspective, top three user expectations
3. Key technical components with risk levels
4. An architecture, and
5. Short-term plan and assignments towards the simplest demonstration.

In contrast, the business learning path is intended to result in

1. An industry ecosystem of customers, partners, suppliers, etc. and
2. The discovery of a working business model or fulfillment of a mission in a government organization.

These learning paths converge when the business model/mission and the technology are all working and integrated. Only after this step can the innovation be scaled via execution and planning. Innovation Engineering tends to focus more on the technical path as required for successful implementation, but must include the broader process as described to be successful.

While all of this is a very quick overview of the process, it does set the context for a set of important principles that are required for the process to be successful. Like with any other organizational activity, Innovation Engineering requires a set of shared beliefs and behaviors to be successful. These 'Guiding Principles' for Innovation Engineering are outlined in the section below are intended to be synergistic with the process flow explained in the Figure 1.2.

1.3   Guiding Principles for Innovation Engineering

1. Start with Story: Virtually all successful projects start with a story narrative. The story is the means of validation, consensus building, and collecting stakeholders. Any project that starts without a validated story likely jumps to an invalidated conclusion about the problem. Stories can vary in length and complexity, *i.e.* the problem of a user and its resolution, or the famous NABC story developed at SRI which stands for Needs, Approach, Benefit, and Competition. However, the key to a good story is that there is an insight that others have

not seen and that there is substantial benefit of the solution to at least some segment or stakeholder.

2. Scale or Invent: Determine if the project is about creating something new (i.e. a new product, new service, new technology, new customer, etc.) then it's a learning process, and in that case it requires a team with corresponding behaviors. If the project is about scaling something that already works (i.e. serving more customers, increasing the capacity of a system, etc.) then it's an execution process best accomplished by someone who has done it or something like it before. In this later case, the team can jump immediately to the scaling phase at the end of the process.

3. User-first: The technical story must highlight a solution first from the user's viewpoint. Note that entrepreneurial stories typically explain how a venture will both solve a problem and achieve a working business model, the technical story must explain the user's viewpoint first and only then lead to the system architecture and the implementation.

4. Effectuation: Great technical innovators and entrepreneurs all use "Effectuation Principals" in a natural manner. It roughly means to start with what you have, and sometimes it means you must take inventory of what you have first. To illustrate, if you were to make a dinner, do you first choose an intended dish and then gather the ingredients (not effectuation), or would you look at what you already have in the kitchen and then invent a new recipe from the ingredients you already have (effectuation). This principle can be applied to technical and business projects in the same manner.

5. Break it down: Components, interfaces, and interconnections. Evaluate potential solutions by breaking the proposed system down into simple sub-systems with minimal inter-connections. Understand the interactions and causal relationships between subcomponents. And of course, if a sub-component already exists or can be easily obtained, then there is no need to build or redesign that subcomponent. For example, when Tesla created its battery, it created it from thousands of cells that were already being produced in mass scale, instead of designing a completely new battery architecture.

6. Look for Insight in the technical story: This is related to having insight about the location of value, the power, or "the magic" in the system design. What will make it effective or exciting?

This principal is a technical parallel to the entrepreneurial behavior of understanding the user's true needs or what they actually care about, or what they are willing to pay for.

7. Minimal Viable System Architecture: Get as quickly as possible to a 1.0 version. Distill the story as quickly as possible to the simplest possible implementation. From this, a more complex system can be evolved using an agile, iterative model to develop greater capability. This is parallel to the entrepreneurial approach of building a Minimum Viable Product (MVP) for testing product market fit, but in this case the focus is the system architecture for testing technical feasibility.

8. Agile increments: After developing a minimal demonstrable solution, use agile increments to prioritize further development.
   a. Start with the simplest possible demonstration on the path to the best solution.
   b. Use a technology strategy that allows easiest adaptation.
   c. Be agile driven. We can't predict final product in advance.

9. Keep it Simple: The focus of the project should be on keeping the design simple, easy to explain, easy to verify, and easy to debug. Technical architects and designers are often interested in technically brilliant and complex solutions, but true elegance lies in simplicity. As quoted from a historical Apple advertisement, "Simplicity is the ultimate sophistication." You might think of this in parallel to timeless works of art, which are characterized by having exactly what is needed to convey the message, but never a single extra music notes or an extra paint stroke.

10. Reduce the Downside: Optimize to reduce downside risk and failure, not to maximize performance/cost. Always evaluate corner cases. This is the parallel of broad vs narrow thinking within engineering. The broad thinking version in business would be used to avoid business risk as well as a predict the expected outcome in the broadest terms.

11. Measurable Objectives: Develop measurable objectives to know when goals are being achieved because you cannot improve what you cannot measure. For example, in a data science algorithm, how will you know that the prediction is good enough? Having both a measure and a target allows you to estimate whether the marginal (extra) work to get a better result is worth the expense of doing that extra work. To understand this more, learn about the concept of "Value of Perfect Information".

12. Create a support ecosystem: Build a support ecosystem with the highest quality partners that you can both reach and trust. Many technical leaders are tempted to reach out to the lower quality contacts (as team members, suppliers, partners, and customers) who are easiest to contact, but it is better to push our comfort zones to find the best people and organizations that you can — as long as trust can still be generated.

1.4   Introduction to Artificial Intelligence

Artificial intelligence (AI) is the science and engineering of creating intelligent machines, with the goal of providing machines the ability to comprehend, reach, and outperform human intelligence. This chapter begins with an overview of AI's fundamentals, then moves on to the birth, history, and future of AI in inventive engineering. Then we'll look at the primary runnel in the field, as well as its evolution and uses in different aspects of our lives. The wrapper will cover the most important and contemporary AI research, such as reinforcement learning [2–7], robotics, computer vision, and symbolic logic.

To better perceive the term AI, we must always comprehend the term intelligence in an equation shown in Figure 1.3. Intelligence is that the ability to find out and solve issues. The foremost common answer that one expects is "to build computers intelligent in order that they will act intelligently!", however the question is what proportion intelligent? However will one decide the intelligence?

- Intelligence is the ability to acquire and apply the knowledge.
- Knowledge is the information acquired through experience.
- Experience is the knowledge gained through exposure (training).

Summing the terms up, we tend to get artificial intelligence because the "copy of something natural (i.e., human beings) 'WHO' is capable of exploit and applying the data it's gained through exposure."

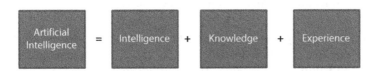

Figure 1.3 Artificial intelligence equation.

Artificial intelligence was first suggested by John Mc Carthy in 1956. According to the John McCarthy, father of Artificial Intelligence (AI): AI is *"The science and engineering of developing intelligent machines using brilliant computer programs"*. Artificial Intelligence is the way of developing computers, computer-controlled robots, intelligent thinking software's, which is similar to humans think. AI have been developed an intelligent software's and system based on the outcomes of how the human brain thinks, learn, decide, and work while trying to solve a problem. When developing the power of computer systems using AI, the anxiety of human lead him to wonder, *"Can a machine think and behave as humans do?"* In AI implementations start with producing common intelligence in machine, which see high regards of humans. AI is the branch of science that helps machines to find solutions of complex problems for different sectors such as humans, industries, researchers, etc.

So we can say that Artificial Intelligence (AI) [11] is the simulation of human intelligence by machines.

1. The ability to solve problems.
2. The ability to act rationally.
3. The ability to act like humans.

1.4.1   History of Artificial Intelligence

The history of Artificial Intelligence in 20th century is given in Table 1.1 [10].

1.4.2   Need for Artificial Intelligence

- To create expert systems which exhibit intelligent behavior with the capability to learn, demonstrate, explain and advice its users.
- Helping machines find solutions to complex problems like humans do and applying them as algorithms in a computer-friendly manner.

1.4.3   Applications of AI

AI has been leading in many domains like [15, 16]:

- Astronomy: Artificial Intelligence can be very convenient to solve complex universe problems. AI mechanization can be helpful for recognize the universe such as how it works, origin, etc.

Table 1.1 History of artificial intelligence.

Year	Milestone/Innovation
1923	The word "robot" in English firstly introduced by Karel Capek using "Rossum's Universal Robots" (RUR) in London.
1943	Foundations of Neural networks (Artificial Intelligence).
1945	The term "Robotics" was continued by Isaac Asimov, alumni of Columbia University.
1950	Turing Testing [12], the word Turing was introduced by Alan Turing for evaluate intelligence and also published Computing Machinery and Intelligence. Claude Shannon was published detailed Analysis of Chess Playing as a search.
1956	John McCarthy was introduced the term "Artificial Intelligence" demonstrated the first AI running program at Carnegie Mellon University.
1958	John McCarthy again invented LISP programming language for AI [14].
1964	Danny Bobrow's presented in dissertation report the computers could recognize natural language well enough to solve algebra word problems efficiently at MIT.
1965	Joseph Weizenbaum developed ELIZA: an interactive problem that carries on a dialogue in English at MIT.
1969	The Scientists of Stanford Research Institute developed a robot equipped with locomotion, perception, and problem solving, which was named Shakey.
1973	The Famous Scottish Robot called Freddy can use vision to locate and assemble models under the Assembly Robotics group at Edinburgh University.
1979	In Stanford Cart, the first computer controlled autonomous vehicle was developed.
1985	In Aaron, The drawing program was created and also demonstrated by Harold Cohen.

(Continued)

Table 1.1 History of artificial intelligence. (*Continued*)

Year	Milestone/Innovation
1990	• Important improvements in all areas of AI • Implementations in machine learning • Case based reasoning • Multi agent planning • Arrangement • Data mining • Web Crawler • Natural languages understands and translations • Vision and Virtual Reality • Games
1997	The "World chess championship" named after beating the Deep Blue Chess Program by Garry Kasparov.
2000	• The Interactive robot pets become available commercially. • "Kismet" the robot with expresses emotions displayed at MIT. • "Nomad" the robot explores remote regions of Antarctica and locates meteorites.

- Healthcare: Healthcare Industries are soliciting AI to make a preferable and turbo diagnosis than humans.
- Gaming: AI plays a vital role in tactical games such as poker, chess, tic-tac-toe, etc., In these games play on the basis of heuristic knowledge i.e. a machine can think of the huge number of possible positions.
- Natural Language Processing: The interaction with computer which understands humans' natural language are possible through NLP.
- Finance: AI and investment production are the best fixture for each other. The investment production is enacting automation, chatbot adaptive intelligence, algorithm trading, and machine learning into action.
- Expert Systems: The integrate machine, software and particular information which can impart reasoning and advising are provides expert system. The applications are facilitates, explanations and advice to the users as well.
- Vision Systems: In this system recognize, apprehend and realize the visual input on computer. The examples are:
  a. Figure out the spatial information or map of areas, the spying aeroplane is used for taking the photographs.

b. For diagnoses the patient, doctors are using a clinical expert system.

c. For recognizing the faces of criminals in forensic artist's stored portrait, police use the computer software.

- Speech Recognition: Generally, the knowledgeable systems can listen and understand the languages in form of the sentences with significances in human interact to it. Which can be managed using slang words, various pronunciations sound in the background, change in human's noise due to cough and cold, etc.?

- Handwriting Recognition: In handwriting detection software, reads text present in the piece of paper though a pen or on-screen by the stylus. Which also identify the outlines of letters and translate it into editable text.

- Data Security: The reliability of data is climacteric for every venture and cyber-attacks are extending very swiftly in the multi-channel world.

- Agriculture: In this also AI are starting setting up its field by agriculture robotics, solid and crop monitoring, predictive analysis.

- E-Commerce: AI is helping all user/client to know about its associated products with recommended size, color, or even brand detail.

- Education: AI can self-closing grading so that the teacher can have more time to teach.

- Social Media: Social Media websites hold billions of customer profiles, which require be storing and managing in a very well-planned way. AI can organize and manage massive amounts of data.

- Entertainment: AI help in entertainment sector by prime videos which are watched through the NET system.

- Transport: AI is fetching extremely demanding for travel industries.

- Automotive: Automotive fabrication is using AI to provide real world virtual assistant to their user for better staging.

- Intelligent Robots: The Robots can be execute the jobs which given through a human. These devices to notice the substantial data from the actual world like heat, light, motion, bump, sound, temperature and pressure. In this they have well organized processors, several sensors and large amount of memory to display knowledge and intelligence. Also, they can understand from their blunders and adjust to the new environment.

- Heuristic Classification: The Heuristic Classifications is one of the most realistic kinds of skilled system, which gives the current knowledge of AI for set information in stable set of categories using in forms of various information. The example of heuristic classification, it advising whether to accept purchase of proposed credit card or not, the proprietor of the credit card information are present, his status of payment, the purchasing item and its creation of buying items (whether there has been past credit card scams in this establishment).

1.4.4   Comprised Elements of Intelligence

The intelligence is insubstantial and contains (shown in Figure 1.4):

1. Reasoning
2. Learning
3. Problem Solving
4. Perception
5. Linguistic Intelligence

1. Reasoning: It is the collection of processes, which makes an ability to deliver on the basis for judgment, decisions making, and prediction. The followings are broad categories of reasoning:

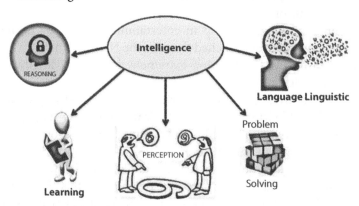

Figure 1.4 Elements of intelligence.

i. Inductive Reasoning
- The broad general statements are made using particular observations.
- Inductive reasoning allows conclusions to be false, whether all the properties are true in the statements.
- Example is: When Nita is a teacher and she is studious as well. Therefore, all teachers are intellectual.

ii. Deductive Reasoning
- Deductive reasoning starts with a usual statements and observation to the potential to reach specific or conceptual conclusions.
- The statements are assumed to be true for all class members whenever any general thing in class is right.
- Examples are: When Shibha is a grandmother because all women of age above 60 years are considered to be as grandmothers but Shibha is in 65 years.

2. Learning: It is the process of developing knowledge or skill using practicing, studying, taught or experiencing something. The Learning also increases the mindfulness of the themes of the study. The capabilities of learning are determined by humans, some animals and AI empowered systems.

The Learning are classified in the followings:
- Auditory Learning: The Auditory Learning is defined by the skills of listening as well as hearing. The example are recorded audio lectures are listened to by students.
- Episodic Learning: The Episodic learning is the linear and orderly learning method using memorizing the arrangements of events which one has viewed or experienced.
- Motor Learning: The Accurate movements of muscles are called motor learning like picking objects, Writing, etc.
- Observational Learning: The Learning comes through watching and imitating others such as a child tried to learn using mimicry of her parent.
- Perceptual Learning: The learning skills for identifying stimulate that one has been observed before like, identifying and classifying objects and situations.
- Relational Learning: In this learning to distinguish between the various stimuli based on relational facts

instead of basic properties such as, Adding 'little less' salt at the time of cooking, potatoes that salty last time, when cooked with adding a table spoon of salt.

- Spatial Learning: The Learning capability through the visual stimuli like images, colors, maps, etc. The example is a person can create a roadmap in mind before actually following the road.
- Stimulus Response Learning: The Learning ability to execute a specific behavior when a particular stimulus is present. The examples are a dog raises its ear on the hearing doorbell.

3. Problem Solving: In this method one's observes and attempts to reaches the preferred outcomes from current circumstances through taking some track congested by known or unknown obstacles. The problem solving was also involved in decision making, which is the approaches of choosing optimum alternative, out of different available alternatives for obtain the desired goal.

4. Perception: It is a mechanism of obtaining, understanding, picking and establishing sensory information. The Perception is assumes to sense [13]. In humans, perception is supported by sensory organs. However in the AI domain, the perception approach sets the data generated by the sensors and collectively in a significant style.

5. Linguistic Intelligence: It's defined as one's capacity to use, understand, speak, and write the vocal and written language. It is essential in the relational statement.

1.4.5   AI Tools

AI has developed an outsized variety of tools to unravel the foremost troublesome issues in engineering, like:

- Search and optimization
- Logic
- Probabilistic methods for uncertain reasoning
- Classifiers and statistical learning methods
- Neural networks
- Control theory
- Languages

1.4.6   AI Future in 2035

AI is striking the subsequent of virtually every industry and every mortal. AI has acted as the main driver of make an appearance technologies like big data, robotics and IoT, and it will pursue to act as a technological innovator for the foreseeable (predictable) subsequent.

- Looking at the features and its wide application we may definitely follow AI. Seeing at the event of Al is it that the future world is changing into artificial.
- Biological intelligence is fixed, as a result of its associate previous, mature paradigm however the new paradigm of non-biological computation and intelligence is growing exponentially.
- The memory capability of the human brain is perhaps of the order usually thousand million binary digits. However most of this is often most likely utilized in memory visual impressions, and alternative relatively wasteful ways that.
- Hence we will say that as natural intelligence is restricted and volatile too world could currently rely on computers for smooth operating.

1.4.7   Humanoid Robot and AI

- Sophia may be a social android golem developed by Hong Kong based mostly company Hanson artificial intelligence.
- Sophia was activated on April 19, 2015.
- She created her initial public look at South by Southwest festival in period of time 2016 in United States.
- In October 2017 Sophia became a Saudi subject, the primary golem to receive citizenship in any country.

1.4.8   The Explosive Growth of AI

- Since Al is applicable in most fields, they become the needs of our life. It's the rationale behind the explosive growth of AI.
- The growth are often divided into two components based on the application area and what purpose they serve, they're as follows:
  - Growth in positive sense (useful to society)
  - Growth in negative sense (harmful to society)

1.5 Types of Learning

Figure 1.5 shows the types of learning.

1. Artificial Narrow Intelligence (ANI)
2. Artificial General Intelligence (AGI)
3. Artificial Super Intelligence (ASI)

1. Artificial Narrow Intelligence (ANI)
   Artificial narrow Intelligence is also referred to as Weak AI, ANI is that the stage of artificial intelligence involving machines that can perform solely a narrowly outlined set of specific tasks. At this stage, the machine doesn't possess any thinking ability; it simply performs a group of pre-defined functions.

   Examples of Weak AI embody Siri, Alexa, Self-driving cars, Alpha-Go, Sophia the humanoid then on. The majority the AI-based systems engineered until this date fall under the class of Weak AI.

2. Artificial General Intelligence (AGI)
   Artificial General Intelligence is also known as strong AI, AGI is that the stage within the evolution of AI whereby machines can possess the flexibility to suppose and build strong a bit like North American country humans.

   There are presently no existing samples of strong AI, however, it's believed that presently be able to create machines that are as good as humans.

   Strong AI is taken into account a threat to human existence by several scientists, as well as Stephen William Hawking UN agency expressed that: "The development of full AI may spell the tip of the human race.... it'd commence on its own, associate degreed re-design itself at an ever-increasing rate.

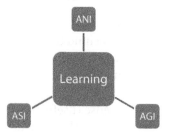

Figure 1.5 Types of learning.

Humans, UN agency are restricted by slow biological evolution, couldn't contend and would be outdated."

3. Artificial Super Intelligence (ASI)

Artificial Super Intelligence is that the stage of AI once the potential of computers can surpass persons. ASI is presently a theoretic situation as portrayed in movies and science fiction books, wherever machines have taken over the world.

Machines are not very far from reaching this stage taking into considerations our current pace.

"The pace of progress in AI is incredibly fast. Unless you've direct exposure to teams. Teams like Deep mind, have gotten no organize but quick. it's growing at a pace getting ready to exponential. The danger of 1 issue seriously dangerous happening is at intervals the five-year timeframe. 10 years at the foremost." —Elon Musk quoted.

So, these were the various stages of intelligence that a machine will acquire. Currently let's perceive the categories of AI, supported their functionality.

1.6   Categories of AI

Based on the functionality of AI-based systems, AI can be categorized into the following types:

1. Reactive Machine AI
2. Limited Memory AI
3. Theory of Mind AI
4. Self-aware AI

1. Reactive Machine AI

This type of AI includes machines that operate only supported the current knowledge, taking into consideration solely this scenario. Reactive AI machines cannot type inferences from the info to judge their future actions. they'll perform a narrowed range of pre-defined tasks.

An example of Reactive AI is the famous IBM Chess program that beat the world champion, Garry Kasparov.

2. Limited Memory AI

Like the name suggests restricted Memory AI, can build conversant and improved selections by learning the past knowledge from its memory. Such an AI contains a short-lived or a temporary memory which will be accustomed store past experiences and therefore measure future actions.

Self-driving cars are limited Memory AI, that uses the information collected within the recent past to form immediate selections. As an example, self-driving cars use sensors to spot civilians crossing the road, steep roads, traffic signals so on to form higher driving selections. This helps to stop any future accidents.

3. Theory of Mind AI

The Theory of Mind AI may be an additional advanced form of computing. This class of machines is alleged to play a serious role in psychology. This kind of AI can focus in the main on emotional intelligence in order that human believes and thoughts are often higher appreciated.

4. Self-Aware AI

Let's simply pray that we tend to don't reach the state of AI, wherever machines have their own consciousness and become conscious. This kind of AI may be a very little so much fetched given this circumstance. However, within the future, achieving a stage of super intelligence may be attainable.

Geniuses like Elon Musk and Sir Leslie Stephen Hawking's have systematically warned us regarding the evolution of AI. AI may be a terribly vast field that covers several domains like Machine Learning, Deep Learning so on.

1.7   Branches of Artificial Intelligence

Artificial Intelligence can be used to solve real-world problems by implementing the following processes/techniques (Figure 1.6 shows the elements of intelligence):

1. Machine Learning
2. Deep Learning
3. Natural Language Processing
4. Robotics
5. Expert Systems
6. Fuzzy Logic

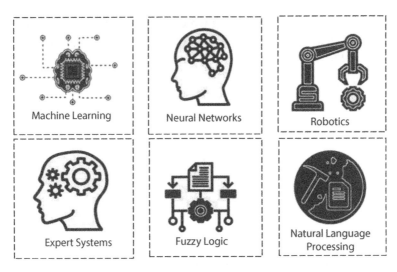

Figure 1.6 Branches of artificial intelligence.

1. Machine Learning
   Machine Learning is that the science of obtaining machines to interpret, method and analyze knowledge so as to solve real-world issues. Figure 1.7 shows the machine learning layout.

Figure 1.7 Machine learning layout.

Under Machine Learning there are three categories:
   1. Supervised Learning
   2. Unsupervised Learning
   3. Reinforcement Learning

2. Deep Learning
   Deep Learning is that the method of implementing Neural Networks [9] on high dimensional knowledge to achieve insights and type solutions. Deep Learning is a complicated

field of Machine Learning which will be used to solve additional advanced issues. The layout of deep learning is shown in Figure 1.8.

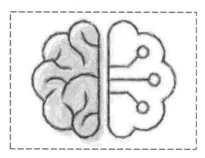

Figure 1.8 Deep learning layout.

Deep Learning is that the logic behind the face verification algorithmic program on Facebook, self-driving cars, virtual assistants like; Siri, Alexa.

3. Natural Language Processing

Natural Language processing (NLP) refers to the science of drawing insights from natural human language so as to speak with machines and grow businesses. We can see the layout of Natural Language Processing in Figure 1.9.

Figure 1.9 Natural language processing layout.

Twitter uses natural language process to filter terroristic language in their tweets, Amazon uses natural language process to grasp consumer reviews and improve user experience.

4. Robotics

Robotics may be a branch of computing that focuses on completely different branches and application of robots. AI Robots are artificial agents acting in a very real-world setting to provide results by taking responsible actions.

Sophia the humanoid is a good example of AI in robotics.

5. Fuzzy Logic

Fuzzy logic could be a computing approach supported the principles of "degrees of truth" rather than the same old trendy computer logic i.e. Boolean in nature.

Fuzzy logic is used within the medical fields to resolve complicated issues that involve higher cognitive process. They're conjointly utilized in automatic gearboxes, vehicle environment control so on.

6. Expert Systems

A professional system is expert AI-based computing system that learns and reciprocates the decision-making ability of a person's expert.

Expert systems use if-then logical notations to unravel advanced issues. It doesn't admit standard procedural programming. knowledgeable systems are principally employed in info management, medical facilities, loan analysis, virus detection so on.

1.8   Conclusion

With the help of numerous innovation engineering guiding principles, this chapter aims to focus on an overview of innovation engineering in artificial intelligence. The history, necessity, and applications of artificial intelligence are discussed in this chapter. It consists of a number of cognitive elements, including language intelligence, learning, thinking, and problem-solving. A wide range of tools, including search and optimization, logic, probabilistic methods for uncertain reasoning, classifiers and statistical learning techniques, neural networks, control theory, and languages, have been developed by AI to solve the most challenging engineering problems. Artificial intelligence in the year 2035. Artificial intelligence subfields are also explained in this chapter.

References

1. Borges, A.F.S. *et al.*, The strategic use of artificial intelligence in the digital era: Systematic literature review and future research directions. *Int. J. Inf. Manage.*, 57, 102225, April 2021. https://doi.org/10.1016/j.ijinfomgt.2020.102225.

2. Chen, D. *et al.*, *Autonomous Driving Using Safe Reinforcement Learning by Incorporating A Regret-Based Human Lane-Changing Decision Model*, 2019, arXiv: 1910.04803 [cs.RO].

3. Palanisamy, P., *Multi-Agent Connected Autonomous Driving Using Deep Reinforcement Learning*, 2019, arXiv: 1911.04175 [cs.LG].

4. Wang, S., *et al.*, *Deep Reinforcement Learning for Autonomous Driving.* arXiv preprint arXiv:1811.11329v1 [cs.CV] 28 Nov 2018.

5. Xu, Z. *et al.*, Zero-shot deep reinforcement learning driving policy transfer for autonomous vehicles based on robust control. *21st International Conference on Intelligent Transportation Systems (ITSC)*, IEEE, 2018, pp. 2865–2871.

6. Ferdowsi, A. *et al.*, Robust deep reinforcement learning for security and safety in autonomous vehicle systems. *21st International Conference on Intelligent Transportation Systems (ITSC)*, 2018.

7. Sallab, A.E. *et al.*, Deep reinforcement learning framework for autonomous driving. *Electron. Imag.*, 2017, 19, 70–76, 2017.

8. Kour, N. and Gondhi, N.K., Recent trends & innovations in artificial intelligence based applications. *Int. J. Emerg. Technol.*, Special Issue (NCETST-2017), 8, 1, 334–339, 2017.

9. Silver, D. *et al.*, Mastering the game of Go with deep neural networks and tree search. *Nature*, 529, 7587, 484, 2016.

10. Nilsson, N., The quest for artificial intelligence: A history of ideas and achievements, Cambridge University Press. 2010.

11. Russell, S., *et al.*, Artificial intelligence: A modern approach, 3rd ed, Prentice Hall. Copyright 2010, 2003, 1995 by Pearson Education, Inc., Upper Saddle River, New Jersey 07458.

12. Turing, A.M. Computing machinery and intelligence. Epstein, R., Roberts, G., Beber, G. (Eds.) *Parsing the Turing Test*, Springer, Dordrecht. https://doi.org/10.1007/978-1-4020-6710-5_3, 2009.

13. McCarthy, J, Artificial intelligence, logic and formalizing common sense. Thomason, R.H. (Eds.) *Philosophical Logic and Artificial Intelligence*, Springer, Dordrecht. https://doi.org/10.1007/978-94-009-2448-2_6, 1989.

14. McCarthy, J,. Artificial intelligence: A paper symposium: Professor Sir James Lighthill, FRS. Artificial Intelligence: A general survey. In: *Science Research Council*, 1973.

15. https://www.javatpoint.com/application-of-ai

16. https://beebom.com/examples-of-artificial-intelligence/

## 2

An Analytical Review of Deep Learning Algorithms for Stress Prediction in Teaching Professionals

Ruby Bhatt

Department of Computer Science, Medicaps University, Indore, India

Abstract

Latest statistical figures on human health show that hypertension, cardiac disease, renal failure etc. along with all sorts of popular diseases are overpassed by mental illness. The graph for mental health shows an exponential increase. It shows that 51% of adults who felt stressed resulted in depression, 61% reported feeling anxious, a big group of teenagers said that they had suicidal thoughts and feelings etc. Seeing a present scenario, mental illness, stress, depression etc. has become a fundamental and inescapable part of our lives. It has created a distressing situation for the psychological health of teenagers and youth internationally. At the dangerous stage of teenage to adulthood transition, many challenges are faced by teenagers. These may be because of the excessive exposure to social networking sites and devices. Hence, it is a need of an hour to know about the various aspects that can be the source of stress among teenagers, working professionals, homemakers, actually every person of the society; knowing the reasons, recognizing the factors that are more substantial reasons and to take appropriate measures to handle up the worst situation excellently. This chapter is a small step towards analyzing the stress among teaching professionals using deep learning algorithms.

Keywords: Deep learning, deep neural network, environmental stress, physiological stressor

Email: profrubybhatt15@gmail.com

Anamika Ahirwar, Piyush Kumar Shukla, Manish Shrivastava, Priti Maheshwary and Bhupesh Gour (eds.) Innovative Engineering with AI Applications, (23–40) © 2023 Scrivener Publishing LLC

2.1 Introduction

The health of masses and living conditions of many all over the globe is directly affected by the coronavirus pandemic. The biggest impact of this infection that resulted worldwide is in the form of various types of mental illnesses. There are different sources of stress like external stress, environmental stress, and physical stress [1]. The external stress occurs because of the environmental stressor when the person is unable to respond to the external and internal stimulus or situation. Even the environment disorder, big gatherings, heavy traffic, a high number of crimes in the societies, pollution can be the cause for external stress. Every individual lives in a society and interact with many people in their day to day life. This can lead to social stress. The external stressor can become the source of stress an individual's life which includes- hot and cold climate, natural disasters, criminal offenses, contamination, and death. These kinds of stressors happen to the earth and humans have no control over these kinds of stressors. Every individual suffers from a different kind of stressful situation in their lives may be because of Physiological Stressor. Every individual also plays a social role in their lives by playing multiple characters with different people. Each person does their jobs to live in a society and with family, such as brother, parents, friends, boss, life partners, and many more social roles they play.

Deep Learning Algorithms are now a days playing crucial role in training machines to behave like a human mind [5]. To drive such a human-like ability to adapt and learn and to function accordingly, there have to be some strong forces which we popularly called algorithms. Deep learning algorithms are dynamically made to run through several layers of neural networks, which are nothing but a set of decision-making networks that are pre-trained to serve a task. Later, each of these is passed through simple layered representations and move on to the next layer. However, most machine learning is trained to work fairly well on datasets that have to deal with hundreds of features or columns. For a data set to be structured or unstructured, machine learning tends to fail mostly because they fail to recognize a simple image having a dimension of 800×1000 in RGB. It becomes quite unfeasible for a traditional machine learning algorithm to handle such depths. This is where deep learning.

It is a very important data science element that channels its modeling based on data-driven techniques under predictive modeling and statistics. This is one of the main reasons deep learning is not considered effective as linear or boosted tree models. Simple models aim to churn out custom data, track fraudulent transactions, and deal with less complex datasets with fewer features [9]. Also, there are various cases like multiclass classification where deep learning can be effective because it involves smaller but more structured datasets but is not preferred usually.

The various types of algorithms used in Deep Learning are [7]:

1. Convolutional Neural Networks (CNNs) [7]: ConvNets majorly consists of several layers and are specifically used for image processing and detection of objects.
2. Long Short Term Memory Networks (LSTMs) [7]: It can memorize and recall past data for a greater period and by default, it is its sole behavior.
3. Recurrent Neural Networks (RNNs): RNNs consist of some directed connections that form a cycle that allow the input provided from the LSTMs to be used as input in the current phase of RNNs.
4. Generative Adversarial Networks (GANs) [7]: GANs are defined as deep learning algorithms that are used to generate new instances of data that match the training data. GAN usually consists of two components namely a generator that learns to generate false data and a discriminator that adapts itself by learning from this false data.
5. Radial Basis Function Networks (RBFNs) [7]: RBFNs are specific types of neural networks that follow a feed-forward approach and make use of radial functions as activation functions. They consist of three layers namely the input layer, hidden layer, and output layer which are mostly used for time-series prediction, regression testing, and classification.
6. Multilayer Perceptrons (MLPs) [7]: MLPs are the base of deep learning technology. It belongs to a class of feed-forward neural networks having various layers of perceptrons.
7. Self-Organizing Maps (SOMs): SOMs help in visualizing the data by initializing weights of different nodes and then choose random vectors from the given training data. They examine each node to find the relative weights so that dependencies can be understood. The winning node is decided and that is called Best Matching Unit (BMU).
8. Deep Belief Networks (DBNs) [7]: DBNs are called generative models because they have various layers of latent as well as stochastic variables.

9. Restricted Boltzmann Machines (RBMs): This algorithm is mainly used in the field of dimension reduction, regression and classification, topic modeling and are considered the building blocks of DBNs.
10. Autoencoders [7]: Autoencoders are a special type of neural network where inputs are outputs are found usually identical. It was designed to primarily solve the problems related to unsupervised learning. Autoencoders are highly trained neural networks that replicate the data.

2.2   Literature Review

In this chapter [1], the authors used a performance parameter to find true positive rate, false positive rate, recall, and F-Score. Different types of Machine Learning technique were applied to predict the stress level of the students. With the help of questionnaires dataset, student's different circumstances and conditions were recognized. With the help of these, the proposed model included PSS and adult Adha questionnaires dataset collection, pre-processing, cleaning, feature extraction and comparison on the basis of their performance parameter.

In [2], the authors used a decision tree algorithm which was then applied to the data which was collected from the two tests to say that these tests are unsatisfactory: the stress level among the students at the starting of the term or semester and the end of the semester. The study reveals that the level of stress among students at the starting of the semester was less and at the end of the semester the level of stress is increased.

In [3], the research introduces a novel self-supervised deep learning model for stress detection using an intelligent solution that detects the stress state using the physiological parameters. It represents a concise review of different intelligent techniques for processing physiological data and the emotional states of humans. Also, for all covered methods, special attention is made to semi-supervised learning algorithms. Lastly, a novel semi-supervised deep learning model for predicting the stress state is proposed.

In this paper [4], predictions of anxiety, depression, and stress were made using machine learning algorithms. In order to apply these algorithms, data were collected from employed and unemployed individuals across different cultures and communities through the Depression, Anxiety, and Stress Scale questionnaire. It was named – DASS 21. Anxiety, depression and stress were predicted as occurring on five levels of severity by five different machine learning algorithms – because these are highly accurate, they are particularly suited to predicting psychological problems. After applying the different methods, it was found that classes were imbalanced in the confusion matrix. Thus, the f1 score measure was added, which helped identify the best accuracy model among the five applied algorithms as the Random Forest classifier. Furthermore, the specificity parameter revealed that the algorithms were also especially sensitive to negative results.

Reece *et al.* [4] focused on the predictors of depression and Post Traumatic Stress Disorder (PTSD) among Twitter users. The Hidden Markov Model (HMM) was used to recognize increases in the probability of PTSD. Of the entire dataset, 31.4% and 24% were observed to be affected by depression and PTSD.

Braithwaite *et al.* [10] collected tweets from 135 participants recruited from Amazon Mechanical Turk (MTurk) and applied decision tree classification to measure suicide risk. The accuracy level for the prediction of suicide rate was observed to be 92%.

Du *et al.* [4] extracted streaming data from Twitter and used psychiatric stressors to annotate tweets that had been deemed suicidal. The Convolution Neural Network (CNN) outperformed the Support Vector Machine (SVM) and extra trees (ET) etc. with a precision of 78% in recognizing tweets with suicidal tendencies. The audio-text approach can also be used to model depression, where the researcher collects data from individuals with depression. The long short-term memory neural network model was used for detecting depression in [4], which observed that the context-free model produced the best results for audio (weighted, sequence and multi-model).

Depression was also predicted in [4] in the early stages through social media content. Data collection was carried out using CLEF eRisk. After evaluating five systems, it was discovered that a combination of machine learning and information retrieval gave the optimum result.

In Hou *et al.* [4], a big data approach was used to predict depression based on a person's reading habits. The features of Chinese text were extracted in order to develop a book classifier and after applying five classifications, naïve Bayes was found to be the most appropriate [4].

2.3 Dataset Pre-Processing

One questionnaires dataset was taken from more than 20 teaching professionals of the University. Data set were collected through a primary and secondary source like mails on Gmail, data shared through Google drive,

Google Survey Form etc. PSS Scale was used on the collected dataset. The different types of questions on the PSS scales were related to mood burst, uncontrolled emotions, joyous feelings etc. The dataset was collected for PSS, a test which incorporates various inquiries by large including the whole enthusiastic inquiry.

This type of questions has three option answers like (a) Happens Many Times (b) Does Not Happen and (c) Cannot Comment.

Every selection has its points for calculation of stress. It was asked from by straightforward questions about their moods, sentiment, and the current states that they might have come across in the last few months and their response to it. The stress divided into basically three categories like regular, modest, and highest. The found dataset is converted into numeric data [3]. The dataset is then split into training and testing data.

PSS Scale [1]: The Perceived Stress Scale (PSS) is a stress pressure assessment instrument. This was established by a physiological researcher by Sheldon Cohen in 1983. [1] This scaled show presents about your emotions, feelings during the previous many month and present [1].

Adult Adha Self-Report Scale: Adult Adha is a self- report scale is known as a stress assessment instrument. There are different types of questions ask on this scale which is related to emotions, feelings, history, during previous many month and present [1].

Weka [1]: It is an Open Source Data Mining programming included as part inside Pentaho that gives techniques to pre-handling content, It is very helpful for mining of various opinions of people, so it is highly used in the opinion mining field also used for other areas, for example, drawing data from a database and perusing CSV records, and a lot of programmed learning calculations.

2.4 Machine Learning Techniques Used

Machine learning is one of the domains of Artificial Intelligence that provides computers and computing systems the ability to independently learn and improve from previous experience without being explicitly programmed by a human. Machine learning is based on the development of computing programs that can retrieve data and learn for themselves.

This is highly effective in healthcare as there is enormous amount of data and if this is properly fed to an intelligent system and trained accordingly, the resulting prediction model will be unparalleled and free from human errors and reduce the time required for diagnostics. Hence, the responses of the dataset that were used to train the following study are tested in healthcare based classification problems [6].

A. Logistic Regression [6]: Like all regression methods, the logistic regression is a predictive analysis. It is used in scenarios where one binary variable is dependent on one or more independent variables. Here, we take the 14 relevant attributes to be independent variables and the possibility of an employee having stress and needing treatment as the dependent variable which is to be predicted by the trained model.

B. KNN Classifier [6]: K-Nearest Neighbor (KNN) classifier is a supervised learning algorithm that can be implemented on labeled data. It was used here for predicting if a person needs treatment or not. KNN classifies the dependent variable based on how similar its independent variables are to a similar instance from the already know data.

C. Decision Trees [6]: A decision tree can be used to model multiple choices or if-else statements/decisions in a tree-like fashion. Here, decision trees are used to find the most contributing factors among the 14 features that are used. This is highly helpful, as now more attention can be given to these areas and necessary steps are taken on those lines.

D. Random Forest Classifier [6]: Random Forests are a cluster of decision trees working together with each other and it has proved to be more effective than a single decision tree. Random Forest is a flexible, easy to use ML algorithm that produces a good result persistently, even without hyper tuning.

E. Boosting [6]: We also implemented ensembled methods that augment the performance of existing models. Boosting is a highly effective and commonly used ensemble classifier. The main motive for boosting is to reduce bias in the model.

F. Bagging [6]: Another effective ensemble method is, Bootstrap Aggregating (or bagging). It involves training of a model using the same algorithm but on different subsets of data from the dataset. This not only helps in improving the stability and accuracy of the model but also in reducing the variance of the model.

2.5 Performance Parameter

In this research we are using different types of parameters are:-
True Positive Rate [1]: It is also known as Sensitivity (TP) [8]. It calculates the values which are correctly classified the accuracy and formula is:-

TP = True Positive / True Positive + False Negative

False Positive: It is also known as Specificity [1]. It calculates the values which are incorrectly classified as true and formula is:-

FP = False Positive / False Positive + False Negative

Recall: Normally, we can use recall for wholeness what percentage of positive tuple did the classifier label as positive. In recall 1.0 is best Score. In others Words we can say that Inverse connection between recall and precision.

RECALL [1] = True Positive / False Positive + True Positive

F-Score [1]: F-score is also known as F – measure. It is used to calculate by detecting out the harmonic mean of recall and precision and formula is:-

F-Score = 2 + Precision + RECALL / Precision - RECALL

MCC [1]: MCC is known as Matthews's correlation [1] coefficient. It is used in machine learning technique and used to measure the quality of binary (two-class) classifications. It generally gives the value between + 1 and −1.
Precision: Precision compares the quantity of effective magnificence predictions that truly belong to the high quality elegance [1]. Formula is-:

Precision = True Positive / True Positive - False Positive

Classification Accuracy: It is a measure of the effectiveness of the classification model. Classification accuracy is the percentage of successful predictions out of the total predictions made. It can be used as a rank of performance among different models.

2.6   Proposed Methodology

In this chapter, different types of Machine Learning technique are used to predict the stress level of the faculty members. In the questionnaires dataset, the faculty data in different ways, circumstances, and conditions are evaluated. This includes PSS and adult Adha questionnaires dataset collection, pre-processing, cleaning, feature extraction [3] and comparison on the basis of their performance parameter as shown in Figure 2.1.

The raw data is collected from questionnaires and other datasets, it is the faculty data in different ways. But, the main intension behind collection of data remains the same for more and more accuracy and acquainted data. The raw data becomes useful only after cleaning and preprocessing. Cleansing of data is done to extract meaningful information out of it. Data cleansing is the process of identifying and resolving corrupt, inaccurate, or irrelevant data. This critical stage of data processing — also referred to as data scrubbing or data cleaning — boosts the consistency, reliability, and value of your company's data. Common inaccuracies in data include missing values, misplaced entries, and typographical errors. In some cases, data cleansing requires certain values to be filled in or corrected, while in other instances, the values will need to be removed altogether. The dataset is given to many cleansing algorithms for better preparation of meaningful information out of it. Use Data Cleansing to fix common data quality issues. You can replace null values, remove punctuation, modify

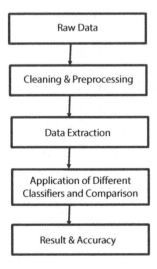

Figure 2.1 Process of data extraction from dataset.

capitalization, and more! The Data Cleansing tool is not dynamic. Few of these tools are free, while others may be priced with free trial available on their website. OpenRefine: Formerly known as Google Refine, this powerful tool comes handy for dealing with messy data, cleaning and transforming it. It's a good solution for those looking for free and open source data cleansing tools and software programs. The consequence of extracting data can be that it can have loss of some meaningful information out of it. Efficiency, especially if you're planning to execute the extraction manually. Hand-coding can be a painstaking process that is prone to errors and difficult to replicate across multiple extractions. When the raw data is in the raw format, no pattern can be interpreted out of it. So, in order to extract meaningful pattern out of the raw data, data is extracted using different Classifiers and Comparison operators. They are then interpreted and the meaningful information is extracted out of it.

A decision is only as good as the data that informs it. And with massive amounts of data streaming in from multiple sources, a data cleansing tool is more important than ever for ensuring accuracy of information, process efficiency, and driving your company's competitive edge. Some of the primary benefits of data scrubbing include:

Improved Decision Making — Data quality is critical because it directly affects your company's ability to make sound decisions and calculate effective strategies. No company can afford wasting time and energy correcting errors brought about by dirty data.

Consider a business that relies on customer-generated data to develop each new generation of its online and mobile ordering systems, such as AnyWare from Domino's Pizza. Without a data cleansing program, changes and revisions to the app may not be based on precise or accurate information. As a result, the new version of the app may miss its target and fail to meet customer needs or expectations.

Boosted Efficiency — Utilizing clean data isn't just beneficial for your company's external needs — it can also improve in-house efficiency and productivity. When information is cleaned properly, it reveals valuable insights into internal needs and processes. For example, a company may use data to track employee productivity or job satisfaction in an effort to predict and reduce turnover. Cleansing data from performance reviews, employee feedback, and other related HR documents may help quickly identify employees who are at a higher risk of attrition.

Competitive Edge — The better a company meets its customers' needs, the faster it will rise above its competitors. A data cleansing tool helps provide reliable, complete insights so that you can identify evolving customer needs and stay on top of emerging trends. Data cleansing can produce faster response rates, generate quality leads, and improve the customer experience. A data cleansing tool can automate most aspects of a company's overall data cleansing program, but a tool is only one part of an ongoing, long-term solution to data cleaning. The steps needed to take to make sure data is clean and usable:

Identify the Critical Data Fields — Companies have access to more data now than ever before, but not all of it is equally useful. The first step in data cleansing is to determine which types of data or data fields are critical for a given project or process.

Collect the Data — After the relevant data fields are identified, the data they contain is collected, sorted, and organized.

Discard Duplicate Values — After the data has been collected, the process of resolving inaccuracies begins. Duplicate values are identified and removed.

Resolve Empty Values — Data cleansing tools search each field for missing values, and can then fill in those values to create a complete data set and avoid gaps in information.

Standardize the Cleansing Process — For a data cleansing process to be effective, it should be standardized so that it can be easily replicated for consistency. In order to do so, it's important to determine which data is used most often, when it will be needed, and who will be responsible for maintaining the process. Finally, you'll need to determine how often you'll need to scrub your data. Daily? Weekly? Monthly?

Review, Adapt, Repeat — Set time aside each week or month to review the data cleansing process. What has been working well? Where is there room for improvement? Are there any obvious glitches or bugs that seem to be occurring? Include members of different teams who are affected by data cleansing in the conversation for a well-rounded account of your company's process.

Data Extraction retrieves and extracts data from various sources for data processing and analyzing purposes. The extracted data may be structured or unstructured data. The extracted data is migrated and stored into a data warehouse from which it is further analyzed and interpreted for business cases. One of the most extensively used web scraping and Data Extraction tools in the market, OutWit Hub browses the Web and automatically collects and organizes relevant data from online sources. The tool first segregates web pages into separate elements and then navigates them individually to extract the most relevant data from them. Extraction also allows you to share data in a common, usable format. Accuracy and precision. Manual processes and hand-coding increase opportunities for errors, and the requirements of entering, editing, and re-enter large volumes of data take their toll on data integrity. Extraction allows many different kinds of data to be combined and ultimately mined for business intelligence. Transformation: Once the data has been successfully extracted, it is ready to be refined. During the transformation phase, data is sorted, organized, and cleansed.

2.7 Result and Experiment

In this chapter, own developed questionnaire dataset from survey form is used. Data set holds more than 20 instances and has 6 attributes. The data set has: Instances = 210 and Attributes = 6. Different tables for the values of true positive rates, false-positive rates, recall, F-Score, MCC, Precision etc. are created. These give different speculation values and calculations with different specifications are evaluated. These values are then used for the evaluation of numeric values in between +1 and -1 and results interpreted. With the help of accuracy and classifier, an accuracy graph is generated. Machine-learning framework compared with classifiers using accuracy, TP, FP is also evaluated. These results helped to interpret the conclusion out of it. Data collection from dataset is collected and shown in Table 2.1.

Table 2.1 Data collection from dataset.

Able to give 100% in my performance	Regular and on time in my class	Students gets satisfy with the content	Students' Queries are sorted out efficiently	Satisfied with the time and work load assigned	Monetary gains is in proportion to assigned work
Happens Many Times	Does Not Happen	Happens Many Times	Does Not Happen	Happens Many Times	Happens Many Times
Does Not Happen	Does Not Happen	Does Not Happen	Does Not Happen	Does Not Happen	Does Not Happen
Happens Many Times	Does Not Happen	Happens Many Times	Does Not Happen	Happens Many Times	Does Not Happen
Does Not Happen	Cannot Comment	Does Not Happen	Cannot Comment	Does Not Happen	Cannot Comment
Happens Many Times	Happens Many Times	Happens Many Times	Happens Many Times	Happens Many Times	Happens Many Times
Cannot Comment	Does Not Happen	Cannot Comment	Does Not Happen	Cannot Comment	Does Not Happen
Does Not Happen	Does Not Happen	Does Not Happen	Does Not Happen	Does Not Happen	Does Not Happen
Happens Many Times	Happens Many Times	Happens Many Times	Happens Many Times	Happens Many Times	Happens Many Times
Does Not Happen	Cannot Comment	Does Not Happen	Cannot Comment	Does Not Happen	Cannot Comment
Happens Many Times	Happens Many Times	Happens Many Times	Happens Many Times	Happens Many Times	Happens Many Times

(Continued)

Table 2.1 Data collection from dataset. (*Continued*)

Able to give 100% in my performance	Regular and on time in my class	Students gets satisfy with the content	Students' Queries are sorted out efficiently	Satisfied with the time and work load assigned	Monetary gains is in proportion to assigned work
Does Not Happen	Does Not Happen	Does Not Happen	Does Not Happen	Does Not Happen	Does Not Happen
Happens Many Times	Does Not Happen	Happens Many Times	Does Not Happen	Happens Many Times	Does Not Happen
Cannot Comment	Happens Many Times	Cannot Comment	Happens Many Times	Cannot Comment	Happens Many Times
Does Not Happen	Does Not Happen	Does Not Happen	Does Not Happen	Does Not Happen	Does Not Happen
Happens Many Times	Happens Many Times	Happens Many Times	Happens Many Times	Happens Many Times	Happens Many Times
Cannot Comment	Cannot Comment	Cannot Comment	Cannot Comment	Cannot Comment	Cannot Comment
Does Not Happen	Happens Many Times	Does Not Happen	Happens Many Times	Does Not Happen	Happens Many Times
Cannot Comment	Does Not Happen	Does Not Happen	Does Not Happen	Does Not Happen	Does Not Happen
Happens Many Times	Happens Many Times	Happens Many Times	Happens Many Times	Happens Many Times	Happens Many Times

2.8 Comparison of Six Different Approaches For Stress Detection

Table 2.2 Comparison of six different approaches for stress detection.

Serial number	Method	Advantages	Limitations	Exploited data	Results, accuracy
1	Feature based ML approach [3]	Speed, interpretability, low compute power	Required expert knowledge of the features	All the sensors	93% (stress detection)
2	ML approach, per subject [3]	Same as 1 + tailored to a single subject	Same as 1 + need to be retrained for each subject	All the sensors	88–99% (per subject)
3	ML approach [3]	Same as 1 + applicable to commercial smart watches	Same as 1	Smart watch compatible data: wrist only without EDA	87% (stress detection, balanced accuracy)
4	DL approach [3]	High-accuracy no expert knowledge	High compute, complex model	All sensors	85% (3 classes)
5	DL, Self-supervised learning [3]	Very high accuracy no expert knowledge	High compute, complex method	ECG only + additional data sets	97% (4 classes)
6	DL, Self-supervised learning [3]	Can leverage unlabeled data	More complex than supervised learning	New research WESAD smart watch data (all wrist data without EDA as in 3	85% (stress detection)

2.9   Conclusions

Stress is a not a problem, it's a pandemic. It is increasing day by day. It is also affecting the individual physical and psychological health. This chapter is proposed for stress prediction based on the faculty data-set of a university. After comparing the six methods in Table 2.2 it can be very well stated that DL, self-supervised learning is the best in accuracy. It uses PSS (perceived stress scale) to calculate stress level on student dataset. The classification techniques that are used in this study are Baye's Net, Logistic Regression, Naïve Bayes, J48, Random Forest and Multilayer perceptron techniques for the prediction of stress. With the help of Weka tool, the accuracy of different techniques is calculated and compared. According to this paper we observe the Kappa statistic, F-measure, mean absolute error, MCC, ROC Area, False positive (FP), True positive (TP), RMSE and Recall and Random Forest classifier gives the best accuracy of 94.73 %.

2.10   Future Scope

The proposed work has lot of scope for future and it can be extended further. In this study, the case of a university faculty is taken. It can be extended to get the stress prediction for college faculties and can be extended to know how well the students those who belong to university, college or school even. This study will surely help us to know that the university faculties are facing a stress levels to some extent and needs proper intervention for better lifestyle.

Additional methods like the Naïve Bayes classifier can be used to test the efficiency of the model. One can implement deep learning techniques like CNN (Convoluted Neural Networks) and verify how the model performs for the given dataset. A much more specific and vast dataset can be used as a training model since the number of responses is limited in our case.

References

1. Sharma, D., Kapoor, N., Kang, S.S., Stress prediction of students using machine learning. *IJMPERD*, 10, 3, 5609–5620, July 2020.
2. Norizam, S., *Determination and Classification of Human Stress Index Using Nonparametric Analysis of EEG Signals*, Diss. Universiti Teknologi MARA, Malaysia, 2015.

3. Alshamrani, M., Semi-supervised deep learning for stress prediction: A review and novel solutions. *Int. J. Adv. Comput. Sci. Appl.*, 12, 9, 426, 2021.
4. Priyaa, A., Garga, S., Tigga, N.P., Predicting anxiety, depression and stress in modern life using machine learning algorithms. *Sci. Direct Proc. Comput. Sci., Elsevier*, 167, 1258–1267, 2020.
5. Jiang, H., Nie, Z., Yeo, R., Farimani, A.B., Kara, L.B., StressGAN: A generative deep learning model for 2D stress distribution prediction. *J. Appl. Mech.*, 234–243, January 2021.
6. Reddy, S., Thota, A.V., Dharun, A., *Machine Learning Techniques for Stress Prediction in Working Employees*, Conference Paper, December 2018.
7. Java Point, Deep learning algorithms, https://www.javatpoint.com/.
8. https://www.simplilearn.com/
9. Tutorial Point, Deep learning algorithms, https://www.javatpoint.com/.
10. Zhuang, X., Nguyen, L.C., Nguyen-Xuan, H., Alajlan, N., Rabczuk, T., Efficient deep learning for gradient-enhanced stress dependent damage model. *Appl. Sci. MDPI*, 1002–1011, April 8, 2020.

## 3

Deep Learning: Tools and Models

Brijesh K. Soni and Akhilesh A. Waoo*

Department of Computer Science and Technology, AKS University, Satna, MP, India

Abstract

Now in this modern era, we are exploring technology and science, in the same scenarios, we are also trying to explore a popular technology named "Deep-Learning", which is a giant technology in the software industry around the world. Here in this chapter, we start with the basic concept of deep learning including the framework and library frequently used to develop such types of applications. Further, in the middle part various deep learning models were discussed with a practical approach using the MNIST dataset. These models are used for solving various complex problems in the domain of computer vision and natural language processing. At the end of this chapter, we are also trying to introduce some emerging and interdisciplinary domains associated with deep learning and artificial intelligence. However, this chapter contains only the core concept of deep learning technology, and it might be fruitful for a beginner in this area.

Keywords: Deep-learning, deep neural network, DBN, RNN, CNN, GAN, MNIST, Keras, TensorFlow, phenotyping, human visual system

3.1 Introduction

Deep learning is the most prominent technology nowadays in most industrial applications. Techniques and methods invented in this domain are broadly applicable in the software industry, automobile industry, gaming industry, agriculture industry, medical industry, telecom industry, etc. [1]. This manuscript covers the core components of deep learning technology. Two concepts are precisely described here, the first one is 'TensorFlow: Keras', and the second one is 'Deep-Learning-Model'.

Corresponding author: akhileshwaoo@gmail.com

Anamika Ahirwar, Piyush Kumar Shukla, Manish Shrivastava, Priti Maheshwary and Bhupesh Gour (eds.) Innovative Engineering with AI Applications, (41–64) © 2023 Scrivener Publishing LLC

- Keras is a software development framework or sometimes also considered a library. Keras was initially designed for developing algorithms for natural language processing and computer vision using the python programming language [2].
- Deep-learning-Models are artificially implemented neural networks.

3.1.1 Definition

Deep learning can be observed in such a manner defined below –

"A way of artificial learning in machines by mimicking biological nervous system for solving complex problems"

Scientists and researchers all around the world believe that learning is the process of gaining skills in living creatures. Now in this modern era technologies are growing at an exponential rate; artificial intelligence is also one of them having huge applications in software industries. These hi-tech industries continuously develop more advanced software-enabled machines possessing self-learning capability [3]. Deep learning is the most significant and popular technique for developing such kinds of self-learning machines. Deep learning is the sub-domain of machine learning, which is further a sub-domain of artificial intelligence [4].

How a human mind solves critical problems, in the same manner, researchers trying to develop artificial models of the nervous system using software technologies in computerized machines with the intent of going more and more depth for solving critical problems. These models are known as artificial neural network that contains multiple numbers of artificial neuron units and appropriate transition paths. These artificial neuron units interact as a fully connected network on the transition path [5]. These artificial neurons are organized in a layered structure, having more than one layer in a single network. The number of layers depends on the problem size, which means for a more complex problem many numbers of layers are required. Ultimately the size of the network depends on the depth of the problem. Now it is understood that for solving more critical problems by going into more depth, a multilayered neural network (Multilayered Perceptron) is required to have the facility of deep learning [6]. These types of neural networks are known as deep neural networks or deep neural network models. These models are the core components of this chapter to be discussed in detail in Section 3.2.

3.1.2   Elements of Neural Networks

A deep learning model or deep neural network may have common building blocks and terminologies [7]. Some of them are briefly described here and are frequently used-

- *Node* – This is the artificial neuron for holding a value in a neural network. In a network, there may be multiple nodes available. Generally, these nodes are composed in the form of layers and every layer has one or more nodes.
- *Connection* – This is the transition path between neurons for transferring value from one node to another node, starting from the input node to the output node. Like nodes, connections are also used in multiple numbers for transferring appropriate values and relating nodes to each other.
- *Layer* – This is the most significant component of a neural network. Each layer has one or more neurons having similar or different values. Generally, layers are categorized as the input layer, hidden layer, and output layer. Primarily input and output layers must be single, and hidden layers may be in n-numbers. These multiple numbers of hidden layers create a deep neural network and facilitate the deep learning process [8].
- *Input* – This is the input value given to the model which will be further processed for generating appropriate output. Values may be random or predefined and are taken by nodes available in the input layer.
- *Output* – After processing, this is the final output generated by the model using the activation specified function. Ideally, the output will be equivalent to the target output, but in practice, it's not possible to generate the exact targeted output. There might be a difference between actual output and target output, which will further deal with backpropagation.
- *Weight* – Weight is a numeric value multiplied by the input values received from the input layer. It will use for upgrading the input to propagate into the next layer. The weight value continuously changes during the training period for getting the targeted output at the output layer.
- *Bias* – This is the constant value applied during the processing of original inputs. This value will be ideal for all input

values. Unlike weight value, this is the constant value and it never changes even during the training period.

- *Activation* – This is a very important function in a neural network model. Without this function whole model works like a simple pipeline. The activation function mathematically operates the summation of original inputs and a weight value, just before the final output is generated. Some common and frequently used activation functions are sigmoid, ReLU function, binary function, and linear function [9].

- *Threshold* – The threshold value is associated with the activation function which directly affects the output to be generated, whether the neuron fires or not fires. It will be decided according to the desired output.

3.1.3 Tool: Keras

This is the most frequently used tensor flow-based library tool for implementing deep learning models. This is originally developed by the world-renowned company Google.

Nowadays most popular companies are using this tool for developing artificially intelligent machines and models. Keras allows building, training, and evaluation of deep neural networks. [10] Here in this section, the fundamental architecture of Keras having three-pillar components (Figure 3.1) will be briefly described-

Models – Models are data structures in Keras. These models shape the core structure of a neural network model and specify internal connections among the neurons and the transition path of the model. In Keras, there are two types of models' namely the sequential model and functional model which are briefly described below-

- *Sequential API Model* – This is the simplest data structure in Keras, where multiple layers are organized linearly or sequentially. That means there are not any direct connections between input and output in the case of a multilayer perceptron. This type of model can be easily created and understood.

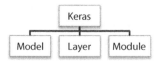

Figure 3.1 Major components of Keras.

- *Functional API Model* – This is the advanced data structure in Keras, where all the layers of a network are randomly connected. This is a hybrid data structure where a network can have sequential and random connections. This is a very complex structure in nature; it couldn't be easily implemented, unlike sequential structure [11].

Layers – Layers are core elements of a neural network that contains one or more neurons in the layered organization. Each layer is further connected to other layers of the same network. A simple network has two or more layers that are responsible for the complexity of the network. In Keras, multiple types of layers are available for solving problems in different types of network models. Some common categories and examples of Keras layers are briefly described here-

- *Core-Layers* – This is the fundamental category of Keras layers, where some important and frequently used layers are included. Without using these layers, it couldn't be possible to implement any neural network. Some important core layers are Dense, Activation, Dropout, Flatten, Input, Reshape, Permute, Lambda, and Masking.
- *Convolution-Layers* – This is the category where important layers are included which are applicable in the convolutional neural network. The convolutional neural network is a very important and popular model for image processing. Conv1D and Conv2D layers are most frequently used in the convolutional neural network. These layers are used for convoluting or filtering the original input values for generating a more optimized output.
- *Pooling-Layers* – This is also a category where included layers are used in the convolutional neural network. MaxPooling1D, MaxPooling2D, and AveragePooling1D, AveragePooling2D, are popular layers that are used for resizing the original inputs in a convolutional neural network.
- *Recurrent-Layers* – This is the category having important layers frequently used in a recurrent neural network. A recurrent neural network is popular for text processing (NLP) among researchers and engineers around the world. Simple RNN and LSTM are two important layers applicable in a recurrent neural network for implementing its various variant models [12].

Modules – Modules are built-in APIs available in TensorFlow and Keras. Sometimes these APIs are also known as the library. By using these APIs, we can solve complex problems easily without paying more time and effort. These APIs or modules can be directly imported into our program and further functions and classes available in these imported APIs can be used in the program for processing data and generating appropriate output in different network models. Keras has multiple modules some of them are described here in this section:

- *Losses* – This module provides various loss functions to compute the quantity that a model should minimize during training. All losses are available both via a class handle and via a function handle. The class handles enable you to pass configuration arguments to the constructor and they perform reduction by default when used in a standalone way.
- *Metrics* – This module provides functions for the jugging performance of the neural network. Metric functions are similar to loss functions, except that the results from evaluating a metric are not used when training the model. Note that you may use any loss function as a metric.
- *Utilities* – This package provides utilities for Keras, such as model plotting utilities, Serialization utilities, Python & NumPy utilities, and Backend utilities.
- *Backend* – This module handles backend operations in Keras. Generally, Keras runs on the top of the TensorFlow backend. But if required it can be changed from TensorFlow to Theano or CNTK backend.
- *Callback* – This module provides functions to analyze immediate results. The callback can perform actions at various stages of training such as at the start or end of an epoch, before or after a single batch, etc.
- *Activations* – This module provides various activation functions for transforming summation input into the final output. These functions decide whether the neuron is active or inactive, which directly affects the final output.
- *Constraints* – This module provides functions to apply weight parameters during optimization.
- *Initializers* – This module provides functions to set the initial weight. During the training period weight will be assigned to each input value. This task is performed by the initializer functions available in this module.

- *Optimizers* – This module provides functions to change weight and learning rates for reducing loss. An optimizer is one of the two arguments required for compiling a Keras model. You can either instantiate an optimizer before passing it to model.compile(), as in the above example, or you can pass it by its string identifier. In the latter case, the default parameters for the optimizer will be used.
- *Regularizers* – This module provides functions for applying some penalties on the layers during the optimization. Regularization is a technique used in an attempt to solve the overfitting problem in statistical models. As the name implies, they use L1 and L2 norms respectively which are added to your loss function by multiplying it with parameter lambda. This penalizes the network's aggressive pattern memorizing behavior which can be detrimental while training since the network will just learn to mimic the given data rather than learning to approximate any useful functions.
- *Text Processing* – This module provides functions to convert normal text input value into an array so that it can be easily processed. These functions are frequently used with recurrent neural networks for text processing and pattern recognition.
- *Image Processing* – This module provides a function to convert normal image input pixels into an array so that they can be simply analyzed. These functions are mostly used with a convolutional neural network for image processing and classification.
- *Sequence Processing* – This module provides functions for converting normal input values into time-based data. These functions can be used in data preparation [13].

3.2   Deep Learning Models

Deep Learning Models are artificially implemented neural networks inspired by the human nervous system.

This section elaborates on four fundamental deep learning models, explored with their practical implementation in the MNIST dataset using TensorFlow: Keras library and python programming language. These models are Deep Belief Network (DBN), Recurrent Neural Network (RNN), Convolutional Neural Network (CNN), and Gradient Adversarial Network (GAN) [14], shown in Figure 3.2.

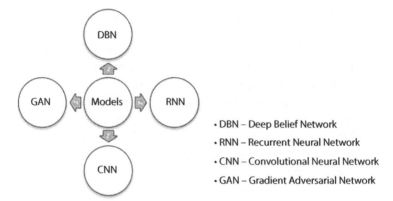

Figure 3.2 Deep learning models.

3.2.1   Deep Belief Network [DBN]

This is a deep neural network model developed at an early age in deep learning. It has hybrid compositions of a set of Restricted Boltzmann Machines (RBN). That means multiple RBNs are stacked within a single network. These RBNs are working on the concept of probability applicable in belief networks. Each RBN has a visible layer and a hidden layer. This is a generative and unsupervised neural network. It uses a greedy unsupervised learning algorithm for the training of intermediate layers, but finally, the whole network will train using a supervised fine-tuning method. Nowadays Restricted Belief Machines and Deep Belief Networks are rarely used for data processing [15]. This section explores the simple architecture of the deep belief network.

3.2.1.1   Fundamental Architecture of DBN

There are two types of layers (Figure 3.3) available in deep belief network architecture. The overall network will be trained in two phases pre-training phase and fine-tuning phase.

- *Visible Layer* – This is the primary layer of Restricted Boltzmann Machines which will be further available in the Deep Belief Network. It looks like an input layer in a simple neural network. It takes input from external sources and further provides it to the next layer. There is only a single visible layer in an RBM, where each neuron is directly connected

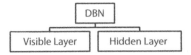

Figure 3.3 Layers in the deep belief network.

to each neuron of the hidden layer. There is no connection among neurons belonging to the same layer [16].

- *Hidden-Layer* – This is the next layer after the visible layer, which takes input from the visible layer. Like the visible layer, there is also a single hidden layer in an RBM. However, this layer is completely responsible for performing computations and generating the desired output, because there is no output layer separately in this type of machine model [17].

3.2.1.2   Implementing DBN Using MNIST Dataset

```
#Importing Libray
import numpy as np
import pandas as pd
from sklearn.model_selection import train_test_
split
from sklearn.metrics.classification import accuracy_
score
from sklearn.preprocessing import standardscaler
#Loading Dataset
digits = pd.read_csv("train.csv")
#Preprocess Dataset
X = np.array(digits.drop(["label"], axis=1))
Y = np.array(digits["label"])
ss=standardscaler()
X = ss.fit_transform(X)
X_train, X_test, Y_train, Y_test = train_test_
split(X, Y, test_size=0.2, random_state=0)
#Developing Model
classifier = SupervisedDBNClassification(hidden_
layers_structure = [256, 256],
learning_rate_rbm=0.05, learning_rate=0.1, n_
epochs_rbm=10, n_iter_backprop=100,
```

```
batch_size=32, activation_function='relu', drop-
out_p=0.2)
#Evaluating Model
classifier.fit(X_train, Y_train)
Y_pred = classifier.predict(X_test)
print('Done.\nAccuracy: %f' % accuracy_score(Y_
test, Y_pred))
```

3.2.2   Recurrent Neural Network [RNN]

This is one of the most popular deep neural network models. Recurrent Neural Network was originally developed for text processing, but nowadays it has various other similar applications like speech recognition, handwriting recognition, and natural language processing. It can store the previous state in memory for predicting the next state, by using the backpropagation method [18].

3.2.2.1   Fundamental Architecture of RNN

This model has a traditional structure which means there are ordinary neurons and layers used for data computation. The key point which makes it unique is its recursive nature. Its hidden layer is responsible for the recursive process following the backpropagation method [19]. Here in this section basic layers as shown in Figure 3.4, are briefly described.

- *Input-Layer* – The input layer is responsible for receiving the inputs. These inputs can be loaded from an external source such as a web service or a CSV file. There must always be one input layer in a neural network. The input layer takes in the inputs, performs the calculations via its neurons, and then the output is transmitted onto the subsequent layers [20].
- *Hidden-Layer* – The introduction of hidden layers makes neural networks superior to most machine learning algorithms.

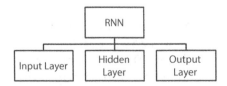

Figure 3.4 Layers in RNN.

Hidden layers reside in-between input and output layers and this is the primary reason why they are referred to as hidden. The word "hidden" implies that they are not visible to the external systems and are "private" to the neural network. There could be zero or more hidden layers in a neural network. Usually, each hidden layer contains the same number of neurons. The neurons simply calculate the weighted sum and add the bias, to execute an activation function [21].

- *Output-Layer* – The output layer is responsible for producing the final result. There must always be one output layer in a neural network. The output layer takes in the inputs which are passed in from the layers before it, performs the calculations via its neurons, and then the output is computed. In a complex neural network with multiple hidden layers, the output layer receives inputs from the previously hidden layer [22].

3.2.2.2   Implementing RNN Using MNIST Dataset

```
import keras
from keras.datasets import mnist
from keras.models import Sequential
from keras.layers import CuDNNLSTM, Dense, Dropout,
LSTM
from keras.optimizers import Adam
#Loading Dataset
(X_train, Y_train),(X_test, Y_test) = mnist.load_
data() # unpacks images to x_train/x_test and
labels to y_train/y_test
#Preprocess Dataset
X_train = X_train.astype('float32') / 255.0
X_test = X_test.astype('float32') / 255.0
#Initializing Classifier Model
classifier = Sequential()
#Adding Input LSTM Layer
classifier.add(CuDNNLSTM(128, input_shape=(X_train.
shape[1:]),return_sequences=True))
classifier.add(Dropout(0.2))
```

```
#Adding Second LSTM Layer
classifier.add(CuDNNLSTM(128))
#Adding Dense Hidden Layer
classifier.add(Dense(64, activation='relu'))
classifier.add(Dropout(0.2))
#Adding Output Layer
classifier.add(Dense(10, activation='softmax'))
classifier.add(LSTM(128, input_shape=(X_train.
shape[1:]), return_sequences=True))
#Compiling Model
classifier.compile(loss='sparse_categorical_
crossentropy', optimizer=Adam(lr=0.001, decay=1e-6),
metrics=['accuracy'] )
#Fitting Model
classifier.fit(X_train, Y_train, epochs=3,
validation_data=(X_test, Y_test))
test_loss, test_acc = classifier.evaluate(X_test,
Y_test)
print('Test Loss: {}'.format(test_loss))
print('Test Accuracy: {}'.format(test_acc))
```

3.2.3   Convolutional Neural Network [CNN]

Convolutional Neural Network is another most important and popular deep neural network model. This is a feed-forward neural network. There are various applications of this model in the domain of image processing for analyzing visual imagery. Convolutional Neural Network is inspired by the human visual cortex [23].

3.2.3.1   Fundamental Architecture of CNN

This deep learning model has a unique and little complex architecture compared to a traditional neural network. It has three types of layers (Figure 3.5) a convolution layer, a pooling layer, and a fully connected or dense layer [24]. Here in this section, these layers will be briefly described.

- *Convolution Layer* – This layer is responsible for extracting features from the input image. Here inputs are small square pixel of an image, which relatively represents the features of

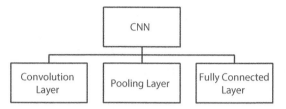

Figure 3.5 Layers in CNN.

that image. Mathematically, convolution is a function that takes two input items and produces an output item. Here, a matrix is used for containing image pixels that provide the first input; another input is taken from the filter or kernel matrix. The image pixel matrix and filter matrix are multiplied and produce an output matrix which is known as a feature map. Different types of filters deal with different features of the image such as edge detection blur and sharpen etc [25].

- *Pooling Layer* – This layer is responsible for reducing the image parameters, which means it removes unnecessary features of the images and represents only essential features. A special type of pooling, spatial pooling which is also known as down-sampling or sub-sampling most frequently used in this type of deep learning model. Some common types of pooling are Max-Pooling, Average-Pooling, and Sum-Pooling [26].

- *Fully Connected Layer* – This is the next layer after the convolution and pooling layer. It takes input from the pooling layer and, analyzes and predicts the preferred pattern for final output. One more important work of this layer is to flatten input from the previous layer [27].

3.2.3.2 Implementing CNN Using MNIST Dataset

```
# baseline cnn model for mnist
from numpy import mean
from numpy import std
from matplotlib import pyplot
from sklearn.model_selection import KFold
```

```python
from keras.datasets import mnist
from keras.utils import to_categorical
from keras.models import Sequential
from keras.layers import Conv2D
from keras.layers import MaxPooling2D
from keras.layers import Dense
from keras.layers import Flatten
from keras.optimizers import SGD

# load train and test dataset
def load_dataset():
# load dataset
(trainX, trainY), (testX, testY) = mnist.load_data()
# reshape dataset to have a single channel
trainX = trainX.reshape((trainX.shape[0], 28,
28, 1))
testX = testX.reshape((testX.shape[0], 28, 28,
1))
# one hot encode target values
trainY = to_categorical(trainY)
testY = to_categorical(testY)
return trainX, trainY, testX, testY

# scale pixels
def prep_pixels(train, test):
# convert from integers to floats
train_norm = train.astype('float32')
test_norm = test.astype('float32')
# normalize to range 0-1
train_norm = train_norm / 255.0
test_norm = test_norm / 255.0
# return normalized images
return train_norm, test_norm

# define cnn model
def define_model():
model = Sequential()
model.add(Conv2D(32, (3, 3), activation='relu',
kernel_initializer='he_uniform', input_shape=(28,
28, 1)))
```

```
model.add(MaxPooling2D((2, 2)))
model.add(Flatten())
model.add(Dense(100, activation='relu', kernel_
initializer='he_uniform'))
model.add(Dense(10, activation='softmax'))
# compile model
opt = SGD(lr=0.01, momentum=0.9)
model.compile(optimizer=opt, loss='categorical_
crossentropy', metrics=['accuracy'])
return model

# evaluate a model using k-fold cross-validation
def evaluate_model(dataX, dataY, n_folds=5):
scores, histories = list(), list()
# prepare cross validation
kfold=KFold(n_folds, shuffle=True, random_state=1)
# enumerate splits
for train_ix, test_ix in kfold.split(dataX):
# define model
model = define_model()
# select rows for train and test
trainX, trainY, testX, testY = dataX[train_ix],
dataY[train_ix], dataX[test_ix], dataY[test_ix]
# fit model
history = model.fit(trainX, trainY, epochs=10,
batch_size=32, validation_data=(testX, testY),
verbose=0)
# evaluate model
_, acc = model.evaluate(testX, testY, verbose=0)
print('> %.3f' % (acc * 100.0))
# stores scores
scores.append(acc)
histories.append(history)
return scores, histories

# plot diagnostic learning curves
def summarize_diagnostics(histories):
for i in range(len(histories)):
# plot loss
pyplot.subplot(2, 1, 1)
```

```
pyplot.title('Cross Entropy Loss')
pyplot.plot(histories[i].history['loss'], color=
'blue', label='train')
pyplot.plot(histories[i].history['val_loss'],
color='orange', label='test')
# plot accuracy
pyplot.subplot(2, 1, 2)
pyplot.title('Classification Accuracy')
pyplot.plot(histories[i].history['accuracy'],
color='blue', label='train')
pyplot.plot(histories[i].history['val_accu-
racy'], color='orange', label='test')
pyplot.show()

# summarize model performance
def summarize_performance(scores):
# print summary
print('Accuracy: mean=%.3f std=%.3f, n=%d' %
(mean(scores)*100, std(scores)*100, len(scores)))

# box and whisker plots of results
pyplot.boxplot(scores)
pyplot.show()

# run the test harness for evaluating a model
def run_test_harness():
# load dataset
trainX, trainY, testX, testY = load_dataset()
# prepare pixel data
trainX, testX = prep_pixels(trainX, testX)
# evaluate model
scores,   histories   =   evaluate_model(trainX,
trainY)
# learning curves
summarize_diagnostics(histories)
# summarize estimated performance
summarize_performance(scores)

# entry point, run the test harness
run_test_harness()
```

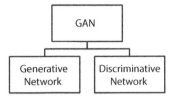

Figure 3.6 Layers in GAN.

3.2.4   Gradient Adversarial Network [GAN]

This is a relatively new member of the family of deep learning models. It is a hybrid system having two combined networks. These two network components are known as generative network and discriminative network, where the generative network generates output, and the discriminative network evaluates that output [28].

3.2.4.1   Fundamental Architecture of GAN

The overall architecture of the gradient adversarial network is divided into two parts (Figure 3.6) generative and discriminative. Mostly these parts are considered an individual network that works in combinations. However, by design generative network is a deconvolutional network whereas the discriminative network is a convolutional network [29].

- *Generative-Network* – The prime intention of this network is to generate plausible output. However, the generated output shows a negative impact on the discriminator [30].
- *Discriminative-Network* – The overall objective of this network is to work as a classifier and distinguish the generator's fake output from the real output. Ultimately this network aims to realize the mistakes of the generator network. It also penalizes the generator network for producing implausible output [31].

3.2.4.2   Implementing GAN Using MNIST Dataset

```
# importing the necessary libraries and the MNIST
dataset
import
import numpy as np
tensorflow as tf import matplotlib.pyplot as plt
```

```
from tensorflow.examples.tutorials.mnist import
input_data

mnist = input_data.read_data_sets("MNIST_data")

# defining functions for the two networks.
# Both the networks have two hidden layers
# and an output layer which are densely or
# fully connected layers defining the
# Generator network function
def generator(z, reuse = None):
    with tf.variable_scope(‹gen›, reuse = reuse):
        hidden1 = tf.layers.dense(inputs = z, units = 128,
                        activation = tf.nn.leaky_relu)

        hidden2 = tf.layers.dense(inputs = hidden1,
            units = 128, activation = tf.nn.leaky_relu)

        output = tf.layers.dense(inputs = hidden2,
            units = 784, activation = tf.nn.tanh)

        return output

# defining the Discriminator network function
def discriminator(X, reuse = None):
    with tf.variable_scope(‹dis›, reuse = reuse):
        hidden1 = tf.layers.dense(inputs = X, units = 128,
                        activation = tf.nn.leaky_relu)

        hidden2 = tf.layers.dense(inputs = hidden1,
            units = 128, activation = tf.nn.leaky_relu)

        logits = tf.layers.dense(hidden2, units = 1)
        output = tf.sigmoid(logits)

        return output, logits

# creating placeholders for the outputs
tf.reset_default_graph()

real_images = tf.placeholder(tf.float32, shape
=[None, 784])
z = tf.placeholder(tf.float32, shape =[None, 100])
```

```
G = generator(z)
D_output_real, D_logits_real = discriminator
(real_images)
D_output_fake, D_logits_fake = discriminator(G,
reuse = True)

# defining the loss function
def loss_func(logits_in, labels_in):
    return tf.reduce_mean(tf.nn.sigmoid_cross_entropy_
    with_logits(
            logits = logits_in, labels = labels_in))

# Smoothing for generalization
D_real_loss = loss_func(D_logits_real, tf.ones_
like(D_logits_real)*0.9)
D_fake_loss = loss_func(D_logits_fake, tf.zeros_
like(D_logits_real))
D_loss = D_real_loss + D_fake_loss

G_loss = loss_func(D_logits_fake, tf.ones_like
(D_logits_fake))

# defining the learning rate, batch size,
# number of epochs and using the Adam optimizer
lr = 0.001 # learning rate

# Do this when multiple networks
# interact with each other

# returns all variables created(the two
# variable scopes) and makes trainable true
tvars = tf.trainable_variables()
d_vars =[var for var in tvars if 'dis' in var.
name]
g_vars =[var for var in tvars if 'gen' in var.
name]

D_trainer = tf.train.AdamOptimizer(lr).mini-
mize(D_loss, var_list = d_vars)
G_trainer = tf.train.AdamOptimizer(lr).minimize
(G_loss, var_list = g_vars)
```

```
batch_size = 100 # batch size
epochs = 500 # number of epochs. The higher the
better the result
init = tf.global_variables_initializer()

# creating a session to train the networks
samples =[] # generator examples

with tf.Session() as sess:

    sess.run(init)
    for epoch in range(epochs):
        num_batches = mnist.train.num_examples//
        batch_size

        for i in range(num_batches):
            batch    =    mnist.train.next_batch
            (batch_size)
            batch_images = batch[0].reshape((batch_
            size, 784))
            batch_images = batch_images * 2-1
            batch_z = np.random.uniform(-1, 1,
            size =(batch_size, 100))
            _= sess.run(D_trainer, feed_dict
={real_images:batch_images, z:batch_z})
            _= sess.run(G_trainer, feed_dict
={z:batch_z})

        print(«on epoch{}».format(epoch))

        sample_z = np.random.uniform(-1, 1, size =
        (1, 100))
        gen_sample = sess.run(generator(z, reuse =
        True),
                        feed_dict={z:sample_z})

        samples.append(gen_sample)

# result after 0th epoch
plt.imshow(samples[0].reshape(28, 28))

# result after 499th epoch
plt.imshow(samples[49].reshape(28, 28))
```

3.3   Research Perspective of Deep Learning

The ideology of anything never being limited, in the same sense, there are some current research trends, where exploration is possible. This section deals with some latest research hypotheses in the domain of deep learning in brief.

3.3.1   Multi-Agent System: Argumentation

This is a research project in which researchers are trying to develop the Multi-agent System for argumentation among law professionals [32]. I believe this will very helpful for analyzing and handling criminal cases under the law and jurisdiction [33]. Researchers are using Conditional Probability and Bayesian-Network for implementing this model. They are trying to design and train a deep neural network in the domain of deep learning [34].

3.3.2   Image Processor: Phenotyping

In this project, researchers are trying to develop an algorithm that provides a better result in Phenotyping [35]. Most agriculture-based countries trying to improve crop quality and secure plants from various types of diseases [36]. They are trying to improve spatial resolution and pattern classification in the existing algorithm. Some researchers are using drones for taking real-time images for further processing [37].

3.3.3   Saliency Map: Visualization

There is a huge amount of opportunity in brain research associated with deep learning because the phenomenon of deep learning originated from the human nervous system [38]. This project is directly related to the human visual system, which means scientists are trying to apply the saliency technique for mapping visual stimuli [39]. Researchers striving to develop a model for the human visual cortex for mapping images artificially [40].

3.4   Conclusion

The human nervous system is fully responsible for how critically we can think and dive into the depth of the problem domain. It is well known that we have lots of alternative tools and technology for solving general problems, but we have to find a unique phenomenon for exploring the edge of unsolvable problems. Deep learning is one of those techniques by using which we can solve critical problems with more accuracy. This chapter covered most of the popular and important deep learning neural network models.

All the models described in this chapter are now pillars in the domain of deep learning. RNN and CNN are two siblings born from mother deep learning, where RNN is popular for text-processing and CNN is known for image-processing. GAN is the most significant and popular model among modern researchers and laboratories around the globe. This is comparable to a strategic technique between an expert and a novice mind in a particular domain for improving knowledge and experience. However, these are the only concepts, but if we want to convert them into the products, we must require a framework, that's why we used TensorFlow and Keras with a python programming language for converting conceptual models into a software product, by taking an example dataset provided by Kaggle partner. The last section of this chapter provided some research ideology for future perspectives in this domain. There were three subdomains in my digital phenotyping in crops, argumentation using multiagent, and the last one is saliency mapping for visual signal processing in the human visual system. Finally, we tried to represent the fundamentals of deep learning having more emphasis on deep learning models.

References

1. Vargas, R. and Obudai Egyetem, Deep learning: Previous and present applications. *J. Aware.*, 2, 12–17, 2017.
2. About Keras. Retrieved from Keras website: https://keras.io/about/.
3. Georgevici, A., II and Terblanche, M., Neural networks and deep learning: A brief introduction. *Intensive Care Med.*, Springer Verlag, 45, 712–714, 2019.
4. Serokell, Artificial intelligence vs. Machine learning vs. Deep learning: What's the difference, 2020. Retrieved from Medium website: https://medium.com/ai-in-plain-english/artificial-intelligence-vs-machine-learning-vs-deep-learning-whats-the-difference-dccce18efe7f.
5. Zhang, Z., A gentle introduction to artificial neural networks. *Ann. Transl. Med.* AME Publishing Company, 4, 370, 2016.
6. Neural network: Architecture, components & top algorithms, 2020. https://www.upgrad.com/blog/neural-network-architecture-components-algorithms.
7. Basheer, I.A. and Hajmeer, M.N., Artificial neural networks: Fundamentals, computing, design, and application. *J. Microbiol. Methods* Elsevier, 43, 3–31, 2001.

8. Smith, S.W., *Neural network architecture*, Hard Cover 1997, Soft Cover 2002, *The Scientist and Engineer's Guide to, Digital Signal Processing Published by Newnes*, https://www.dspguide.com/ch26/2.htm.

9. Sharma, S., Activation functions in neural networks, 2017. https://towardsdatascience.com/activation-functions-neural-networks-1cbd9f8d91d6.

10. Keras API reference, https://keras.io/api/.

11. Keras API reference: Models API, https://keras.io/api/models/.

12. Keras API reference: Layers API, https://keras.io/api/layers/.

13. Keras-modules, https://www.tutorialspoint.com/keras/keras_modules.htm.

14. Sk, S., Jabez, J., Anu, V.M., The power of deep learning models: Applications. *Int. J. Recent Technol. Eng.*, 8, 3700–3704, 2019.

15. Hua, Y., Guo, J., Zhao, H., Deep belief networks and deep learning. *International Conference on Intelligent Computing and Internet of Things*, IEEE Xplore, 2015.

16. Restricted Boltzmann machines, http://docs.goodai.com/brainsimulator/guides/rbm/index.html.

17. Fischer, A. and Igel, C., An introduction to restricted Boltzmann machines. *Iberoamerican Congress on Pattern Recognition*, 2012.

18. Sherstinsky, A., Fundamentals of recurrent neural network (RNN) and long short-term memory (LSTM) network. *Phys. D Nonlinear Phenom.* Elsevier, 404, 1–43, 2020.

19. Nayak, M., Introduction to the architecture of recurrent neural networks (RNNs), 2019. https://medium.com/towards-artificial-intelligence/introduction-to-the-architecture-of-recurrent-neural-networks-rnns-a277007984b7.

20. Recurrent neural networks explanation. https://www.geeksforgeeks.org/recurrent-neural-networks-explanation/?ref=lbp.

21. Recurrent neural networks (RNN) with Keras. https://www.tensorflow.org/guide/keras/rnn.

22. Amidi, A. and Amidi, S., Recurrent neural networks cheatsheet. https://stanford.edu/~shervine/teaching/cs-230/cheatsheet-recurrent-neural-networks.

23. Teuwen, J. and Moriakov, N., *Convolutional neural networks*, Handbook of Medical Image Computing and Computer Assisted Intervention, Elsevier Inc., https://doi.org/10.1016/B978-0-12-816176-0.00025-9, 2020, https://www.sciencedirect.com/topics/engineering/convolutional-neural-networks.

24. Gupta, D., Architecture of convolutional neural networks (CNNs) demystified, 2017. https://www.analyticsvidhya.com/blog/2017/06/architecture-of-convolutional-neural-networks-simplified-demystified.

25. Sakib, S.; Ahmed, N.; Kabir, A.J.; Ahmed, H. *An Overview of Convolutional Neural Network: Its Architecture and Applications*. Preprints 2018, 2018110546 (doi: 10.20944/preprints201811.0546.v4).

26. Jmour, N., Zayen, S., Abdelkrim, A., Convolutional neural networks for image classification. *International Conference on Advanced Systems and Electric Technologies*, 2018.

27. Chauhan, R., Ghanshala, K.K., Joshi, R.C., Convolutional neural network (CNN) for image detection and recognition. *International Conference on Secure Cyber Computing and Communication*, 2018.
28. Creswell, A. and White, T., Generative adversarial networks: An overview. *IEEE Signal Process. Mag.*, 35, 1–14, 2017.
29. Pouget-Abadie, J. and Goodfellow, I., Generative adversarial networks, in: *Advances in Neural Information Processing Systems*, MIT, *Proceedings of the 27th International Conference on Neural Information Processing Systems*, 2, 2672–2680, 2014.
30. The generator. https://developers.google.com/machine-learning/gan/generator.
31. The discriminator. https://developers.google.com/machine-learning/gan/discreminator.
32. Maudet, N., Parsons, S., Rahwan, I., Argumentation in multi-agent systems: Context and recent developments. *International Workshop on Argumentation in Multi-Agent Systems*, 2006.
33. Chow, H.K.H. and Siu, W., An argumentation-oriented multi-agent system for automating the freight planning process. *Expert Syst. Appl.*, Elsevier, 40, 3858–3871, 2013.
34. Panisson, A.R. and Meneguzzi, F., Towards practical argumentation-based dialogues in multi-agent systems. *International Conference on Web Intelligence and Intelligent Agent Technology*, IEEE Xplore, 2015.
35. Namin, S.T., Brown, T.B., Borevitz, J.O., Deep phenotyping: Deep learning for temporal phenotype/genotype classification. *Plant Methods*, Springer Nature, 14, 1–22, 2018.
36. Tsaftaris, S., Minervini, M., Scharr, H., Machine learning for plant phenotyping needs image processing. *Trends Plant Sci.* Elsevier, 21, 989–991, 2016.
37. Singh, A.K. and Ganapathysubramanian, B., Deep learning for plant stress phenotyping: Trends and future perspectives. *Trends Plant Sci.* Science Direct, 23, 883–898, 2018.
38. Weiden, M., Deepak, K., Keegan, M., Electroencephalographic detection of visual saliency of motion towards a practical brain-computer interface for video analysis. *ACM International Conference on Multimodal Interaction*, 2012.
39. Schreiber, A., Saliency maps for deep learning part 1: Vanilla gradient, 2019. https://medium.com/@thelastalias/saliency-maps-for-deep-learning-part-1-vanilla-gradient-1d0665de3284.
40. What is saliency map, 2000. https://www.geeksforgeeks.org/what-is-saliency-map.

## 4

Web Service Composition Using an AI Planning Technique

Lalit Purohit[1]* and Satyendra Singh Chouhan[2]

[1]Shri G. S. Institute of Tech & Science, Indore, India
[2]Dept. of Computer Engineering, Malviya National Institute of Technology (MNIT), Jaipur, India

Abstract

The concept of web service has become an emerging paradigm with the fast development of the Internet and number of applications increasing over the Web. It provides another way to distributed computing by the interoperability between the heterogeneous applications regardless of the implementation language and platform. Each web service offers functionality of its own. If a single service is not sufficient to offer the required functionality, multiple web services offering different functionalities are threaded together to offer desired functionality by the end user. With the increase in growth of the web services and web service based applications from various organizations, clustering of web services is desired to enable efficient web services searching. This leads to improving the performance of the overall composition process. The composition of services involves efficient and effective arrangement of services to complete the given customized tasks as per the needs of the end user. Nowadays, user's needs are changing from time to time. To deal with the dynamically changing requirements from the end user, a need of dynamic composition of web services arises. In this work, the clustering process has been employed for reduction in the search space and AI planning based technique is used to deal with the problem of dynamic composition of web services. To achieve dynamic and automatic composition, a plan based on the user's request is to be generated that describes the execution sequence of web services. The AI planning is helpful in achieving this objective. Planning is defined as a process of finding a sequence of actions (plan) such that if an agent performs the plan on the given initial state, it will achieve the goal state. By considering web service

Corresponding author: purohit.lalit@gmail.com

Anamika Ahirwar, Piyush Kumar Shukla, Manish Shrivastava, Priti Maheshwary and Bhupesh Gour (eds.) Innovative Engineering with AI Applications, (65–82) © 2023 Scrivener Publishing LLC

composition as a planning problem, the web services are the task/functionality provided and the composition as a goal.

Keywords: Artificial intelligence planning, web services, dynamic web service composition, clustering

4.1 Introduction

In the present scenario, a large number of service providers are offering Web Services over the Internet. The enterprise business applications are taking advantage of these services and offering specific services to the end users. The web services are software components with the property of loose coupling, modular, self-described, and are interoperable. Over the Web these components can be easily published, discovered, and invoked by other software components [1]. The applications available over the Web take the advantage of available web services to easily exchange the data with other web applications. This is primarily due to the basic nature of web services of being programming language and platform independent. This has motivated many enterprises to publish their business models as service(s) and can be accessed over the Web [2]. The web services are designed with a goal to offer a specific service to the end user. The primary advantage of web service is that they are reusable i.e. can be used multiple times by any software component. A web service offers limited functionality on its own. However, if a single web service is not able to fulfill the requirements of the application/end user, multiple such web services can be combined together. This process of aggregating various web services together to offer a value added service to the application is termed as Web Service Composition [3].

A large number of web services available over the Web. For business-to-business interaction, the potential of web services can only be realized when many services and businesses are composed together and executed to form a value added composite service [3]. It also enables customers to compose services automatically and on demand. For example, in the travel domain, a tour planning web service can be obtained by integrating a book flight web service, hotel booking service, cab booking service, travel insurance service, payment gateway web service, etc., together.

Web service compositions are of two types – (I) Static composition (II) Dynamic composition. These two types of compositions are defined based on time of composition of web services. The composition is known as static when the task of composition is performed offline i.e. before the start of execution of composite web service. The dynamic composition of web services is achieved when the order of web service execution is determined dynamically (at run time) and automatically. The dynamic composition is highly flexible and is most suitable for a continuously growing web repository [2]. However, the task of composing web services dynamically is a challenging task and this chapter focuses on this approach of composition.

In today's times, the Web environment has become dynamic in nature with the drastic increase in the number of services and constant updates. The user's goals might change during the run time due to these ongoing updates in the web service environment. Then, the composition should adapt to these changes and make decisions according to the up to date information. The task of effective and efficient arrangement of web services according to the changing requirements from the end user introduces the need for dynamic web service composition. Many solutions are available from existing state-of-the-art for web service composition. Figure 4.1 represents a broad categorization of various approaches used in the past to efficiently achieve web service composition.

The existing techniques of composition are aggregating the web services with a static approach [4]. In the static composition, a pre-evaluated composition plan is generated offline. Whenever the end user requests for

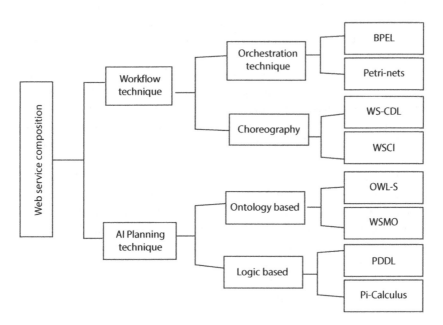

Figure 4.1 Categorization of web service composition techniques.

composite service, the pre-computed composition plan is executed. The composition plan execution remains the same for each end user request. But, many times there is a need to change the plan of composition as per the request of the end user. In such cases, web services are to be composed dynamically. The dynamic composition of web service offers flexibility to the end user in terms of generating output as per the input provided.

For the composition process, a huge repository of web services has to be searched for choosing the required web services. While finding the services relevant to the user's requested query, one needs to check each and every web service present in the huge search space. To deal with this huge task, a clustering approach is applied before applying the composition. The clustering approach help in reducing the workload by not matching each web service with the requested query [5–7]. The dynamic web service composition mainly involves arrangement or ordering of tasks automatically and dynamically to fulfill the user's goal. A plan of web services needs to be generated to achieve the required composite service as output. Thus, the problem of service composition can be modeled as a planning problem.

The primary objective here is to obtain the composition which is able to adapt itself with modifications in customer's requirement and with minimal user intervention. Since, static approaches are suitable for the process in which the business partners are fixed and the functionalities are unlikely to get modified in the short term. Therefore, to overcome this problem we perform the dynamic composition of web services. The clustering technique used in the proposed approach improves the performance of the composition process. This can be observed by the fact that the web services are large in number and on applying clustering, the search of web services for composition tasks is performed on the clusters and not on each and every web service. The planning task involved in the composition process also aims to generate the concurrent plan but not a predefined sequence of tasks [8, 9].

In this chapter, we discuss web service composition using AI planning techniques. First, we present the background information that contains formal definitions and planning related terminologies. It also discusses the service composition as AI planning with a suitable example (Section 4.2). In Section 4.3, we discuss the methodology for web service composition using AI planning. Next we present the performance evaluation of the proposed methodology with respect to a case study in Section 4.4. Conclusions and possible future directions are given in Section 4.5.

4.2   Background

This Section gives a brief introduction to Artificial Intelligence (AI), AI planning, formal definitions related to AI planning and formal introduction of web service composition problems as AI planning problems.

4.2.1   Introduction to AI

Artificial Intelligence (AI) is the study of automated machines or devices with the capability of automatic adoption with respect to changing environments. The machines or devices can discern the external environment and take more effective actions to maximize the chances of successfully achieving the goal. A typical AI based system is shown in Figure 4.2. Any typical AI system has a rule base to take action. The feedback obtained by accessing external environment data is used by AI systems to improve the rule base. This further improves the action taken and decisions made by the AI system [10].

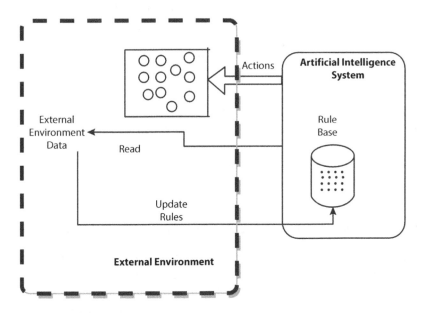

Figure 4.2 Artificial intelligence system.

4.2.2   AI Planning

AI Agents are robots or automatic programs with the capability of interacting with each other and other resources over the Web. The way an artificial agent acts in an environment is called its behavior. The reasoning side of action is known as planning and it is an important ingredient of rational behavior of an agent [9]. The planning problem in AI is considered as decision making accomplished by an intelligent agent [11, 12]. Agents are usually robots or computer programs which are trying to achieve some goal. Planning comes before the acting and in a fully observable environment planning can be done offline and beforehand. Planning is one of the key research areas in AI. The inputs to a planning problem are: Planning has found various real-world applications in robotics [13], games [14], logistics [15], search and exploration, military operations, and web services [15]. The notations and formal definitions are as follows.

Definition 1 (*Plan*) Given a set of action 'A', a plan is represented by a sequence of actions of 'A'. Formally, if 'P' represents the plan then where each $a_i \in A$, is a transition from a state in S to any other state in S, for any $s \in S$. Moreover, for, P=*null*, and otherwise. P holding the *null* value represents the empty plan.

Definition 2 (Action) An action "a" can be defined as a mapping from and 'A' represents the set of actions by any agent such that $a \in A$. An agent can build a plan from the set of actions 'A'. Each of the action has associated precondition (P) and effect (E). Preconditions are necessary conditions for executing an action. Effects are the conditions (facts/fluents) that will be true after executing the action.

Definition 3 (*Planning problem*) In AI domain, a planning problem is represented as - where set of fluents (also called predicates) is symbolized as F, I is the initial state (a subset of predicates that are true), set of actions *are denoted by* 'A', and goal state *as* 'G' (a subset of predicates that are desired to be true).

4.2.3   AI Planning for Effective Composition of Web Services

The Web Service composition problem is considered as a planning problem. The dynamic composition method is required for generating the plan automatically. Such methods can be accomplished using AI planning. AI planning and service composition is much similar. The problem is to determine a flow of actions which leads to the desired goal upon execution and this is common in both. AI planning focuses on the preconditions and effects of the actions and the same goes with service composition [8].

Before applying composition, web service clustering is applied as it helps in pre-processing required before the composition process. Clustering Technique is applied for reducing the search space while searching for web services which are needed for composition [16–18]. It helps in minimizing the total number of services available for finding the services relevant to a user's query. A suitable example is given below.

Example 1. (*The traveling domain* [19]) A researcher is required to travel to another city to present a research paper in an international conference. She needs to plan a tour using a web service based system which satisfies all the constraints such as cost, time, dates, preference of a particular hotel type, airlines, etc. For this purpose, various web services from the travel domains are available such as air tickets booking, accommodation service, cab booking service, insurance service, etc. These web services can be integrated/composed together in such a manner that all the end user constraints are also satisfied by the tour planning web service. This can be done by modeling web service composition problems as an AI planning problem. In this case, for the given request from the application/end user, 'I' represents the initial states and 'G' denotes the goal states. The available services are represented as the set 'A'.

4.3 Proposed Methodology for AI Planning-Based Composition of Web Services

The proposed approach for achieving web service composition using AI planning is presented in Figure 4.3. The actor is the end user/application program to request service. Candidate web services are assumed to be available and are accessible from the repository. Each step in the proposed approach is discussed in detail.

4.3.1 Clustering Web Services

The task of grouping the objects such that the more similar ones are in the same group (i.e. cluster) and less similar ones are in other groups. Clustering of web services can be performed by using QoS parameters. For clustering web services, Partition based Clustering (such as K-means and Self Organizing Feature Maps (SOM)), and Model based Clustering are popular techniques. In this work, K-Means clustering is used to perform clustering of web services. K-means needs the cluster number (K) and the selection of centroids [7]. The points (Web services in this case) which are nearest to the centroids are placed in the same cluster. To measure the

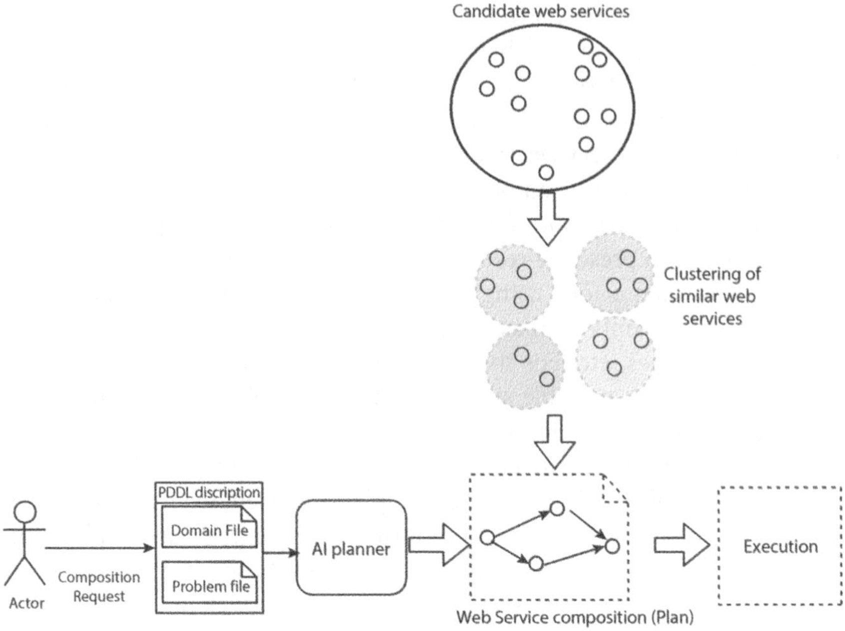

Figure 4.3 Overview of the proposed solution approach.

distance between points and centroids, Euclidean distance is used. The web services in multi-dimensional space are represented using various associated QoS parameters. The Euclidean distance among web services is obtained by using QoS parameters. Based on the Euclidean distance values and 'K', clusters of web services are formed [5].

The web services are organized in such a way that web services with similar QoS parameter values are in a cluster. When the request of the desired web service from the end user is made, the web services with similar QoS parameter values can be found in a cluster. With this, the web services can be accessed quickly. As the number of web services is growing rapidly in the repositories, it becomes a challenge to find a web service of interest. Clustering helps in categorizing the web services which allow consumers to find related services easily.

4.3.2 OWL-S: Semantic Markup for Web Services (*For Composition Request*)

OWL-S is the ontologically descriptive language to descriptive semantic web services. It was developed to describe services using Web Ontology

Language (OWL). The OWL-S enables automatic discovery, compose, invoke and monitor a particular web service offering service. The web services can be described in a way amenable to planning. It consists of a service profile, process model and groundings. It describes the inputs, outputs, preconditions, and effects. Inputs are input needed by the web service, outputs are output produced by the web service, and Preconditions are the logical conditions which should be satisfied before the service begins its execution. Effects are the changes brought in the database/files/associated resource/etc., after the execution of the web service. In OWL-S, operations can be represented as processes. The web services are either atomic process, composite process or simple process. In this work an AI planner is used for web service composition. OWL-S representation is transformed into a PDDL (Planning Domain Description Language) description. PDDL is widely used as an input description language for AI planners.

4.3.3   PDDL: Planning Domain Description Language

To formally describe a planning problem, PDDL is the standard encoding language. It is supported by almost every planner. Planning domain and problem are specified using PDDL and given as input to the planner. Component of PDDL language are;

- Objects: Things in the domain which will be used.
- Predicates: Properties of objects that can be false or true.
- Initial state
- Goal state
- Actions/Operators: through which we can change the state of the system.

PDDL is mainly based on the STRIPS [20] syntax and also represents the actions, using pre-conditions, post-conditions and the effects. Here, the action's applicability is represented using pre-conditions i.e., a particular action is applicable on a state if and only if preconditions are satisfied.
Planning task is generally described in two separate PDDL files.

1. A domain file for specifying predicate and actions
2. A problem file for specifying objects, initial state, and goal state

The separation of domain and problem description is useful because we can have multiple problem files with the same domain file. The domain file contains the types of objects, describes a set of predicates and actions each has some parameters, a pre-condition (P) and effect (E). From the web service composition perspective, each action can be assumed to be a web service. Thus, domain files consist of all the web services offered in the domain. The problem files consist of the initial state, user's query, and the goal state of the problem.

Given below an example of domain and problem definition:

Domain	Problem
(define (domain travel)	(define (problem travel-1))
(:requirements :strips)	(:domain travel)
(:predicates	(:objects p1-person
(road ?from ?to)	home oce- location
(person ?p)	car bus- vehicle)
(vehicle ?v)	(:init (at p1 home) (road home office))
(at ?thing ?place)	(:goal (at p1 office))
(travel ?p ?v))	
(:action goto	
:parameters (?p ?from ?to)	
:precondition (and (road ?from ?to)	
(at ?p ?from) (not (?from ?to))	
(person ?p))	
:effect (and (at ?p ?to) (not (at ?p	
?from))))	

In the above example, "road" is a route from one place(?from) to another(?to). The predicate "at" tells that something (?thing) is present on place(?place). Other predicates like "person" is for any person and "vehicle" is for car, bike etc. The predicate "travel" shows that a person(?p) travels by vehicle(?v). The action "goto" means that a person needs to go from a place(?from) to another(?to). The problem file consists of a set of objects and description of initial and goal states. The propositions listed in the initial state description are true and the one's which are not present are assumed as false. The goal is a logical expression similar to the precondition and it is a conjunction of positive propositions.

In the problem part (example), "p1", "home", "oce", "car", "bus" are all objects of the problem file. In the initial state, person 'p1' is present at home and there is a road from home to office. The goal of the problem is that person 'p1' is at the office.

4.3.4   AI Planner

The presented methodology uses Blackbox AI planning system for planning [21]. The blackbox planner uses two approaches: planning as satisfiability and planning as graph. First, Blackbox converts the web service composition problem, described in PDDL, into a Boolean satisfiability problem. Next, it solves using various satisfiability approaches that are specified during execution. The front-end of the planner uses the graph plan system [22]. The Graph plan generates a planning graph. Graph plan is a compact structure where the encoding of all possible plans is done up to a predefined length. Next, the search process is guided by planning graph. Planning graph approach take a mid-path in between state-space search based and partial order planning (POP) techniques and explore the search space defined by the planning graph. The planning graph structure has been an influencing approach in state-based heuristic planning. In satisfiability based approach, a planning problem is converted into a propositional satisfiability (SAT) problem. The problem is represented as a propositional logic formula and then gives as an input to a SAT solver. SAT solver solves it by determining that there existing a model for the propositional logic formula or not.

Blackbox planner provides a lot of flexibility in such a way that we can use WALKSET for 30 seconds and if it fails, then can use SATZ for 900 seconds. Due to this, it is capable of solving a wide range of problems efficiently.

Mapping to Web Service Composition. The plan generated by the Blackbox planner is used and web services are mapped according to that plan. Hence, the web service composition is achieved.

4.3.5   Flowchart of Proposed Approach

The process of composition starts with the input of WSDL documents. These documents are parsed so as to obtain the feature that is 'web service name' for further process. In the next step the feature is used for the purpose of similarity calculation of web services. With the help of this calculation, a similarity score gets generated. K-means clustering techniques are applied on the web services similarity scores. After this, the web services are chosen for the process of composing the PDDL files. These PDDL files are fed as input to the AI planner and in the end the plan gets generated. The plan is then mapped to the web services and the process of composition gets completed. Figure 4.4 shows the flowchart of the proposed approach.

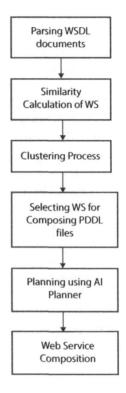

Figure 4.4 Flowchart.

4.4 Implementation Details

The implementation work is performed in various steps which include parsing of WSDL files, similarity calculation between web services, applying clustering process over the web services, PDDL les generation, plan generation and lastly the composition of web services. The presented approach is implemented using JAVA language. All the experiments were performed using Intel Core i7-6300 2.7 GHz with 8 GB RAM. Blackbox planner is used for planning purposes.

4.4.1 Domain Used

We use the travel domain as a case study for the implementation of the presented approach. The domain and problem description is as given below. It is defined in terms of different entities such as person, locations etc. The example travel domain has several locations such as restaurant, ATM, airport, national park, hotel, beach, and researcher's home. The domain has the following actions:

-gotohotel(p,x,y) : person 'p' goes from location 'x'to hotel 'y'

-gotohome(p,x,y) : 'p'goes from any location 'x'to researcher's home 'y'

-gotorestro(p,x,y) :'p' goes from any location 'x' to restaurant 'y'

-gotoatm(p,x,y) : 'p' goes from any location 'x' to atm 'y'

-gotobeach(p,x,y) :'p' goes from any location 'x'to hotel 'y'

-gotopark(p,x,y) :'p' goes from any location 'x' to hotel 'y'

-orderfood(p,x) : 'p' orders food at location 'x'

-withdrawmoney(p,x) : person 'p' withdraws money at location 'x'

Based on the above description of the domain, problem instances described in the next section are used.

4.4.2   Case Studies on AI Planning

In this section, two case studies are described which leads to two different execution sequences.

Case Study 1
A student P (referred as person) is conducting research work. She is willing to visit another city to meet another researcher. The visit is to be planned so that she can explore the knowledge and research field by interacting with the researcher by duly considering the mentioned constraints. Following sequence of actions (inputs) are considered to plan a tour.

The visit to another city is to be planned by flight. From the airport of the destination city, she wants to go to the hotel of her choice using a cab. After reaching the hotel, she will immediately get ready to visit the researcher at home by 11 AM. By 1:00 PM, her meeting with the researcher will be finished. She will leave the researcher's home to have lunch at the restaurant. Her return flight is scheduled at 11 PM on the same day, thus, for the remaining time she would like to explore various tourist spots across the city. To visit various spots of interest around the city, firstly an ATM close to the restaurant for withdrawing some money is to be visited. Since she likes water-sports, a nearby beach is also to be visited. A famous national park in the city for sightseeing is also to be visited at last, in the evening. By observing the available inputs, the initial states and goal states, a possible plan is generated as follows.

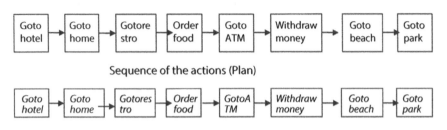

Sequence of the actions (Plan)

Sequence of the actions (Plan)

Similarly case 2 with different scenario can be taken as:

Case Study 2: A student (referred as person P) is doing research work. She wants to visit another city to meet another researcher. The visit is to be planned so that she can explore the knowledge and research field by interacting with the researcher by duly considering the mentioned constraints. Following sequence of actions (inputs) are considered to plan a tour.

The visit to another city is to be planned by flight. From the airport of the destination city, she wants to go to the hotel of her choice using a cab. Her meeting with the researcher is scheduled in the evening at 8:30 P.M. Meanwhile, after reaching the hotel at 9:00 AM, she decided to visit various famous places of interest across the city after getting ready. To visit various places of interest around the city, firstly an ATM close to the restaurant for withdrawing some money is to be visited. Since she likes water sports, a nearby beach is also to be visited. A famous national park in the city with a beautiful sun set view is also to be visited at last, in the evening. Afterwards, she visited the researcher at home by 7:00PM. Afterwards, she went to the restaurant to have dinner.

4.4.2.1 Experiments and Results on Case 1 and Case 2

For experimental purposes, we changed the requirements of the user in each case by changing the initial state, goal states and the actions to be performed during the traveling of the person. Also, in each case, we have experimented by increasing the number of each instance in the problem. For example, the problem instance is defined as (P, A, H, RH, R, AL, B, NP) where 'P denotes person, A is airport, H is hotel, RH is home of researcher,

R represents restaurant, *AL* is the location of ATM, *B* is beach and *NP* is national park. While performing the experiments, we have increased the number of instances for each of *P, A, H, RH, R, AL, B,* and *NP*. The problem instances are denoted by 1 to 6. For each of the problem instances, the experiments are repeatedly performed '*n*' times and reported the average results for each metrics. The results show the various performance metrics of Blackbox planner such as: planning time, total elapsed time, Nodes created (in the graph created by Blackbox planner), No. of grounded action variables, Total no. of variables, no of actions in the plan.

The results of experiments performed by using Blackbox for the Travel domain are presented in Figure 4.5. It can be observed from the experiment that the numbers of objects are increasing with the increasing number of combinations. In order to obtain the results, each combination on the planner is executed 20 times and then averaged. In Figure 4.5, the first figure shows the average time taken for each case. Second figure represents the total number of nodes created by Blackbox planning in the planning graph. This metric is associated with the size of the graph and it is directly proportional to memory use in the system. Fourth figure shows the number

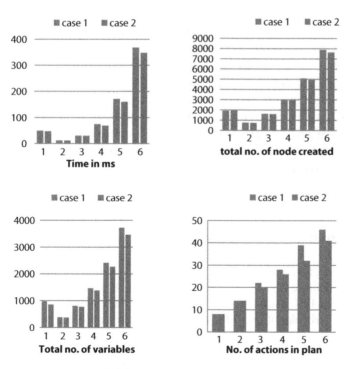

Figure 4.5 Experimental results of Blackbox planner with respect to various metrics.

of actions in a plan generated by the Blackbox planner. In summary we can observe that by increasing the number of instances such that *A, H, RH, R, AL, B,* and *NP* the complexity of the proposed approach increases. Moreover, from the experimental analysis we observe that the proposed approach is effective in case of small size problems.

4.5   Conclusions and Future Directions

In this chapter, we reviewed the research being done previously in dynamic web service composition and after knowing the various techniques and work done. We performed the project in two steps: first to have an effective and efficient selection of web services based on the user's query, and a concept of clustering is applied in this step. Clustering helps in reducing the efforts required to search for the web services in the huge repository. K-means Clustering is used to prune the dataset and reduce the search space of the repository. After getting the clusters we created the scenario according to the user's query and in the next step, we performed the overall web service composition. In the second phase we have performed experimental evaluation by using some domains available such as travel, food, geography and using them to obtain the PDDL domain and problem files. For an example we took a travel scenario domain description and created the PDDL files of this domain problem. We worked on various problem instances of the different case studies. We attempted to work on Blackbox planner which mainly uses planning as satisfiability and planning as graph. The PDDL domain and problem files were given as input to the Blackbox planner. We also noted the resultant plan generated and various other variations in the output when given different problem instances. In future we would like to see the applicability of other state-of-the-art planners for dynamic web service decomposition.

References

1. Hwang, S.Y., Hsu, C.C., Lee, C.H., Service selection for web services with probabilistic QoS. *IEEE Trans. Serv. Comput.*, 8, 3, 467–480, 2015.
2. Cui, L., Li, J., Zheng, Y., A dynamic web service composition method based on viterbi algorithm. *IEEE 19th International Conference on Web Services*, 2012.
3. Purohit, L. and Kumar, S., A classification based web service selection approach. *IEEE Trans. Serv. Comput.*, 14, 2, 315–328, 2021.

4. Lemos, A.L., Daniel, F., Benatallah, B., Web service composition: A survey of techniques and tools. *ACM Comput. Surv. (CSUR)*, 48, 3, 1–41, 20152015.

5. Ratnakar, A., Sharma, P., Gupta, S., Purohit, L., Web service clustering on the basis of QoS parameters. *2019 1st International Conference on Artificial Intelligence and Data Sciences (AiDAS)*, Ipoh, Perak, Malaysia, pp. 12–17, 2019.

6. Purohit, L. and Kumar, S., Clustering based approach for web service selection using skyline computation. *IEEE International Conference on Web Services (ICWS)*, Milan, Italy, pp. 260–264, 2019.

7. Kumar, S. and Purohit, L., *Exploring K-Means Clustering and Skyline for Web Service Selection*, pp. 603–607, 2016.

8. Kuzu, M. and Cicekli, N.K., Dynamic planning approach to automated web service composition. *Appl. Intell.*, 36, 1, 1–28, 2010.

9. Ghallab, M., Nau, D., Traverso, P., *Automated Planning: Theory and Practice*, Elsevier, Amsterdam, Netherlands, 2004.

10. Ertel, W., *Introduction to Artificial Intelligence*, 2nd ed., Springer, Cham, Switzerland, 2017.

11. Wooldridge, M., *An Introduction to Multiagent Systems*, John Wiley & Sons, West Sussex, England, 2009.

12. Chouhan, S.S. and Niyogi, R., Multi-agent planning with collaborative actions, in: *Australasian Joint Conference on Artificial Intelligence*, pp. 609–620, 2016.

13. Parker, L.E., Distributed intelligence: Overview of the field and its application in multi-robot systems. *J. Phys. Agents*, 2, 1, 5–14, 2008.

14. Brafman, R., II, Domshlak, C., Engel, Y., Tennenholtz, M., Planning games, in: *International Joint Conference on Artificial Intelligence (IJCAI)*, pp. 73–78, 2009.

15. Cirillo, M., Pecora, F., Andreasson, H., Uras, T., Koenig, S., Integrated motion planning and coordination for industrial vehicles, in: *Proceedings of the 24th International Conference on Automated Planning and Scheduling (ICAPS)*, vol. 2126, 2014.

16. Chouhan, S.S. and Niyogi, R., MAPJA: Multi-agent planning with joint actions. *Appl. Intell.*, 47, 4, 1044–1058, 2017.

17. Zheng, K., Xiong, H., Cui, Y., Chen, J., Han, L., User clustering based web service discovery, in: *Proceedings of International Conference on Internet Computing for Science and Engineering*, pp. 276–279, April 2012.

18. Peer, J., *Web Service Composition as AI Planning: A Survey*, pp. 1–63, University of St. Gallen, Switzerland, 2005.

19. Purohit, L. and Kumar, S., Web services in the internet of things and smart cities: A case study on classification techniques. *IEEE Consum. Electron. Mag.*, 8, 2, 39–43, March 2019.

20. Strips: A new approach to the application of theorem proving to problem solving. *Artif. Intell.*, 2, 3, 189–208, 1971.

21. Blackbox: A new approach to the application of theorem proving to problem solving, in: *Workshop on Planning as Combinatorial Search (AIPS98)*, vol. 58260, pp. 58–60, 1998.
22. Blum, A.L. and Furst, M.L., Fast planning through planning graph analysis. *Artif. Intell.*, 90, 1, 281–300, 1997.

## 5

Artificial Intelligence in Agricultural Engineering

Ashwini A. Waoo[1], Jyoti Pandey[2] and Akhilesh A. Waoo[3]*

[1]Department of Biotechnology, AKS University, Satna, MP, India
[2]Department of Agriculture, AKS University, Satna, MP, India
[3]Department of CS/IT, AKS University, Satna, MP, India

Abstract

Agriculture plays a significant role in the sector of the economy. Computerization in agriculture is the most important concern and an emerging subject across the world. The population is growing exponentially and with this increase, the demand for food and employment is also increasing. The conventional methods which were utilized by the farmers were not enough to complete these requirements. Thus, computerized automated methods were introduced. These new methods assure the food requirements and also provided many employment opportunities to billions of people.

Artificial Intelligence (AI) involves computer science in agriculture and resulted in an agricultural revolution. This type of technology has played a major role in the security of crop yield from various factors like climate changes, growth of population, issues in employment, and the security of food. The main concern of this chapter is to compile the various applications of Artificial intelligence in agriculture as irrigation, weeding, spraying with sensors, and other means embedded in robots and drones. These technologies are very valuable for the conservation of water as well as to reduce the excessive use of pesticides, herbicides, in maintaining soil fertility, it also helps in the efficient use of manpower and promote productivity and also improve quality.

Keywords: Artificial intelligence, climate change, impact of AI in agriculture, applications of AI

Corresponding author: akhileshwaoo@gmail.com

Anamika Ahirwar, Piyush Kumar Shukla, Manish Shrivastava, Priti Maheshwary and Bhupesh Gour (eds.) Innovative Engineering with AI Applications, (83–100) © 2023 Scrivener Publishing LLC

5.1 Introduction

Artificial intelligence is changing various things in our life; including the mode in which our food is produced. Technologies like machine learning, image identification, and analytical modeling are being ready to apply in industries related to agriculture and to boost productivity and effectiveness. These approaches could be significant steps in the effort to produce more food for an increasing global population by serving farmers, decreasing chemical inputs, identifying diseases in advance, solving the problem of labor shortages, and managing all weather conditions with climate change. Artificial agriculture has two types of direction (Figure 5.1) given below-

- Systems that think like humans
  - o The Cognitive modeling
  - o Replicates human thought processes
  - o Make the same decisions as humans
  - o Uses purely logical reasoning
- Systems that act like humans
  - o The natural language processing for communication with human
  - o Knowledge representation to store information effectively and efficiently
  - o The automated reasoning to retrieve and answer questions using the stored information
  - o Machine learning to adapt to new circumstances
  - o The computer vision to perceive objects
  - o The robotics to move objects

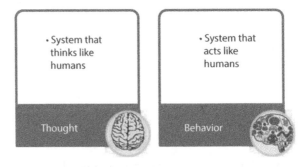

Figure 5.1 Approaches to artificial intelligence.

The world's population is understood to be nearly 10 billion by 2050, boosting agricultural order in a condition of humble financial progress by somewhere in the range of 50 percent contrasted with 2013 [1]. At present, ~37.7% of the total land surface is useful for crop production. From employment creation to involvement in National Income, agriculture is very important. It is contributing an extensive part to the economic success of the developed nations and is playing a vigorous part in the economy of the developing countries as well. The growth of agriculture has resulted in a significant enhancement in the per-capita earnings of the rural community [2].

Development in the field of the agricultural area will progress the rural development, further leading in the direction of rural transformation and finally resulting in the transformation based on structure [3, 4]. Among the foundation of new technology, there has been observed an impressive transformation in various industries across the world [5]. Unexpectedly, agriculture, although being the most digitized, has seen energy for the progress and commercialization of agricultural technologies.

Artificial Intelligence (AI) has begun to play a most important role in daily life, extending our perceptions and capability to modify the environment around us [6–8]. Plessen, (2019) gave a perfect method for harvest with planning based on the pairing of crop assignment with vehicle direction-finding is presented [9].

Artificial Intelligence makes computers able to think. Automated computerization of activities and connections with human thinking, like decision-making, learning, etc. The art of creating machines that perform functions that necessitate intelligence when performed by people.

Artificial Intelligence has four major components as shown in Figure 5.2:

- Data: Artificial intelligence involves Data, it is defined as symbols that represent properties of objects, events, and their environment.
- Information: Data gives information, it is a message that contains related meaning, implication, or input for a decision and/or action.
- Knowledge: It is the (1) cognition or recognition (know-what), (2) capacity to act, and (3) understanding (know-why) that resides or is contained within the mind or in the brain.
- Intelligence: It requires the ability to sense the environment, make decisions, and control the action.

Figure 5.2 Components of artificial intelligence.

5.2   Artificial Intelligence in Agriculture

In the agricultural field, AI is an advanced technology for the progress of farmers. Artificial intelligence based on pieces of equipment and many machines has taken the agriculture system to a different level. This technology has very important for better crop production and enhanced real-time monitoring, observation, harvesting, processing, and marketing. The newest technologies of computerized systems by using agricultural robots and drones have made an unbelievable contribution in all agro-based areas. Different hi-technical computer-based automated systems are designed to confirmation of different important parameters like the detection of weeds, detection of yield and crop quality, and other different techniques [10].

Nowadays agriculture growing up with advanced techniques for smart work which means traditional farming to Modern farming as shown in Figure 5.3. In contrast to traditional farming, Modern farming is based on Automated machines, given by Artificial intelligence.

The low output-to-input ratio points to the enormous systemic flaws in India's agronomy that bring severe hardship to farmers and agricultural laborers, who bear the impact of rising input costs, falling productivity, climate change, poor market access, technological stagnation, and so on. Although the agricultural predicament in India is required to be addressed at various levels, this article discusses the role of technology – in particular,

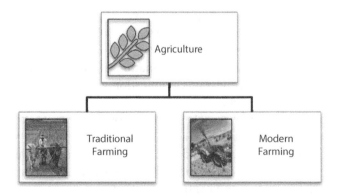

Figure 5.3 Agricultural technologies.

artificial intelligence (AI) in rising agricultural output, and therefore, farmer incomes in India. Artificial Intelligence can develop agricultural productivity by recognizing diseases in different plants and doing pest management. with around 98% accuracy. Also, AI gives growers a weapon against cereal-hungry bugs. Sensors monitor the fruit's growth in the direction of perfect ripeness, the light adjusting to speed up or slow the rapidity of maturation, this kind of farming requires substantial processing power.

It is used in *several* industries in the world today; finance, transport, healthcare and now agriculture, farmers can monitor the well-being of their crops or the progress of animals without any demand of going to the farm, and agriculture is undergoing a fundamental transformation. Now a day, development in artificial intelligence technology is less labor-intensive and more efficient.

The powered solution will improve the quality and make the sure faster market for crops. Agriculture plays a major role in both, industries and the organization of the economy. But the change in climate, population growth, and security of food are the concerns that have propelled the industry into looking for innovative approaches for improvement of crop yield. Thus, artificial intelligence is increasingly emerging as part of the industry's evolution of technology.

Artificial intelligence provides many sources for data collection such as temperature, precipitation, wind, speed, and radiation of solar, with comparisons to historical values on the agricultural earth Though artificial intelligence won't eliminate the job of farmers (Figure 5.4), it will observe the progress and which provide them more efficient to produce, harvest and sell off essential crops

Fundamentally, Artificial intelligence in the agriculture field is segmented into robotics, crop management, and husbandry of the animal. It is planned to build farming easier, more accurately, more valuable, and

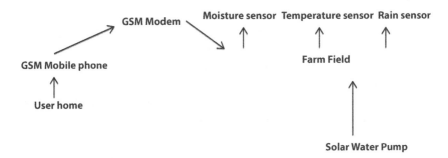

Figure 5.4 Soil/moisture/temperature analysis in smart agriculture.

more productive use for the growth of farmers. It is predicted that AI and associated farm services can impact 70 million Indian farmers by 2020, thus adding US$ 9 billion to farmer incomes. In 2017, the global AI in the agriculture market size was US$ 240 million, and is possible to reach US$ 1.1 billion by 2025 [11]. Furthermore, issues for example population growth, climate change, and security of food demand innovative ways to improve crop yield and agriculture business by livestock's using traditional farming to modern farming techniques.

It's referring to the model of human intelligence technology i.e., programmed to assume like humans and copy their actions. The term may apply to any instrument that exhibits traits connected with the mind of humans for knowledge and problem-solving. Artificial intelligence can take measures that have the best possibility of achieving a specific goal.

Artificial intelligence is based on the human intelligence principle. It can be defined that, a machine that can without any problems mimic it and complete tasks, from the very simple to those that are still more complex. The goals of artificial intelligence consist of learning, reasoning, and perception.

5.2.1   AI Startups in Agriculture

AI was founded in 2014. This Israeli introduction has revolutionized agriculture farming. AI has developed a solution based on cloud-based obtainable data like soil/water sensors, images of aerial, etc. for farmers. This data is then combined with in-field devices that make sense of it all. These devices are used in greenhouses or fields. It is powered by types of sensors and many technologies like computer vision. The input from these sensors is used to find a correlation between different data labels and build predictions.

Blue River Technology, is founded in 2011. This is based on a California startup that combines artificial intelligence, the vision of the computer, and robotics to make next-generation agriculture tools that reduce chemicals' effect and saves costs. Computer vision is used for the identification of the individual plant, and how to treat these individual plants and robotics enables the smart machinery to get action.

Farm Bot, it founded in 2011. This company has to take accurate farming to a different level by enabling environmental awareness with precision farming technology. The product, Farm Bot comes at a price and helps the owner to do end-to-end farming methods. Range of seed plantation, the detection of weed, testing of soil, and plants watering, all work done by physical Bot used with an open-source software system.

5.2.2   Challenges in AI Adoption

Although Artificial Intelligence offers opportunities for applications in the agriculture field, there is a lack of awareness of hi-tech machine learning solutions on farms across most parts of the world. The revelation of farming to outer factors like the condition weather, the condition of the soil, and the presence of pests is quite a lot. AI systems also require a lot of data from machines to make accurate predictions. In the case of agricultural land, although data can be gathered easily, temporary data is hard to get. For example, crop-specific data can be obtained only once in one year when the crops are growing continuously. This is only one reason. AI offers a lot of uses in agronomic products like seeds, fertilizer, and pesticides in-field accurate solutions.

5.2.3   Stunning Discoveries of AI

Agriculture is in the central zone of the world's economy. Thousands of years have passed since people first started to work in the land, and now it is a multimillion-dollar industry. At the same time, current global trends have a direct influence on the branch. The protection of the environment, growing population, and healthy food quality need many tools than different fertilizers and combined harvesters are recent issues in the world. The following are some key discoveries of AI in the agricultural field.

5.2.3.1   Precision Technology to Sow Seeds

In the present time, when farmers struggle to feed as many people as possible, they can't permit sowing seeds by the random method in the ground. A single seed is responsible for yielding a lot if planted in the exact place. Everybody can avoid both methods overlapping and skipping a lot of space when planting or protecting crops.

The modern software system can also spread the seed within the place wherever it grows the best form, predict weather conditions, and connect with large data. Thus, human information is mixed with the machine mind to grow plants most effectively.

5.2.3.2   Robots for Harvesting

Harvesting is the foremost harassing and monotonous job. Employees get tired and less productive. Robots, on the opposite hand, without exhaustion can work for the maximum time. Manufacturers build new machines according to the product type. For instance, Harvest crop was determined to focus on strawberries and to apply machine vision in agriculture. Nowadays you cannot pick only strawberries but also remove their leaves and inspect fruits with different robotic components. It requires highly specific activities, and it works like the behavior of humans.

5.2.3.3   Field Inspection Using Drones

Imagine that you just will get a vehicle in the air, and it'll send you a report on everything you wish to grasp about field inspection. This is not just a fantasy- you have the opportunity to use agricultural drone technology right away in smart agriculture (Figure 5.5).

Most significantly, drones will analyze the plant's condition and also the level of harm caused by pests and weeds. Having a drone report in hand, farmers understand what steps to be taken next.

5.2.3.4   "See and Spray" Model for Pest and Weed Control

Should farmers pay their days and nights during a constant battle with pests and weeds? The supernatural dance orchestra of AI and laptop vision creates the "See and Spray" (Figure 5.6) model.

Smart sees and spray machines direct their efforts to a particular plant. Machines will distinguish the variation between "good" plants and "bad" weeds. At the instant, this technology is employed specifically for cotton fields, however, it is a nice potential for the entire trade.

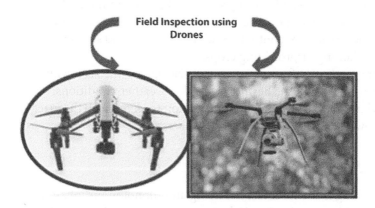

Figure 5.5 Inspection using drones

Figure 5.6 See and spray model.

Figure 5.7 Chatbot.

This is the latest development widely discussed by engineers. The idea is to generate a chatbot specifically for farmers, as shown by the schematic representation in Figure 5.7. Just like Alexa helps any of using us to rapidly solve certain tasks, the farmer's chatbot will be adapted to the requests specific to the industry.

5.3   Scope of Artificial Intelligence in Agriculture

Agriculture rapidly accepting the integration of Artificial Intelligence (AI) and Machine Learning (ML) both in terms of agricultural products and

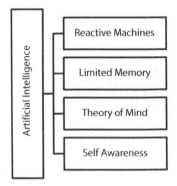

Figure 5.8 Types of artificial intelligence.

in-field farming techniques. There are four types of artificial intelligence as shown in Figure 5.8.

These newer approaches have some advantages such as farmers can produce crops that can resist pests and diseases, improve the nutritional contents of crops, and improve the flavor and texture of crops.

5.3.1   Reactive Machines

These machines are basic types of artificial systems that are purely reactive and have the capability neither to form memories nor to use past experiences to report for current decisions.

5.3.2   Limited Memory

This type of artificial intelligence contains machines that can look into the past. This type of work is already done by self-driving cars. For example, they observe other cars' speeds and paths. That can't be done in just one minute but rather requires identifying specific objects and monitoring them over time.

5.3.3   Theory of Mind

We may stop here and do calls this point the important divide between the machines we have and the machines we will build in the future. Though, it is better to be more specific to talk about the types of representations of machines that need to form and what they need to be about.

5.3.4   Self-Awareness

This is the final type and the process of Artificial intelligence development which builds systems Ultimately, Artificial intelligence researchers will have to not only understand consciousness but build machines that have it. These machines will be smarter than the human mind but self-awareness does not exist in reality still and it is a hypothetical concept in the case of artificial intelligence.

5.4   Applications of Artificial Intelligence in Agriculture

The applications of AI in agriculture fall into three major categories: Agricultural Robots, Predictive Analytics, and Crop and Soil Monitoring. Computer images and deep learning algorithms are used for the progression of data captured by drones or software-based technology to observe crops and health of the soil, Machine learning models are used to track and predict various environmental impacts on crop yield such as weather/climate changes.

5.4.1   Agricultural Robots

It is used to handle important tasks of agriculture like harvesting crops at a higher volume and faster pace than laborers of human, robots are designed to support in picking and Packing of crops while struggle other challenges within the agricultural force labor, Agricultural robots can save from harm crops from harmful weeds that may be resistant to herbicides that are meant to eliminate them.

Automation like robotics can help farmers for getting more resourceful ways to the protection of crops from different weeds, a robot also called See and Spray leverages a computer for visualization to monitor and precision/accurately spray weeds on the plants of cotton, and precision spraying can help to prevent resistance by herbicides.

The robot is capable to harvest approximate 8 acres in a single day and replaced by 30 human laborers, an expected 40 percent of annual costs of the farm is funneled into "income, salaries, and contract for expenses in labor" for crops such as fruits and vegetables where needs of labor are likely to be the highest.

5.4.2 Soil Analysis and Monitoring

Companies are leveraging computers used for visualization and deep-learning of algorithms to process the capture of data by drones or software-based technology to monitor crop and soil health.

5.4.3 Predictive Analysis

Machine learning models are being developed to track and calculate various impacts of the environment on the yield of crops such as weather/climate changes. The following aspects are taken into Consideration for Predictive Analysis.

- Weather and Climatic Conditions Forecasting
- Disaster Prediction
- Crop Analysis
- Rainfall Analysis
- Disease Cycling

5.4.4 Agricultural Industry

Artificial Intelligence is used in many different types of agricultural industries, from manufacturing to automotive. Agriculture is a major source of involvement in the industry and a large part of the establishment of our economy. In changing climates and population growth, AI resulted in a smart innovative technology that is useful for the protection and improvement of crop yield. Agriculture plays a major role in the industry and the foundation of the economy. Factors like climate change, growth of population, and security of food concerns have propelled the industry into looking for more inventive approaches to improving crop yield. AI is progressively emerging as part of the industries for technological evolution.

5.4.5 Blue River Technology – Weed Control

The Blue River Technology can control weeds it is a top priority for farmers and current challenges as resistance to herbicides become more commonplace. Today, an expected 250 species of weeds have become herbicide-resistant.

Companies are using robotics to help farmers find more effective ways to the protection of their crops from different weeds.

5.4.6   Crop Harvesting

Nowadays Automation is also emerging to help with the challenges of the labor force. The industry is predicted to experience a six percent decline in agricultural workers from 2014.

Harvest CROO Robotics has developed a robot to assist strawberry farmers to pick/selecting and pack their crops. The shortage of laborers has led to millions of dollars of revenue losses in key farming regions like California and Arizona.

5.4.7   Plantix App

Plantix app identifies possible defects and deficiencies of nutrients in the soil, the app uses to detect and identify images of plant diseases, the image recognition app can recognize possible defects through images captured by the user's smartphone camera, and the farmers can contribute to the online community to network with other farmers to discuss plant health issues and contact their local weather reports [12].

Plantix can diagnose diseases of plants, damages of pests, and deficiencies of nutrients affecting the crops and provides related treatment measures. This type of analysis is conducted by software algorithms that correlated with particular foliage patterns and with certain defects of soil, pests of plants, and diseases of plants.

5.4.8   Drones

Drones can be used in a variety of agronomic activities such as Spaying, plant counting parameters (plant size, plot statistics, compromised plots, planter skips), plant height and density, vegetation indices: leaf area, anomaly detection treatment efficacy, infestations, water needs: damage/drown out, etc.

5.4.9   Driverless Tractors

A driverless tractor is a self-governing farm vehicle that delivers a high attractive effort with slow speeds, for the tillage purpose and other tasks of agriculture it can operate automatically without the presence of any human inside the tractor, Self-driving tractors have the latent to optimize the on-farm process and recommend a safer also provide a less demanding working environment for the workers of farm and their families.

Driverless tractors are programmed to examine and observe their location, and decide the speed and obstacles to avoid animals, human beings, or objects in the field performing their task; they operate by using the aid of a supervisor monitoring the development at a control station [13, 14].

5.4.10   Precise Farming

Precision farming uses Artificial intelligence to produce correct and restricted techniques that help suggest guidance and considerate about water and management of nutrients, optimal harvesting and times of planting as well as when the right times for the rotation of crop would be, these processes make farming more capable and can help calculate ROI on specific crops based on their costs and margins inside the market.

5.4.11   Return on Investment (RoI)

By including the data, for example, conditions of climate, types of soil, commercial centers, potential invasions, and information in the algorithm, AI can decide on the best seeds to exploit and support to farmers maximize production. This can get better the RoI (Return on Investment) for all farms; AI improvement can process investigations that help farmers minimize losses in the production supply chain of their farms.

5.5   Advantages of AI in Agriculture

Agriculture is smart digital, Artificial intelligence in agriculture is emerging in three categories, agricultural robotics, soil and crop monitoring and predictive analytics, farmers are using a sensor and soil sampling for the collection of data, and this data is stored in on-farm management systems that allow for improved processing and their analysis [15, 16].

Machine learning provides customers with a sense of their soil's strengths and weaknesses the importance is on preventing defective crops and optimizing the potential for the production of healthy crops, the growth in AI technology has strengthened agro-based businesses to run more powerfully. AI systems can solve some of the most challenges, by continuous monitoring parameters (shown in Figure 5.9) such as:

- Land use land cover mapping.
- Crop health monitoring.
- Crop inventory.

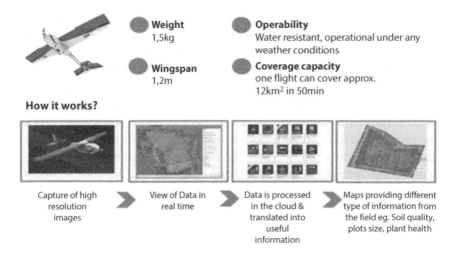

Figure 5.9 Field monitoring.

- Soil resource inventory.
- Water supply management.
- In seasonal agricultural operation.

5.6   Disadvantages of AI in Agriculture

Artificial intelligence improves agriculture manufacturing in many amazing ways; there are many concerns as regards the forthcoming of AI on employment and the labor force of the sectors of agriculture. Droning field tasks can be easily automated this can regularly make certain roles outmoded. Humans will be replaced by smart robots that can safely navigate space, find and move agricultural products as well as make simple and complex field operations.

The cost of technology such as drones has made it engaged outside of the government and research bodies, it is expensive to buy the drones, and the biggest challenge will be funding inside from the government efforts and research institutions.

5.7   Conclusion

Artificial Intelligence (AI) helps improve agricultural productivity. AI has been applied in several aspects of agricultural practices some examples of

AI are obtainable. In this article, we investigate applications of artificial intelligence to offer business leaders an understanding of trends and present representative examples of admired applications. AI/ML techniques help farmers analyze land/soil/health of crops, etc. AI helps farmers to save time and allows farmers to grow the right crop' in each season that has the best yield. Vertical cropping can reduce water usage, and make efficient land' usage can be cultivated in urban areas in buildings. It also reduces the problems associated with labor unavailability. Prediction of next year's crop seasons/weather/climate/rainfall can also be possible. AI technology suggests the appropriate pesticides/crops/places for agriculture according to the current need of India.

References

1. FAO, *The State of Food and Agriculture 2017: Leveraging Food Systems for Inclusive Rural Transformation*, pp. 1–181, Food and Agriculture Organization of the United Nations, Rome, 2017.
2. Talaviya, T., Shah, D., Patel, N., Yagnik, H., Shah, M., Implementation of artificial intelligence in agriculture for optimization of irrigation and application of pesticides and herbicides. *Artif. Intell. Agric.*, 4(1), 58–73, 2020. https://doi.org/10.1016/j.aiia.2020.04.002.
3. Mogili, U.M.R. and Deepak, B.B.V.L., Review on application of drone systems in precision agriculture. *International Conference on Robotics and Smart Manufacturing. Procedia Comput. Sci.*, 133, 502–509, 2018.
4. Shah, G., Shah, A., Shah, M., Panacea of challenges in real-world application of big data analytics in healthcare sector. *JDIM*, volume, 1(2), 107–116, 2019. https://doi. org/10.1007/ s42488-019-00010-1.
5. Kakkad, V., Patel, M., Shah, M., Biometric authentication and image encryption for image security in cloud framework. *Multiscale Multidiscip. Modeling, Experiments Design*, vol. 2, no. 4, pp. 233–248, 2019. 10.1007/s41939-019-00049-y.
6. Kundalia, K., Patel, Y., Shah, M., Multi-label movie genre detection from a movie poster using knowledge transfer learning. *Augment. Hum. Res.*, 5, 11, 20202020. https:// doi.org/10.1007/s41133-019-0029-y.
7. Gandhi, M., Kamdar, J., Shah, M., Preprocessing of non-symmetrical images for edge detection. *Augment. Hum. Res.*, 5, 10, 2020. https://doi.org/10.1007/ s41133-019-0030-5.
8. Ahir, K., Govani, K., Gajera, R., Shah, M., Application on virtual reality for enhanced education learning, military training, and sports. *Augment. Hum. Res.*, 5, 7, 2020.

9. Plessen, M.G., *Freeform Path Fitting for the Minimisation of the Number of Transitions between Headland Path and Interior Lanes within Agricultural Fields*, pp. 1–7, 2019, Arxiv 1910.12034v1.

10. Liakos, K.G., Busato, P., Moshou, D., Pearson, S., Bochtis, D., Machine learning in agriculture: A review. *Sensors (Basel)*, 18, 8, 2674, Aug. 14, 2018.

11. Maher, T., A complete overview of artificial intelligence in agriculture market, 2018. https://krishijagran.com/news/a-complete-overview-of-artificial-intelligence-in-agriculture-market.

12. Khan, M. Y., and Kumar, S., applications of artificial intelligence in agriculture. *International Research Journal of Modernization in Engineering Technology and Science*; Volume: 03/Issue: 01: pp. 1398-1402, January, 2021.

13. Faggella, D., AI in agriculture–present applications and impact. *Emerj*, https://emerj.com/ai-sector-overviews/ai-agriculture-present-applications-impact/, 2020.

14. Anbarasan, V., and Jayalakshmi, V., Artificial Intelligence in Agriculture and its Application. *International Journal of Creative Research Thoughts (IJCRT)*; Volume 10, Issue 6, June 2022 | ISSN: 2320-2882.

15. Irimia, M., Five ways agriculture could benefit from artificial intelligence, AI for the Enterprise, IBM, 2016.

16. Pathan, M., Patel, N., Yagnik, H., Shah, M., Artificial cognition for applications in smart agriculture: A comprehensive review. *Artif. Intell. Agric.*, 4, 81–95, 2020.

## 6

The Potential of Artificial Intelligence in the Healthcare System

Meena Gupta* and Ruchika Kalra

Amity Institute of Physiotherapy, Amity University, Noida, Uttar Pradesh, India

Abstract

AI is a cross-disciplinary field of research that attempts to understand, model and replicate intelligence and cognitive processes by invoking computational, mathematical, logical, mechanical and biological principles and devices. There are various types which comes under AI, as machine learning, natural language processing, artificial neural networks, robots, expert systems and fuzzy logics. The concept behind the artificial intelligence is that to act as the copy of human, thinking, skills, language processing, and other features. AI has the potential to be used in planning and resource allocation in health and social care services. AI has the potential analyse clinical data, research publications, and professional guidelines to aid the diagnosis of disease and could also help to inform decisions about treatment. The sensor technology works as the human machine interaction with devices such as wearable and non-wearable devices which woks separately and have the best transmission with the presence of sensor nodes with this technology there is no use for the repeater and the feedback outcome comes best with the help of technology in the devices like thermal mechanism where the heat is the mediator turning mechanical to electrical energy for wearable device and in case of non-wearable device such as pacemaker in heart will initiate for the electrical energy to stimulate heart pumping. The artificial intelligence not only works privately but also in community and public healthcare which consist of experimental trials outcomes, research, private documentation which needs to be secured hence there are alarming devices named as intrusion devices which also work with sensor networking and Xerox of human immune system so as to save the data so as the T and B cells does. Utility of AI in medicine, surgery, and rehabilitation is specific with every application in the artificial intelligence. Such clinically relevant set of apps are a good example of evidence based clinical answers and skills that

---

*Corresponding author: meenaguptaphysio@gmail.com

Anamika Ahirwar, Piyush Kumar Shukla, Manish Shrivastava, Priti Maheshwary and Bhupesh Gour (eds.) Innovative Engineering with AI Applications, (101–130) © 2023 Scrivener Publishing LLC

can be accessed as and when we need them. AI integrated mobile applications, and wearable fitness trackers, the physiotherapist can track the vitals, physical activity, exercise sessions and other parameters, without the patient having to come into the clinical setting. The future changes and requirement for AI will be increased with increased precision in all aspects which is present as in medicine, pathology, rehabilitation, but future will be facing challenges inclusive of updates in AI should follow the clinical practice as followed by the medical professionals.

Keywords: Artificial intelligence, healthcare, mobile applications, natural language processing, machine learning

6.1   Introduction

Artificial intelligence is defined as the research field of turning and replicating the intelligence and cognitive process by artificial means by computer means such as mathematical, logical, cognitive principles as shown in Figure 6.1. The artificial intelligence is cumulative form of synthesizing and analyzing the agents of computer presenting intellectual behavior [1, 2].

The artificial intelligence is upgraded and in process in the field of healthcare with various systems such as machine learning, natural learning process, expert systems, robotics, fuzzy logics which together have stepped in various diagnostics, healthcare data, clinical treatment, modeling, decision making and other healthcare services which have enhanced the accuracy and precision [3–6]. According to a literature the artificial intelligence is termed as intelligent agent which is composed of a system inclusive of actuators, sensors, agents and environment and are interlinked and terming as perception cycle of artificial intelligence [7–9] as shown in Figures 6.2 and 6.3.

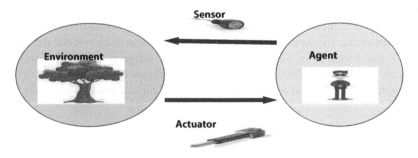

Figure 6.1 Tuning and replication.

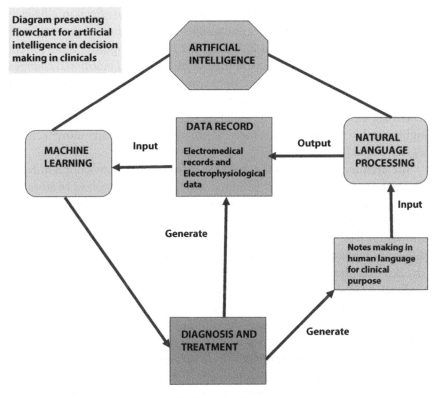

Figure 6.2 Application of artificial intelligence technology.

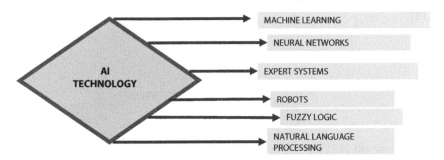

Figure 6.3 AI technologies.

6.2 Machine Learning

The concept of machine learning defines that where the machine learns to present as human and study their behavior, by this they can make the computer intelligent and make the progression of the artificial intelligence faster and precise towards accuracy. The concept of working machine learning travels similar by establishing the human cognitive skills, there thoughts, physiological changes at time of situation and emotional changes occurring at the same time. The significance of machine learning behind artificial intelligence is highly required to be intelligent, it should be consistent for being with learning capabilities. The machine learning itself is highly used in very diagnosis, medical procedures and many more technological works [10, 11].

The architecture behind the machine learning is the environment from where the learning abilities is gathered and the second it comes to learning which the most important factor to gather from environment and classify upon its completeness and incompleteness and quality. The third comes the knowledge base which affects the learning system by account of the expression such as reasoning, modification, presentation as shown in Figure 6.4. The last execution plays a wide role where it improves the learning skill by feedback, transparency and solves issues of complexity [12, 13].

There are types for machine learning algorithms as supervised learning where the expected output and the output came from computer is compared and the error is deleted to come up with expected one. The other is unsupervised where adaptation is done by exploring in the level of input cycle and this algorithm is also termed as cluster algorithm. The third is reinforcement learning where the actions are taken at environment level so as to improve long term output. The recommender systems are the customization process where the alteration is done as required by the usage [14].

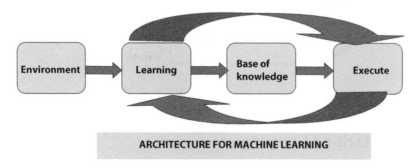

Figure 6.4 Process architecture of machine learning.

6.3   Neural Networks

These are also known as artificial neural networks where they act as the neuron as present in human beings, as the function of neuron consisting of generating input signals from output signal and traveling after creation of threshold in building the bio-electrical signal passing through synapse, these function is also followed by the artificial neuron creating neuron network. The significance for the artificial neuron is to work as parallel processing, memory and signaling, and distributing equal data to every neuron [15, 16] as shown in Figure 6.5.

The structure of the artificial neuron is created with the development of 3 layers with different function such as input layer for input signals and names as "n" neurons whereas the intermediate layers is named after "m" neurons present with many intermediate and hidden channels and the output layers for the output signals and named after "p" neurons [17].

According to the feedback architecture of neural networks explaining the concept of the transferring the input signals as "x" and functioning the signal with "f" and producing output as y, these layers are functional on each step according to the architecture but if there is no feedback architecture the signal will not be exchanged at every neuron but only be transferred to layers [18].

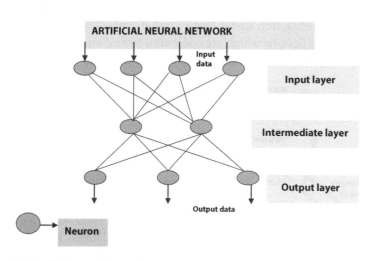

Figure 6.5 Artificial neural network.

6.4   Expert Systems

The expert systems act as the machine memory to enhance utility and provide better intellectual advice. They are solely depended on database large in size providing the justification and the specific knowledge in that context, as the creation of programs structured termed as knowledge based systems also as synonym to expert systems. Th provision of providing the knowledge to human is distinctive as gathered from books, as the information is such that as assembled in the specialists such as doctors, engineers, analysts and many more. The terms of knowledge depend on the level of interaction of the user and expert system. There are various technologies that are task specific to generate better outcomes which follows the rule as goal specific, better problem solving [19–21]. There are benefits behind experts systems are as better precision and accuracy than humans, more cheaper as in contrast to humans, better experience with success results, better in handling monotonous wok and increase expert skills, enable the compatibility with every system where humans aren't, enhances the productive outcome. Nowadays the expert systems are more into the creation and maintaining the health records and manage it [22, 23]. The construction of expert system is flexible to represent the quantitative and qualitative measures, the knowledge base in the expert system is based on the equations working regarding the task where the there are letters headed in terms representing each such as force it as shear stress, D as data and diameter of coil, n is representation of number of coils involved. The rules engine consisting of the units such as length, diameter and other units which design the specific construction under these limited units. The data base present with number of designs which are compared to find and choose according to the optimal one as shown in Figure 6.6. The user interface is working in

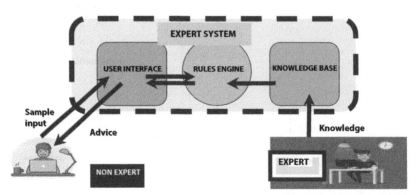

Figure 6.6 Working process of expert systems.

all long the process for creating a design and the expert makes it clear that is there any additional requirement as input. All this process finished the user provides advice for the application usage in this system [24, 25].

6.5 Robots

The robots are the new technology which are proven to be an assistant in human work with the combination of artificial technology the robots have been proven to be the essential in the rehabilitation and other healthcare approach as depicted in the figure below the artificial assistant with the assistive robot which is a source to the patient as attached with sensors gathering all the movements and the needs as sensors present at the patients wrist sending the signals to medical support, family and drafting the assistance with the help of robot turning as commuter and source for physical and social rehabilitation [26, 27].

In robotics there are two types, i.e., physical and social which plays role specifically , such as physical robots are for the cognitive, engaging to encourage to work and assist in activities of daily living, they are also specialized in surgery for the better precision and more coverage with limited exposure [28]. The other social robots are specially to play role in distinctive way such as social friend which pretends to be a coach to rehabilitate and instruct you to follow exercise protocol, play as a role to socialize, talk and be counsellor and allow to manage a psychologist with the human oriented intelligent technology as shown in Figure 6.7 [29–31].

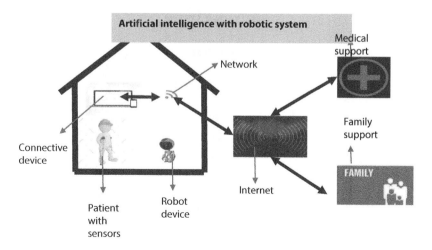

Figure 6.7 Artificial intelligence with robotic system.

There are various benefits as allowing to create a feedback so as to come up with better outcome as with the support of the sensor technology the robots creates a data allowing the doctor to check the improvement and resolve the issue even if the patient is not reachable [32].

6.6   Fuzzy Logic

Fuzzy logic system is defined as technology for mathematics with engineering methodology which is changes the presentation of the human decision making as the difference between the yes and no and making various statements in between with variation [33]. The architecture system of the fuzzy logic work with models such as fuzzification as first where the signals of input are turn to five steps of differentiation from -2 to 2 with required term beside as used in distinct technologies as shown in Figure 6.8.

The second goes with rule setting which is done by the experts at the level of knowledge base. The third level moves to inference engine stimulating the signals to transform it to human reasoning turning from input. The fourth level moves to defuzzification where the fuzzy input is turn in to defuzzed output [34, 35].

The benefits of the fuzzy logic is to obtain easy decision making, better precision, fast conceptualization, making math understanding easier, working best in various fields of healthcare. There are some disadvantage

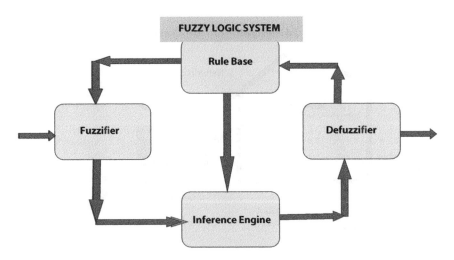

Figure 6.8 Fuzzy logic system.

such as works when the simple problems are there, no specific approach, and does not require high amount of accuracy [36, 37].

The fuzzy logic plays a very less role which in artificial intelligence in healthcare where it plays the role of what human thinks and how they judge and provide the feedback , accordingly the fuzzy logic follows [38].

6.7   Natural Language Processing

Natural language processing (Figure 6.9) is that part of the artificial intelligence playing the role in linguistics, where the computer tries to process the computer language in normal human language so as to make understanding clear in all aspects of different human language making understood by other person who is unable to go through different languages [39, 40].

Natural language processing is composed of various components that make the architecture of the concept better, it is present with term known as phonology that id defined as making arrangement to create a sound that is systematic that is a study of obtaining the sounds and study the sound language, The others is morphology that is defined as the nature of letters and words presenting the morpheme which is in nature that it cannot be divided. Lexical the component which provided the meaning to the words and multiple parts of speech as required in the context, this can be variable according to semantic theory. The syntactic component is for the grammar presentation, as by keeping the sentence structure and equality among the words and their relation. The semantic component provides the meanings

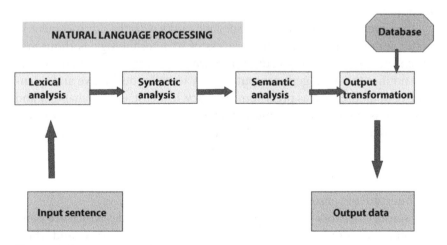

Figure 6.9 Language processing system.

according to the level of sentence incorporation and presenting in different parts of speech. The discourse component work to keep the length of the sentence as required and making it structural. The pragmatic component provides better usage of words in the sentences and providing nub so as to get other meanings from the same sentence [41–44].

The generation takes place with speaker and generator in which the phrase is generated according to the user intention. The components for generation will be including of selection of the context to organization of the material to the source for lingual clarity and then realizing for the outcome, then in last the application and the speaker will be done according to the situation [45].

6.8 Sensor Network Technology in Artificial Intelligence

There are various wireless sensors that play the role in artificial intelligence to just same as the sensory system present in the humans as same as in intelligent computers there are sensory networks, modern sensors, sensory architecture in artificial intelligence [46–48].

The sensory networks are wireless connection that are connected in the computer system such as the bunch of nerves in limbs of human, this is required so as for the place where the wires cannot be deployed such as withe patient while doing activity so as to record the activity, military combat zone, geology places and many more, these are utilized in parameter systems to automatically measure such as by spatial and temporal environment [49, 50].

The modern sensors are in sensory networks with the advancement in better compatibility as with the process of nanotechnology as thousands of sensors are applied in sensory nodes which gathers even a small change and notifies the intelligent computer. They work on qualitative and quantitative in nature such as precision, accuracy, low cost, easy availability and require less energy for the same as shown in Figure 6.10. These sensors are proven to be best for the aspect of environment, communication and easily made by the satellite connection so can be used in area as being wireless [51–53].

Architecture of Sensory Network
The sensory network is mesh space with number of nodes which are point to point in relation where it accesses the geographical measures and where kept. This mesh does not require the transmitter to signal ad transfer the

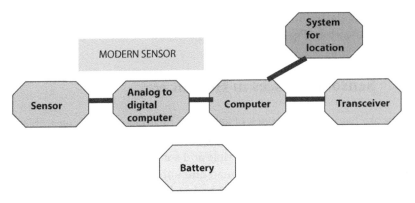

Figure 6.10 Sensor network system.

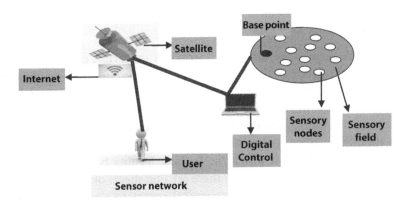

Figure 6.11 Sensor network system.

information as this is having ability to transfer on its own as the nodes are so close in the sensors. The network is equally distributed and placed so as extract, collect and synthesize the data. The data is centrally sent to the nodes to create one center data, due to this the sensors are having the self-configuration that increases its capability. The advantage of this structure is there is no dependency to repeat, better expanding property. The disadvantage is the battery consumption and the signal should be passed from every node [54, 55].

The sensory network architecture is both with static and mobility in nature where the nodes that power to find the exact place of themselves even when distributed unevenly and they are once processed through authentication once employed in work. The nodes are present with ability to store the memory up to hundreds of bytes with the help of cryptography system. There are two points one is key server and other is base station which is connected to laptops and can be controlled through wireless networks as shown in Figure 6.11 [56, 57].

6.9   Sensory Devices in Healthcare

There are basically two types of sensor in healthcare one is wearable and other is implanted and there are energy harvesters that are applied respectively. These devices are quite flexible and soft in nature providing the relation between the device and human and enhancing the output. There are devices which are nowadays researched and made the sensor to be charged by the human contact which can be acted as the energy harvesters [58–61].

6.9.1   Wearable Devices

The wearable devices are such that it works by epidermis and act as e skin which have the property to be as human interaction interface resulting in generation of bio-metric signals which records the acoustic and mechanical signals in the in the body and turns into feedback such as recording heart rate, murmurs, temperature [62–65]. Wearable devices are present with the noninvasive quality hence accepted fast by the patients. There are mechanisms through which the transfer leading to outcome such as piezzo-electric mechanism where there are fine sheets or wires in the sensors which is transmitting the mechanical energy to electrical energy for output, the other is thermo electric mechanism where the temperature is the transmitter for turning the output into electrical energy, triboelectric mechanism where there is the coupling mechanism of the and having triboelectric nanogenerator where the signals are transferred through fabrics and polymer [66–72].

6.9.2   Implantable Devices

These are the devices that are to be placed inside the body which is having main function to stimulate the muscle or organ such as in case of deep brain stimulation which generate or stop the signal so as to control the tremors and pain by controlling the brain signals, it can also be used as the pacemaker in the heart so as to generate the heart signals to pump the heart. These devices are also used to deliver the drug at equal intervals as they are somewhat battery oriented in some device and some as present with the energy harvesters [73–76]. According to the study , as the external power supply is the problem for the implantable device hence can be adjusted and combined with wearable device so as to interact the neural interface and generate the power by different mechanism, such as muscle stimulation, temperature gradient, and use of ultra violet rays that interacts with E skin and leading to power supply without the use of battery. The energy harvesters are like zinc oxygen single wire generator gets triggered by the human heart beat, blood pressure and generates the biomechanical energy to electrical energy. There are also piezo nano-wires that also work on the same principle with the physical vapor deposition technique [77–82].

6.10 Neural Interface for Sensors

The neural interface is between the sensor and the human body interaction where the interaction can be with central nervous system and peripheral nervous system. The study for the nervous system is still difficult to rule out the outcomes and still the research is under procedure [83–86]. The neural interface for central nervous system is for brain, scalp and cortical surface which generates signals which are as the electroencephalogram, electrocorticogram, and local end potential respectively where the electrodes and sensors are placed according to depth so as to get the graph for the same (Figure 6.12). Now the flexibility of the sensors have increased leading to better implantation and better neural interface such as technique of optoelectronic interface through optoelectronic implants, syringe implanted mesh electronics, micro needle electrodes and E dura implant for spinal cord [87–89].

For peripheral nervous system the signaling is from the head to the branches for communication the devices are different such as transverse intrafasicular multi-channel electrode, flat interface nerve electrode, 3D spike ultraneural interface, these all interface communicates through the sensory system and transmitting signals from and to high authorities. This can be useful in case of neuroprosthesis, and nerve stimulation according to the condition (Figure 6.13) [90–94].

6.10.1 Intrusion Devices in Artificial Intelligence

The wireless sensory networks are very useful in all the ways, but there is only the risk of safety and privacy which needs to be taken care for. Hence there are various safety mechanisms but not energy beneficial; hence, the researchers came to the intrusion systems that are possible solution for the safety aspects. The intrusion systems are flexible in determining the

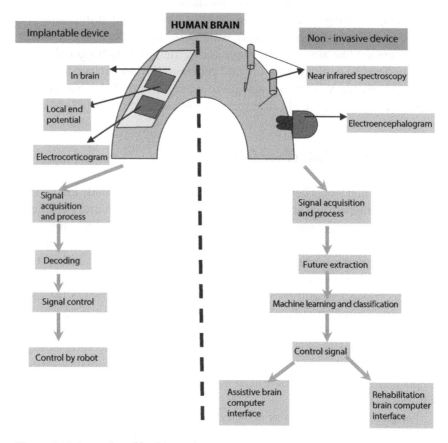

Figure 6.12 Sensor-based healthcare devices.

problems and safety attacks but are unable to diffuse it. There are basically three types of intrusion system that are coping the human system such as the artificial immune intrusion device exactly works as human immunity, the artificial neural networks intrusion works as neurons and genetic intrusion works on the biological criteria of humans [95–98].

The artificial immune intrusion devices are the scanners for upcoming threat same as our D cells T cells and B cell work. The architecture for the artificial systems works as the ruling out the database, monitoring for the logs, checking for the traffic and ruling for the type of attack and alarming and responding accordingly [99–101].

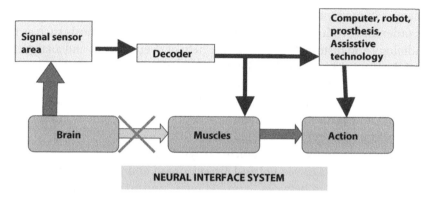

Figure 6.13 Neural interface system.

The artificial neural networks intrusion devices are same as connection of nervous system with neurons, where the artificial neural networks will be capable of identifying for the complex trends. The feed-forward ANN working only in one direction whereas the feedback moves in all direction, here the intrusion devices rule out the normal and abnormal events, determining the exhaustion attacks. Once the attack is identified the robot behind works for the same [102–104].

Genetic algorithms intrusion devices are best for computing solutions, adaptive in nature and for solving the problem. This works on the concept selection naturally, evolution, and mutation theory and inherited genes as in humans. It is useful in intrusion by creating the design and proposition and classifying the rule of attacks and produce new rules to satisfy the attack prevention [105, 106].

6.11 Artificial Intelligence in Healthcare

6.11.1 Role of Artificial Intelligence in Medicine

The medicine is major field of healthcare as nowadays the level of knowledge is increasing so as the level of research hence leading to wide amount of challenges such as adapting, implementing, and analyzing the challenges this where the modern medicine occur which requires artificial intelligence to solve the specialists and physician to resolve by formulation and variable diagnosis [107–110].

The artificial neural networks plays the role as the human nervous system consisting of neurons which analyze, drafts the easier method of changes in more presentable and understanding analytics keeping the data in order and productive. The neural networks work in diagnosis such as in radiology and histopathology with the help of deep analysis and analytical and data presentation such as PAPNET specifically for cervical examination and screening. ANN can interpret all the radiology sheets from plain to MRI and plain graphs from ECG to EEG too. The prognosis is also made very fast and accurate by the neural networks and outcome is interpreted even before and after surgery [111–119].

The fuzzy systems in the medicine plays the role by giving the variation to the medical diagnosis not just by yes or no and black and white but also classification in between them to precise and accurate the results and differentiate the diagnosis. It works best in imaging such as ultrasound, computed tomography and magnetic reasoning imaging [120, 121].

According to the study there is a new concept of the hybrid intelligent system where the there is a relation with artificial neural networks, fuzzy expert system and genetic algorithm which in combination will make the medicine department to another level of outcome with better assessment and outcome and through which prognosis will be easier to be encouraged [122–124].

6.11.2   Role of Artificial Intelligence in Surgery

The artificial intelligence plays the role in surgery by better recognition, cognitive ability, and decision making.

Machine learning in surgery works as predictor and patter recognizer to machines. The machine learning enables to structure to the detected data and predict the programming according to that. It is having the ability to conceptualize the predictive outcomes and, hence can be alarming at the time of surgery. It is developed with multiple algorithms facility that makes it more convenient to statistically present. Natural language processing has the ability to process in the human language. In surgical purpose the natural language processing is used as the comb to utter all the electrical medical records and maintain the language according to surgeon. This makes surgeon to be sure whatever is he doing is exact with the assessment and the NLP generates the condition of the patient according to the situation in the theater. Artificial neural networks helps to classify the data, manage the complex surgery with the problems to be in pattern [125–128].

6.11.3   Role of Artificial Intelligence in Rehabilitation

In rehabilitation the robots work as artificial intelligence where the role of combination works such as sensors, robotic technology and the processing behind as the role of the artificial intelligence can be through virtual, robotic or sensory feedback to the environment linking your day to day activities and charting accordingly, where the robot can act as the trainer, care taker, motivator which in together progress to rehabilitation the devices such as endoskeleton, exoskeleton, and MIT manus are the technology behind it [129–131].

6.12   Why Artificial Intelligence in Healthcare

The artificial intelligence is accepted due to the curation of the data as the basic problem nowadays is absent data that makes difficult to analyze and bring out the documentation as for what and how the diagnosis, prognosis can be manipulated so as to gather the information worldwide [132].

It is required due to presence with management of strategic change in the capacity, as the procedure of the artificial intelligence is not only to reach with algorithmic solutions but also to make aware in healthcare professionals and try with the trials and draw the outcomes which can be easily compared by the data collection and presentation in the device [133].

It plays a great role in accountability by creating thousands of classifications and that will and multiple algorithms where according to the law the explanation is the term for the solution to every problem and justify accordingly, where the accountability for this occurs [134].

The priority of the artificial intelligence comes as the privacy and data management where the data is to be kept in private as the data involves national statistical data which interprets the level of the nation, hence it is secured with the safety guards oriented by side and organization creating the procedure under artificial intelligence [135].

6.13   Advancements of Artificial Intelligence in Healthcare

According to the data reported in a study interprets that the artificial intelligence is the most benefiting in terms for the healthcare systems, there are very recent advances that place a very decent role in healthcare systems.

The role in mobile health where the wireless technologies are grasped by the patient and creates the innovative idea by keeping the health record in hand always wherever and whenever, as the awareness towards the smart phones and fitness is increasing leading to increase in mobile applications not even in patients but in normal person to so s to keep a record and motivate and encourage themselves according the outcome and feedback of daily living. The mobile applications not only help to keep a record but to plan for the further days and keep the genuine record for the medical professional to keep an eye towards his patient [136, 137].

The role of artificial intelligence have come up so far with the technology of keeping the electro medical records which are private healthcare information of every patient in every visit and type of management provided by every healthcare professional. As the data storage s quite high and the prevalence of low resource is there hence the electro medical records can act as placed with multiple safety guards preventing and creating the suitable treatment for the particular condition [138, 139].

The storage devices are quite less and heavy to store hence the information technology have come up with the concept of cloud computing which is secured by the passwords and linked with the accounts as any mishap happens will be on the spot complained, as this will be the matter of security in public health [140].

6.14 Future Challenges

The future challenges are eye opener to artificial intelligence as the points to be covered under the research for the healthcare ad artificial intelligence. The great challenge is the acceptance and adoption the feature for the society of every category according to availability, financially and can be accepted in the large area of scale. The myth to be removed as thought by the people of the society as the technology can remove the healthcare professionals. To come up with the results it will take accordingly 5 to 10 years to overcome and challenge the further challenge on every step [141, 142].

6.15 Discussion

According to the data studied and reviewed interprets the technology of the artificial intelligence, its working, mechanism of machine learning, natural language processing, fuzzy logics, robots, expert system, artificial neural networks where these mechanism ought to act same as the human system of working from cognitive, decision making, action of nervous system, expert mind setting and in terms of memory [143, 144].

According to the study the artificial intelligence is a successful technology with benefits for healthcare sectors specific to medicine, surgery, rehabilitation, and even more specific to the subjects below it such as cardiology, neurology, oncology, orthopedics and many more. The technology is not limited to the treatment but also validated towards all the administration in private, public and community healthcare sectors where the data security, accountability and data presentation is to rectify in case of the experimental trials. This technology gives rise to suitability of research to wide place and accountability towards the sector. The intelligent not only copies the language, areas but also takes the image for the decision according to humans and society which in turns better outcomes [145–147].

6.16   Conclusion

This study concluded with the effects of the artificial intelligence and its potential ability in the healthcare sector and be a hand for healthcare professionals. It can be beneficial in all aspects of healthcare sectors with its different technologies and very structural in aspects of results and outcomes by creation of real data presentation. The AI is motivator for the healthcare sector not the remover for the professionals.

References

1. Frankish, K. and Ramsey, W.M. (Eds.), *The Cambridge Handbook of Artificial Intelligence*, United States of America by Cambridge University Press, New York, 2014.
2. Poole, D.L. and Mackworth, A.K., *Artificial Intelligence: Foundations of Computational Agents*, United States of America by Cambridge University Press, New York, 2010.
3. Yu, K.-H., Beam, A.L., Kohane, I.S., Artificial intelligence in healthcare. *Nat. Biomed. Eng.*, 2, 719–731, 2018.
4. Trivikram, C., Samarpitha, S., Madhavi, K., Moses, D., Evaluation of hybrid face and voice recognition systems for biometric identification in areas requiring high security. *I-Manag. J. Pattern Recognit.*, 4, 9–16, 2017.
5. Hamet, P. and Tremblay, J., Artificial intelligence in medicine. *Metabolism*, 69, S36–S40, 2017.
6. Tran, B.X., Vu, G.T., Ha, G.H., Vuong, Q.H., Ho, M.T., Vuong, T.T., La, V.P., Ho, M.T., Nghiem, K.P., Nguyen, H., Latkin, C.A., Tam, W., Cheung, N.M., Nguyen, H.T., Ho, C., Ho, R., Global evolution of research in artificial intelligence in health and medicine: A bibliometric study. *J. Clin. Med.*, 8, 3, 360, 2019.
7. Begovic, M., Oprunenco, A., Sadiku, L., *Let's Talk about Artificial Intelligence*, vol. 2019, UNDP, New York, NY, USA, 2018.

8. Jiang, F., Jiang, Y., Zhi, H., Dong, Y., Li, H., Ma, S., Wang, Y., Dong, Q., Shen, H., Wang, Y., Artificial intelligence in healthcare: Past, present and future. *Stroke Vasc. Neurol.*, 2, 230–243, 2017.
9. Shaban-Nejad, A., Michalowski, M., Buckeridge, D.L., Health intelligence: How artificial intelligence transforms population and personalized health. *NPJ Digit. Med.*, 1, 53, 2018.
10. Springhead, W. and Jiang, L., *Artificial Intelligence and Expert System*, vol. 160-180, pp. 277–280, National University of Defense Technology Publishing House, 1995.
11. Yongqing, W., *Expert System WMES Research and Realization*, vol. 6, pp. 14–15, The Microcomputer Develops, Springer, 1994.
12. Yangsen, Z., *Artificial Intelligence Principle and Application*, Higher Education Publishing House, 2004.
13. Xue, M. and Zhu, C., A study and application on machine learning of artificial intelligence, in: *2009 International Joint Conference on Artificial Intelligence*, IEEE, pp. 272–274, April 2009.
14. Das, S., Dey, A., Pal, A., Roy, N., Applications of artificial intelligence in machine learning: Review and prospect. *Int. J. Comput. Appl.*, 115, 9, 31–41, 2015.
15. Honkela, T., Duch, W., Girolami, M., Kaski, S. (Eds.), vol. 6792, *Artificial Neural Networks and Machine Learning-ICANN 2011: 21st International Conference on Artificial Neural Networks, Proceedings*, Espoo, Finland, Springer June 14-17, 2011.
16. Gallo, C., Artificial neural networks tutorial, in: *Encyclopedia of Information Science and Technology*, Third Edition, pp. 6369–6378, IGI Global, 2015.
17. McCulloch, W.S. and Pitts, W., A logical calculus of the ideas immanent in nervous activity. *Bull. Math. Biophys.*, 5, 4, 115–133, 1943.
18. Hornik, K., Stinchcombe, M., White, H., Multilayer feedforward networks are universal approximators. *Neural Netw.*, 2, 5, 359–366, 1989.
19. Horvitz, E.J., Breese, J.S., Henrion, M., Decision theory in expert systems and artificial intelligence. *Int. J. Approx. Reason.*, 2, 3, 247–302, 1988.
20. Sol, H.G., Cees, A.T., de Vries Robbé, P.F. (Eds.), *Expert Systems and Artificial Intelligence in Decision Support Systems: Proceedings of the Second Mini Euroconference*, Lunteren, Springer Science & Business Media, The Netherlands, November 17–20, 1985, 2013.
21. Patterson, D.W., *Introduction to Artificial Intelligence and Expert Systems*, Prentice-Hall, India, 1990.
22. Vial, A., Stirling, D., Field, M. *et al.*, The role of deep learning and radiomic feature extraction in cancer-specific predictive modelling: A review. *Transl. Cancer Res.*, 7, 803–16, 2018.
23. Krishnamoorthy, C.S. and Rajeev, S., *Artificial Intelligence and Expert Systems for Engineers (Vol. 11)*, CRC Press, 1996.
24. Alty, J.L. and Coombs, M.J., *Expert Systems: Concepts and Examples*, OSTI Gov U.S. Department of Energy Officeof Scientific and Technical Information, 1984.

25. Duda, R.O. and Shortliffe, E.H., Expert systems research. *Science*, 220, 4594, 261–268, 1983.
26. van den Heuvel, R.J., Lexis, M.A., Gelderblom, G.J., Jansens, R.M., de Witte, L.P., Robots and ICT to support play in children with severe physical disabilities: A systematic review. *Disabil. Rehabil. Assist. Technol.*, 11, 2, 103–116, 2016.
27. Riek, L.D., Healthcare robotics. *Commun. ACM*, 60, 11, 68–78, 2017.
28. Hussain, A., Malik, A., Halim, M.U., Ali, A.M., The use of robotics in surgery: A review. *Int. J. Clin. Pract.*, 68, 1376–82, 2014.
29. Kraft, K., Chu, T., Hansen, P., Smart, W.D., Real-time contamination modeling for robotic healthcare support, in: *2016 IEEE/RSJ International Conference on Intelligent Robots and Systems (IROS)*, IEEE, pp. 2249–2254, October 2016.
30. Luxton, D.D. and Riek, L.D., *Artificial intelligence and robotics in rehabilitation*, APA Psycnet, 2019.
31. Tapus, A. and Mataric, M.J., Emulating empathy in socially assistive robotics, in: *AAAI Spring Symposium: Multidisciplinary Collaboration for Socially Assistive Robotics*, pp. 93–96, March 2007.
32. Davenport, T.H. and Glaser, J., Just-in-time delivery comes to knowledge management. *Harv. Bus. Rev.*, 80(7):107-11, 126, 2002.
33. Dubois, D. and Prade, H., *Fuzzy Sets and Systems: Theory and Applications*, Academic Press, New York, 1980.
34. Biradar, A., *Fuzzy Logic System in Artificial Intelligence*, International Journal of Advance Research in Science, Engineering and Technology, advance journal publications, 2016.
35. Mendel, J., Fuzzy logic systems for engineering: A tutorial. *Proc. IEEE*, 83, 345–377, 1995.
36. Fraleigh, S., Fuzzy logic and neural networks: Practical tools for process management. *PC AI*, 8, 3, 16–21, 1994.
37. Tanaka, K., *An Introduction to Fuzzy Logic for Practical Applications*, Springer, 1997.
38. Cavus, N., The evaluation of Learning Management Systems using an artificial intelligence fuzzy logic algorithm. *Adv. En. Software*, 41, 2, 248–254, 2010.
39. Rospocher, M., van Erp, M., Vossen, P., Fokkens, A., Aldabe, I., Rigau, G., Soroa, A., Ploeger, T., Bogaard, T., Building event-centric knowledge graphs from news. *Web Semant. Science, Serv. Agents World Wide Web, In Press*, 37–38, 2016, 132–151, 2016.
40. Shemtov, H., *Ambiguity Management in Natural Language Generation*, Pennsylvania State University, Stanford, 1997.
41. Nation, K., Snowling, M.J., Clarke, P., Dissecting the relationship between language skills and learning to read: Semantic and phonological contributions to new vocabulary learning in children with poor reading comprehension. *Adv. Speech Lang. Pathol.*, 9, 2, 131–139, 2007.
42. Liddy, E.D., *Natural language processing*, Syracuse University, 2001.

43. Feldman, S., *NLP Meets the Jabberwocky: Natural Language Processing in Information Retrieval*, vol. 23, pp. 62–73, ONLINE-WESTON THEN WILTON-, Eric education, 1999.

44. Kumar, A., Irsoy, O., Ondruska, P., Iyyer, M., Bradbury, J., Gulrajani, I., Socher, R., Ask me anything: Dynamic memory networks for natural language processing, in: *International Conference on Machine Learning*, pp. 1378–1387, June 2016.

45. Natural Language Processing, Natural Language Processing RSS, Web. Mar. Capturing the patient's perspective: A review of advances in natural language processing of health-related text. Yearbook of medical informatics, 26(01), 214–227, 2017.

46. Volosencu, C., Identification of distributed parameter systems, based on sensor networks and artificial intelligence. *WSEAS Trans. Syst.*, 7, 785–801, 2008.

47. Banks, H.T. and Kunish, K., *Estimation Techniques for Distributed Parameter Systems, Systems & Control: Foundation & Applications*, vol. 1, pp. Note(s): XIII–315, Wiley online library, 1989.

48. Volosencu, C. *et al.*, Malicion node detection in sensor network using autoregression based on neural network. *4th IFAC Conf. on Management and Control of Production and Logistics, MCPL2007*, Sibiu, pp. 571–577, 2007.

49. Volosencu, C., Curiac, D.I., Doboli, A., Dranga, O., Knowledge based system for reliable perimeter protection using sensor networks. *Int. Conf. Winsys 2007*, Barcelona, 2007.

50. Krishnamachari, B., *A Wireless Sensor Networks Bibliography*, Technical Report, University of Southern California, 2007.

51. Akyildiz, I.F., Su, W., Sankarasubramaniam, Y., Cayirci, E., Wireless sensor networks: A survey. *Comput. Netw.*, 38, 4, 393–422, March 2002.

52. Tubaishat, M. and Madria, S., Sensor networks: An overview. *IEEE Potentials*, 22, 2, 20–23, Apr. 2003.

53. Demetriou, M.A., Adaptive identification of second-order distributed parameter systems. *Inverse Probl.*, 10, 261–294, 1994.

54. Krishnamachari, B., *A Wireless Sensor Networks Bibliography*, Technical Report, University of Southern California, 2007.

55. Feng, J., Koushanfar, F., Potkonjak, M., System architectures for sensor networks issues, alternatives and directions. *Proc. of the 2002 IEEE Int. Conf. on Computer Design (ICCD'02)*, Freiburg, pp. 226–231, 2002.

56. Volosencu, C., Identification of distributed parameter systems based on sensor networks, in: *New Trends in Technologies: Control, Management, Computational Intelligence and Network Systems*, pp. 369–394, 2010.

57. Volosencu, C., Identification of distributed parameter systems, based on sensor networks and artificial intelligence. *Methods*, 13, 17, 2008.

58. Bariya, M., Nyein, H.Y.Y., Javey, A., Wearable sweat sensors, *Nat. Electron.*, 1, 3, 160–171, 2018.

59. Lissandrello, C.A., Gillis, W.F., Shen, J., Pearre, B.W., Vitale, F., Pasquali, M., Holinski, B.J., Chew, D.J., White, A.E., Gardner, T.J., A micro-scale printable

nano clip for electrical stimulation and recording in small nerves, *J. Neural Eng.*, 14, 3, 036006, 2017.

60. Osborn, L.E., Dragomir, A., Betthauser, J.L., Hunt, C.L., Nguyen, H.H., Kaliki, R.R., Thakor, N.V., Prosthesis with neuromorphic multilayered e-dermis perceives touch and pain, *Sci. Robot.*, 3, 19, eaat3818, 2018.

61. Raspopovic, S., Capogrosso, M., Petrini, F.M., Bonizzato, M., Rigosa, J., Di Pino, G., Carpaneto, J., Controzzi, M., Boretius, T., Fernandez, E., Granata, G., Oddo, C.M., Citi, L., Ciancio, A.L., Cipriani, C., Carrozza, M.C., Jensen, W., Guglielmelli, E., Stieglitz, T., Rossini, P.M., Micera, S., Restoring natural sensory feedback in real-time bidirectional hand prostheses. *Sci. Transl. Med.*, 6, 222, 222ra219, 2014.

62. Kim, D.H., Lu, N., Ma, R., Kim, Y.S., Kim, R.H., Wang, S., Wu, J., Won, S.M., Tao, H., Islam, A., Yu, K.J., Kim, T., II, Chowdhury, R., Ying, M., Xu, L., Li, M.L., Chung, H.J., Keum, H., McCormick, M., Liu, P., Zhang, Y.W., Omenetto, F.G., Huang, Y., Coleman, T., Rogers, J.A., Epidermal electronics, *Science*, 333, 838, 2011.

63. Chortos, A., Liu, J., Bao, Z., Pursuing prosthetic electronic skin, *Nat. Mater.*, 15, 9, 937–950, 2016.

64. Rezai, A.R., Phillips, M., Baker, K.B., Sharan, A.D., Nyenhuis, J., Tkach, J., Henderson, J., Shellock, F.G., Neurostimulation system used for deep brain stimulation (DBS): MR safety issues and implications of failing to follow safety recommendations. *Invest. Radiol.*, 39, 5, 300–303, 2004.

65. Horch, K.W. and Dhillon, G.S., Neuro prosthetics-Theory and practice, World Scientific Publishing Co. Pte. Ltd, 2004.

66. Park, K., II, Lee, M., Liu, Y., Moon, S., Hwang, G.T., Zhu, G., Kim, J.E., Kim, S.O., Kim, D.K., Wang, Z.L., Flexible nanocomposite generator made of $BaTiO_3$ nanoparticles and graphitic carbons. *Adv. Mater.*, 24, 22, 2999–3004, Wiley online library, Deerfield Beach, Fla., 2012

67. Jeong, C.K., Lee, J., Han, S., Ryu, J., Hwang, G.T., Park, D.Y., Park, J.H., Lee, S.S., Byun, M., Ko, S.H., Stretchable piezoelectric nanocomposite generator. *Adv. Mater.*, 27, 18, 2866–2875, 2015.

68. Park, K.-I., Jeong, C.K., Ryu, J., Hwang, G.-T., Lee, K.J., Flexible and large-area nanocomposite generators based on lead zirconate titanate particles and carbon nanotubes, *Adv. Energy Mater.*, 3, 12, 1539–1544, 2013.

69. Zhu, G., Yang, R., Wang, S., Wang, Z.L., Flexible high-output nanogenerator based on lateral ZnO nanowire array, *Nano Lett.*, 10, 8, 3151–3155, 2010.

70. Fattahi, P., Yang, G., Kim, G., Abidian, M.R., Replacing a battery by a nano-generator with 20 V output, *Adv. Mater.*, 26, 12, 1846–1885, 2014.

71. Qi, Y., Kim, J., Nguyen, T.D., Lisko, B., Purohit, P.K., McAlpine, M.C., Enhanced piezoelectricity and stretchability in energy harvesting devices fabricated from buckled PZT ribbons, *Nano Lett.*, 11, 3, 1331–1336, 2011.

72. Hwang, G.T., Annapureddy, V., Han, J.H., Joe, D.J., Baek, C., Park, D.Y., Kim, D.H., Park, J.H., Jeong, C.K., Park, K., II, Self-powered wireless sensor node enabled by an aerosol-deposited PZT flexible energy harvester, *Adv. Energy Mater.*, 6, 13, 1600237, 2016.

73. Lee, S., Wang, H., Wang, J., Shi, Q., Yen, S.-C., Thakor, N.V., Lee, C., Battery-free neuromodulator for peripheral nerve direct stimulation, *Nano Energy*, 50, 148–158, 2018.

74. Hwang, G.T., Kim, Y., Lee, J.H., Oh, S., Jeong, C.K., Park, D.Y., Ryu, J., Kwon, H., Lee, S.G., Joung, B., Kim, D., Lee, K.J., Self-powered deep brain stimulation via a flexible PIMNT energy harvester, *Energy Environ. Sci.*, 8, 9, 2677–2684, 2015.

75. Lee, S., Wang, H., Shi, Q., Dhakar, L., Wang, J., Thakor, N.V., Yen, S.-C., Lee, C., Development of battery-free neural interface and modulated control of tibialis anterior muscle via common peroneal nerve based on triboelectric nanogenerators (TENGs), *Nano Energy*, 33, 1–11, 2017.

76. Ravi, S.K., Wu, T., Udayagiri, V.S., Vu, X.M., Wang, Y., Jones, M.R., Tan, S.C., Photosynthetic bioelectronic sensors for touch perception, UV-detection and nanopower generation: Toward self-powered e-skins, *Adv. Mater.*, 30, 39, e1802290, 2018.

77. Hwang, G.T., Park, H., Lee, J.H., Oh, S., Park, K., II, Byun, M., Park, H., Ahn, G., Jeong, C.K., No, K., Self-powered cardiac pacemaker enabled by flexible single crystalline PMN-PT piezoelectric energy harvester, *Adv. Mater.*, 26, 28, 4880–4887, 2014.

78. Dagdeviren, C., Yang, B.D., Su, Y., Tran, P.L., Joe, P., Anderson, E., Xia, J., Doraiswamy, V., Dehdashti, B., Feng, X., Lu, B., Poston, R., Khalpey, Z., Ghaffari, R., Huang, Y., Slepian, M.J., Rogers, J.A., Conformal piezoelectric energy harvesting and storage from motions of the heart, lung, and diaphragm, *Proc. Natl. Acad. Sci. U. S. A.*, 111, 5, 1927–1932, 2014.

79. Kim, D.H., Shin, H.J., Lee, H., Jeong, C.K., Park, H., Hwang, G.-T., Lee, H.-Y., Joe, D.J., Han, J.H., Lee, S.H., Kim, J., Joung, B., Lee, K.J., *In Vivo* self-powered wireless transmission using biocompatible flexible energy harvesters, *Adv. Funct. Mater.*, 27, 25, 1700341, 2017.

80. Feng, H., Zhao, C., Tan, P., Liu, R., Chen, X., Li, Z., Nanogenerator for biomedical applications, *Adv. Healthc. Mater.*, 7, 10, 1701298, 2018.

81. Shi, B., Li, Z., Fan, Y., Implantable energy-harvesting devices, *Adv. Mater.*, 30, 44, 1801511, 2018.

82. Li, Z., Zhu, G., Yang, R., Wang, A.C., Wang, Z.L., Muscle-driven *in vivo* nanogenerator, *Adv. Mater.*, 22, 23, 2534–2537, 2010.

83. Buzsaki, G., Anastassiou, C.A., Koch, C., The origin of extracellular fields and currents — EEG, ECoG, LFP and spikes, *Nat. Rev. Neurosci.*, 13, 6, 407–420, 2012.

84. Lotte, F., Bougrain, L., Clerc, M., Electroencephalography (EEG)-based brain–computer interfaces, *Wiley Encyclopedia of Electrical and Electronics Engineering*, Wiley, 2015.

85. Kubler, A., Nijboer, F., Mellinger, J., Vaughan, T.M., Pawelzik, H., Schalk, G., McFarland, D.J., Birbaumer, N., Wolpaw, J.R., A review of organic and inorganic biomaterials for neural interfaces, *Neurology*, 64, 1775, 2005. Fattahi, P., Yang, G., Kim, G., Abidian, M.R., *Adv. Mater.*, 26, 12, 1846–1885, 2014.

86. Yang, T., Hakimian, S., Schwartz, T.H., Intraoperative ElectroCorticoGraphy (ECog): Indications, techniques, and utility in epilepsy surgery. *Epileptic Disord.*, Wiley online library, 16, 3, 271–279, 2014.

87. Shin, G., Gomez, A.M., Al-Hasani, R., Jeong, Y.R., Kim, J., Xie, Z., Banks, A., Lee, S.M., Han, S.Y., Yoo, C.J., Lee, J.L., Lee, S.H., Kurniawan, J., Tureb, J., Guo, Z., Yoon, J., Park, S., II, Bang, S.Y., Nam, Y., Walicki, M.C., Samineni, V.K., Mickle, A.D., Lee, K., Heo, S.Y., McCall, J.G., Pan, T., Wang, L., Feng, X., Kim, T., II, Kim, J.K., Li, Y., Huang, Y., Gereau, R.W., Ha, J.S., Bruchas, M.R., Rogers, J.A., Flexible near-field wireless optoelectronics as subdermal implants for broad applications in optogenetics, *Neuron*, 93, 3, 509–521.e3, 2017.

88. Hong, G., Yang, X., Zhou, T., Lieber, C.M., Mesh electronics: A new paradigm for tissue-like brain probes, *Curr. Opin. Neurobiol.*, 50, 33–41, 2017.

89. Jia, Y., Khan, W., Lee, B., Fan, B., Madi, F., Weber, A., Li, W., Ghovanloo, M., Wireless opto-electro neural interface for experiments with small freely behaving animals, *J. Neural Eng.*, 15, 4, 046032, 2018.

90. Lee, S. and Lee, C., Toward advanced neural interfaces for the peripheral nervous system (PNS) and their future applications, *Curr. Opin. Biomed. Eng.*, 6, 130–137, 2018.

91. Wang, J., Thow, X.Y., Wang, H., Lee, S., Voges, K., Thakor, N.V., Yen, S.C., Lee, C., Intelligence toward future implanted body sensor networks, *Adv. Healthc. Mater.*, 7, 5, 1700987, 2018.

92. Clements, I.P., Mukhatyar, V.J., Srinivasan, A., Bentley, J.T., Andreasen, D.S., Bellamkonda, R.V., Regenerative scaffold electrodes for peripheral nerve interfacing. *IEEE Trans. Neural Syst. Rehabil. Eng.*, 21, 4, 554–566, 2013.

93. Delgado-Martinez, I., Righi, M., Santos, D., Cutrone, A., Bossi, S., D'Amico, S., Del Valle, J., Micera, S., Navarro, X., Fascicular nerve stimulation and recording using a novel double-aisle regenerative electrode, *Neural Eng., J.*, 14, 4, 046003, 2017.

94. Rossini, P.M., Micera, S., Benvenuto, A., Carpaneto, J., Cavallo, G., Citi, L., Cipriani, C., Denaro, L., Denaro, V., Pino, G.D., Ferreri, F., Guglielmelli, E., Hoffmann, K.P., Raspopovic, S., Rigosa, J., Rossini, L., Tombini, M., Dario, P., Erratum to implantable neurotechnologies: Bidirectional neural interfaces—Applications and VLSI circuit implementations, *Clin. Neurophysiol.*, 121, 777, 2010.

95. Bri, D., Garcia, M., Lloret, J., Dini, P., Real deployments of wireless sensor networks, in: *Proceedings of the 3rd International Conference on Sensor Technologies and Applications (SENSORCOMM '09)*, Athens, Greece, pp. 415–423, June 2009.

96. Sahadevaiah, K. and Prasad Reddy, P.V.G.D., Impact of security attacks on a new security protocol for mobile ad hoc networks. Network protocols and algorithms, *Network Protoc. Algorithms*, 3, 4, 122–140, 2011.

97. Alrajeh, N.A., Khan, S., Lloret, J., Loo, J., Artificial neural network based detection of energy exhaustion attacks in wireless sensor networks capable of energy harvesting, *Ad Hoc Sens. Wirel. Netw.*, 2013, 1–25, 2013.

98. Sisodia, M.S. and Raghuwanshi, V., Anomaly base network intrusion detection by using random decision tree and random projection a fast network intrusion detection technique. *Network Protoc. Algorithms*, 3, 4, 93–107, 2011.

99. Lim, T.H., *Detecting Anomalies in Wireless Sensor Networks [Qualifying Dissertation]*, Department of Computer Science, University of York, 2010.

100. Kim, J., Bentley, P., Wallenta, C., Ahmed, M., Hailes, S., Danger is ubiquitous: Detecting malicious activities in sensor networks using the dendritic cell algorithm, in: *Artificial Immune Systems, Lecture Notes in Computer Science*, vol. 4163, pp. 390–403, Springer, Berlin, Germany, 2006.

101. Drozda, M., Schaust, S., Szczerbicka, H., AIS for misbehavior detection in wireless sensor networks: Performance and design principles, in: *Proceedings of the IEEE Congress on Evolutionary Computation (CEC '07)*, pp. 3719–3726, September 2007.

102. Alrajeh, N., Khan, S., Lloret, J., Loo, J., Artificial neural network based detection of energy exhaustion attacks in wireless sensor networks capable of energy harvesting. *Ad Hoc Sens. Wirel. Netw.*, 2013, 1–25, 2013.

103. Mukherjee, P. and Sen, S., Using learned data patterns to detect malicious nodes in sensor networks, in: *Distributed Computing and Networking, Lecture Notes in Computer Science*, vol. 4904, pp. 339–344, Springer, Berlin, Germany, 2008.

104. Li, Y.Y. and Parker, L.E., Intruder detection using a wireless sensor network with an intelligent mobile robot response, in: *Proceedings of the IEEE Southeast Conference*, pp. 37–42, April 2008.

105. Abdullah, B., Abd-alghafar, I., Salama, G., II, Abd-alhafez, A., Performance evaluation of a genetic algorithm based approach to network intrusion detection system, in: *Proceedings of the International Conference on Aerospace Sciences and Aviation Technology*, Military Technical College, Cairo, Egypt, 2009.

106. Khanna, R., Liu, H., Chen, H.-H., Reduced complexity intrusion detection in sensor networks using genetic algorithm, in: *Proceedings of the IEEE International Conference on Communications (ICC '09)*, pp. 1–5, June 2009.

107. Lusted, L.B., Medical progress – medical electronics. *N. Engl. J. Med.*, 252, 580–5, 1955.

108. Ledley, R.S. and Lusted, L.B., Reasoning foundations of medical diagnosis. *Science*, 130, 9–21, 1959.

109. Steimann, F., On the use and usefulness of fuzzy sets in medical AI. *Artif. Intell. Med.*, 21, 131–7, 2001.

110. Gunn, A.A., The diagnosis of acute abdominal pain with computer analysis. *J. R. Coll. Surg. Edinb.*, 21, 170–2, 1976.

111. Hopfield, J.J., Neural networks and physical systems with emergent collective computational abilities. *Proc. Natl. Acad. Sci. U.S.A.*, 79, 2554–8, 1982.

112. Boon, M.E. and Kok, L.P., Neural network processing can provide means to catch errors that slip through human screening of pap smears. *Diagn. Cytopathol.*, 9, 411–6, 1993.

113. Downs, J., Harrison, R.F., Kennedy, R.L., Cross, S.S., Application of the fuzzy ARTMAP neural network model to medical pattern classification tasks. *Artif. Intell. Med.*, 8, 403–28, 1996.

114. Ashizawa, K., Ishida, T., Mac Mahon, H., Vyborny, C.J., Katsuragawa, S., Doi, K., Artificial neural networks in chest radiography: Application to the differential diagnosis of interstitial lung disease. *Acad. Radiol.*, 6, 2–9, 1999.

115. Tailor, A., Jurkovic, D., Bourne, T.H., Collins, W.P., Campbell, S., Sonographic prediction of malignancy in adnexal masses using an artificial neural network. *Br. J. Obstet. Gynaecol.*, 106, 21–30, 1999.

116. Lucht, R., Delorme, S., Brix, G., Neural network-based segmentation of dynamic MR mammographic images. *Magn. Reson. Imaging*, 20, 147–54, 2002.

117. Burke, H.B., Hoang, A., Iglehart, J.D., Marks, J.R., Predicting response to adjuvant and radiation therapy in patients with early stage breast carcinoma. *Cancer*, 82, 874–7, 1998.

118. Dybowski, R., Weler, P., Chang, R., Gant, V., Prediction of outcome in critically ill patients using artificial neural network synthesised by genetic algorithm. *Lancet*, 347, 1146–50, 1996.

119. Han, M., Snow, P.B., Epstein, J., II, Chan, T.Y., Jones, K.A., Walsh, P.C. *et al.*, A neural network predicts progression for men with Gleason score 3+4 versus 4+3 tumors after radical prostatectomy. *Urology*, 56, 994–9, 2000.

120. Zadeh, L.A., Fuzzy sets. *Inf. Control*, 8, 338–53, 1965.

121. Halm, U., Rohde, N., Klapdor, R., Reith, H.B., Thiede, A., Etzrodt, G. *et al.*, Improved sensitivity of fuzzy logic based tumor marker profiles for diagnosis of pancreatic carcinoma versus benign pancreatic disease. *Anticancer Res.*, 20, 4957–60, 2000.

122. Verma, B. and Zakos, J., A computer-aided diagnosis system for digital mammograms based on fuzzy-neural and feature extraction techniques. *IEEE Trans. Biomed. Eng.*, 5, 46–54, 2001.

123. Sztandera, L.M., Goodenday, L.S., Cios, K.J., A neuro-fuzzy algorithm for diagnosis of coronary artery stenosis. *Comput. Biol. Med.*, 26, 97–111, 1996.

124. Behloul, F., Lelieveldt, B.P., Boudraa, A., Janier, M.F., Revel, D., Reiber, J.H., Neurofuzzy systems for computer aided myocardial viability assessment. *IEEE Trans. Med. Imaging*, 20, 1302–13, 2001.

125. Bellman, R., *An Introduction to Artificial Intelligence: Can Computers Think?*, Thomson Course Technology, 1978.

126. Deo, R.C., Machine learning in medicine. *Circulation*, 132, 20, 1920–1930, 2015. [PubMed: 26572668].

127. Sutton, R.S. and Barto, A.G., *Reinforcement learning: An introduction. Vol. 1*, MIT Press, Cambridge, 1998.

128. Miller, R.A., Pople, H.E.J., Myers, J.D., Internist-I, an experimental computer-based diagnostic consultant for general internal medicine. *N. Engl. J. Med.*, 307, 8, 468–476, NEJM group, 1982. [PubMed: 7048091].

129. Smith, R.O., The emergence and emergency of assistive technology outcomes research methodology. *Assistive Technol. Outcomes Benefits*, 10, 1, 19–37, 2016.

130. Talbot, T.B., Sagae, K., John, B., Rizzo, A.A., Sorting out the virtual patient: How to exploit artificial intelligence, game technology and sound educational practices to create engaging role-playing simulations. *Int. J. Gaming Comput.-Mediat. Simul.*, 4, 3, 1–19, 2012. http://dx.doi.org/10.4018/jgcms.2012070101.

131. van den Heuvel, R.J., Lexis, M.A., Gelderblom, G.J., Jansens, R.M., de Witte, L.P., Robots and ICT to support play in children with severe physical disabilities: A systematic review. *Disabil. Rehabil. Assist. Technol.*, 11, 103–116, 2016.

132. Celi, L.A., Moseley, E., Moses, C., Ryan, P., Somai, M., Stone, D. *et al.*, From pharmacovigilance to clinical care optimization. *Big Data*, 2, 134–41, 2014.

133. Helpman, E. and Trajtenberg, M., Diffusion of general purpose technologies. *NBER Work. Pap. Ser.*, Working paper series 5773, 1996.

134. Trajtenberg, M., *AI as the next GPT: A Political-Economy Perspective*, NBER Work. Pap. Ser., w24245, 2018.

135. Johnson, A.E., Pollard, T.J., Mark, R.G., Reproducibility in critical care: A mortality prediction case study. *Machine Learning for Healthcare Conference*, November 2017.

136. Gibson, D.G., Ochieng, B., Kagucia, E.W. *et al.*, Mobile phone-delivered reminders and incentives to improve childhood immunisation coverage and timeliness in Kenya (M-SIMU): A cluster randomized controlled trial. *Lancet Glob. Health*, 5, e428–38, 2017.

137. Stockwell, M.S., Kharbanda, E.O., Martinez, R.A. *et al.*, Effect of a text messaging intervention on influenza vaccination in an urban, low-income pediatric and adolescent population: A randomized controlled trial. *JAMA*, 307, 1702–8, 2012.

138. Haskew, J., Rø, G., Saito, K. *et al.*, Implementation of a cloud-based electronic medical record for maternal and child health in rural Kenya. *Int. J. Med. Inform.*, 84, 349–54, 2015.

139. Haskew, J., Ro, G., Turner, K. *et al.*, Implementation of a cloud-based electronic medical record to reduce gaps in the HIV treatment continuum in Rural Kenya. *PloS One*, 10, e0135361, 2015.

140. Piette, J.D., Mendoza-Avelares, M.O., Ganser, M. *et al.*, A preliminary study of a cloud-computing model for chronic illness selfcare support in an underdeveloped country. *Am. J. Prev. Med.*, 40, 629–32, 2011.

141. Utermohlen, K., Four robotic process automation (RPA) applications in the healthcare industry. *Medium*, 2018.

142. UserTesting, *Healthcare Chatbot Apps are on the Rise but the Overall Customer Experience (cx) Falls Short According to a UserTesting Report*, UserTesting, San Francisco, 2019.

143. Lohr, S., IBM is counting on its bet on Watson, and paying big money for it, New York Times, 17, 10, 2016.

144. Otake, T., IBM big data used for rapid diagnosis of rare leukemia case in Japan, *The Japan Times*, 2016.

145. Graham, J., Artificial intelligence, machine learning, and the FDA, 2016.

146. Barber, F., Botti, V.J., Koehler, J., AI: Past, present and future. Upgrade the European Online Magazine for the IT Professional, 3, 5.

147. Savadjiev, P., Chong, J., Dohan, A., Vakalopoulou, M., Reinhold, C., Paragios, N., Gallix, B., Demystification of AI-driven medical image interpretation: Past, present and future. *Eur. Radiol.*, 29, 3, 1616–1624, 2019.

## 7

Improvement of Computer Vision-Based Elephant Intrusion Detection System (EIDS) with Deep Learning Models

Jothibasu M.*, Sowmiya M., Harsha R., Naveen K. S. and Suriyaprakash T. B.

Department of ECE, PSG Institute of Technology and Applied Research, Coimbatore, India

Abstract

The expanding need of wild life behavior and partition of human-wild life strife has guided the researchers to the execution of counteraction and alleviation draws near. The division of boondocks grounds and separation of elephant populaces moves toward the essential driver of Human Elephant Collision (HEC). Human-elephant strife is a troublesome issue since which prompts to territory misfortune, destruction of agribusiness zones, environment misfortune. This demands an intelligent system which predicts and rest the conflict. In this work, Artificial Intelligent based device is developed to detect the presence of elephant into residential areas and provides a warning to the forest rangers. In this counterfeit intelligent gadget, the identification part comprises of the PIR sensor and seismic sensor. Both of the sensor yields trigger the camera module associated with the model created. The camera module catches a video for a specific span which may contain the nearness of the animal. At that point, the recordings are been coordinated to the trained AI algorithm. The AI algorithm forms the video in the succession of the casing and once if the presence of an elephant is available in the video, it triggers the cautioning system. An SSD, YOLO, and Faster RCNN algorithm has been accomplished to locate the ideal one. The model builds up a broad item to distinguish an economical arrangement.

Keywords: Deep learning, human elephant conflict, PIR sensor, YOLO, Faster RCNN

Corresponding author: jothibasu@psgitech.ac.in

Anamika Ahirwar, Piyush Kumar Shukla, Manish Shrivastava, Priti Maheshwary and Bhupesh Gour (eds.) Innovative Engineering with AI Applications, (131–154) © 2023 Scrivener Publishing LLC

7.1   Introduction

In recent times our environment is influenced more regrettable because of numerous external factors. The wellspring of nourishment for creatures in the backwoods isn't adequate as before because of ecological corruption, deforestation which drives the creatures to show up in human local locations. A few administration approaches have been rehearsed at various scales for human-elephant conflict. Elephants can be found in a variety of habitats, such as savannas, forests, deserts, and swamps. Generally, elephants were classified into two species, namely African elephants (*Loxodonta africana*) and Asian elephants (*Elephas maximus*). Under Asian elephants, Indian elephants have specific name *Elephas maximus* indicus. Elephants put through seasonal migration in search of food, water, and spouses. Due to over population and rapid urbanization, the need for land especially for human survival has tremendously increased. So, humans started invading forests. This leads to loss of habitat for the wildlife. The increase in the area of human settlements has resulted in the shrinkage of forests that serve as home for the elephants. Due to the loss of their habitat, the elephants may enter the human survival area that was once a natural habitat [15]. The shortage of food for elephants also leads to crop looting in the nearby farm lands. In recent times there have been several incidents of entry of elephants into residential areas. Every year many humans lose their lives due to human Elephant Conflicts and many elephants die on railway tracks after being hit by a train.

Even though many widespread avoidance techniques are available, still it provides temporary zone-specific solutions. This demands an intelligent system which predicts and rest the conflict. This system should be more efficient in detecting the presence of elephant in the area and alert the public nearby about the presence of the elephant and to perform some repulsive operations against the elephants which infringe into the residential as well as the farming areas [13, 16]. Our system is designed in such a way that once the motion is detected using a sensor, the camera is activated to capture a video of 10 seconds including the frames of object crossed. The captured video is divided into frames then fed to the Deep learning architecture which is pre trained with the images of the elephant. The Deep learning architecture forms feature maps by convolving throughout the frames of the video. The presence of elephant is predicted by classifying the feature maps based on the pre trained model and the accuracy is evaluated. If the accuracy is more and consistent throughout all the frames of the video, then the presence of elephant is confirmed. Once the presence of elephant is confirmed, the system switches over to the alerting and repulsive system which undergoes alarming and an instant message is sent to the forest officers.

7.2 Elephant Intrusion Detection System (EIDS)

7.2.1 Existing Approaches

Elephant detection method is developed using PIR and microwave radar sensors. The system contains two parts, elephant detector, and bee simulator. A bee stimulator contains a vibrating trigger was used to aggravate the bees. The elephants were extruded using the sound and sting of the bee. Wireless RF module is used for communication between the two parts. Ropes tied to a pole were used to trigger the sensor during the arrival of elephants [1].

Authors have proposed an automated unsupervised elephant intrusion detection system (EIDS) [2]. The elephant's image is captured and processed using Haar wavelet and analyzed using image vision algorithms. A message is sent using GSM module indicating that an elephant has been detected in the forest border. Optimized distance metric concepts have been performed which retrieves more images with lesser retrieval time.

Occlusion is a major concern in the forest areas as elephants may be fully or partially hidden due to the plants, trees or any other occluding objects. Furthermore, the size and shape of elephants varies significantly which results in the inability to use shape and size as attributes [14]. Real time video input from the camera is converted into a sequence of images. These images are pre-processed to remove the distortion and noise using filters and enhance the features. The pre-processed image is further segmented to identify the region of interest (ROI), which may have elephant or otherwise. After feature extraction, SVM training is performed with a set of training images collected with two classes [3]. To emphasize the correctness of the detection of elephants in an image, further each of the image in class which contains elephant is considered and applied with color and texture features.

Elephant Intrusion system detect the elephant on the railway track and alerts the driver that the elephant is on the track. The transmitter and receiver start to communicate once the train starts to move, this communication take place only at the moment of the train. Here, prototype model for real-time elephant intrusion is developed and a design model to spot the elephant intrusion. The system automatically sends a SMS through

GSM to the driver if an elephant is detected. Image processing techniques are used to detect whether the object detected is elephant or not [4].

A detection system using deep architectures [5] is developed for animal detection. The system used algorithms such as support vector machine (SVM), k-nearest neighbor (KNN) and ensemble tree for classification. The detection model provided an accuracy of 91.4% on standard camera-trap dataset.

7.2.2   Challenges

The real time detection of the elephant in the forest prone areas is a challenging task. The elephant in the forest may be closer or far from the camera so that when the camera is triggered to take the video, the image of the elephant in the video may differ in size when it moves far and near the camera. So, the same elephant may appear at different sizes in the same video which may lead to false detection. To solve this issue, we use deep learning architecture where the object at different scales and different aspect ratios are detected and there may be no chance for false detection.

Another issue is that, the elephants may enter the residential areas during night times, so that the quality of the captured video may be not clear which may also lead to false detection [6, 12]. As we use Pre trained Deep learning Architecture which is trained with plenty of elephant's images which includes Gray scale, RGB images. So, that the system may perfectly predict the presence of elephant even in the average quality video of the camera.

Time taken for prediction and classification of elephant in the video is another aspect which should be considered [8]. The algorithms used in this system are more time efficient as they predict and classify the object in the video within a second. Processing time is faster and the delay in the system has been reduced.

7.3   Theoretical Framework

7.3.1   Deep Learning Models for EIDS

Deep learning is a subset of machine learning which uses neural networks to learn and perform operations, whereas machine learning is a subset of Artificial intelligence which learns from data and improves the system by experience. In EIDS, we used deep learning methods like Faster RCNN, SSD, YOLO to detect elephants from the surveillance areas. Figure 7.1 signifies the relation between AI, ML and DL.

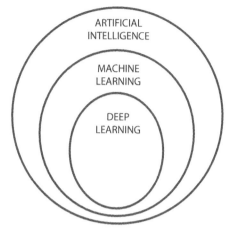

Figure 7.1 Relation between AI, ML, and DL.

7.3.1.1   Fast RCNN

Fast RCNN is one of the Object detection algorithms which takes input of image and feed the image to the CNN, which in turn generates the convolutional feature maps. The feature map generation is same as that of the Faster RCNN algorithm. Using these maps, the regions of proposals are extracted. The region proposals are extracted using the selective search method where the regions are proposed based on the texture, color, size, and shape compatibility. We then use a RoI pooling layer to reshape all the proposed regions and it can be fed into a fully connected network. A SoftMax layer and linear regression layer is used in this algorithm which classifies and bounds the object in the given input image. Since the Fast RCNN uses the selective search algorithm for region proposals, it takes nearly 2 seconds to detect the object in the given frame.

7.3.1.2   Faster RCNN

Faster RCNN is the efficient object detection algorithms which uses the Region proposal Networks to localize the object in the frame and classifies the object, thereby reducing the time consumption for processing the frame of the image [9]. It consists of two modules as shown in Figure 7.2. The first module is fully convolutional network which proposes regions in the image and the second module is the Fast RCNN which works on these proposed regions and detects the object.

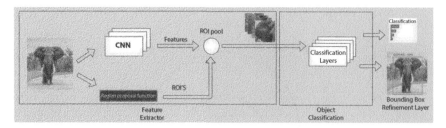

Figure 7.2 Faster RCNN.

7.3.1.2.1   Region Proposal Network (RPN)

Region proposal network gets input of the convolutional feature map where the image is convolved with the sliding window. RPN consists of two stages. The first one is Region Proposal Generator and the second one is bounding box regressor and a classifier. RPN uses a separate network which generates region proposals, by sliding a small network over the convolutional feature map output by the last shared convolutional layer. This small network takes input of an n × n spatial window of the input convolutional feature map. Each sliding window is charted to a lower-dimensional feature. The bounding box regressor uses a relative method where the proposed region is made to actually bind the objects in the image. To ensure that the bounded region contains an object, the classifier is used. The classifier identifies the presence of object using SoftMax classification method. In SoftMax classification method, the confidential scores are normalized and if the output is high, it indicates that the bounding box detected the object on the other hand if the output is low, the bounding box does not bounded the object and the corresponding bounding region is eliminated.

7.3.1.2.2   Anchors

There may be some cases that, multiple objects occur on same sliding window frame. Multiple bounding boxes with object to bounding box ratio of 1:1 for the region proposals are used. These bounding boxes are called anchors. An important property of the anchor boxes is that the center points of all these boxes are same. Figure 7.3 shows the overlapping anchor boxes for a frame.

7.3.1.2.3   Loss Function

In Faster RCNN architecture, each anchor boxes are assigned with binary class label. The anchors with Intersection over Union (IoU) ratio above

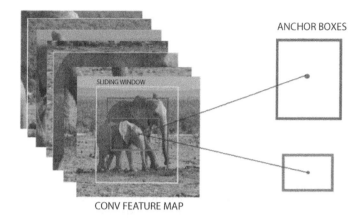

Figure 7.3 Anchor boxes.

0.7 are assigned as positive and the anchor with IoU ratio less than 0.3 is assigned as negative. Anchors with neither positive nor negative do not contribute to this function. Loss is calculated by,

Total Loss function = Classification loss + regression loss

$$L(\{p_i\},\{t_i\})=\{1/N_{cls}\ [\Sigma_i\ L_{cls}\ (p_i,p_i^*)]\} + \measuredangle\{1/N_{reg}\ [\Sigma_i\ (t_i,t_i^*)]\}$$

Where,

i – index of the anchor

p_i – predicted probability

p_i^* – ground truth label of pi

t_i – vector representing co-ordinates of bounding boxes

t_i^* – ground truth values of the co-ordinates

N_{cls} – normalized classification function

N_{reg} – normalized regression function

L_{cls} – classification loss over two classes

$p_i^* L_{reg}$ – regression loss for positive anchor

$\measuredangle$ – balancing parameter

7.3.1.3 *Single-Shot Multibox Detector (SSD)*

Single Shot means that the tasks of object localization and classification are done in a single forward pass of the network. The SSD is a purely convolutional neural network that is organized into three parts,

1. Base convolutions-derived from the input image classification architecture (VGG16) that will provide lower level feature maps.
2. Auxiliary convolutions-added on the top of the base network that will provide higher-level feature maps.
3. Prediction convolutions-it locates and identifies the objects on the feature maps.

7.3.1.3.1 Architecture

SSD is built on a VGG-16 Architecture without the fully connected layers which provides high quality image classification methods. In SSD, a set of auxiliary connected layers are used which enables the extraction of features at multiple scales and progressively decreasing the size of the input image at each layer. Multi box is a method used for fast class agnostic bounding box co-ordinate proposals [10]. Here, Inception type convolutional network is used. Figure 7.4 gives the comprehensive architecture of SSD.

Multibox loss function consists of two components,

- Confidence loss – measures how confident the network detects the object
- Location loss – measures how far the predicted bounding boxes from the actual ground truth values

Features maps are a representation of the dominant features of the image at different scales, therefore running Multibox on multiple feature maps increases the likelihood of any object to be eventually detected, localized and appropriately classified.

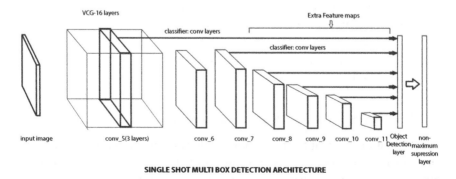

SINGLE SHOT MULTI BOX DETECTION ARCHITECTURE

Figure 7.4 SSD architecture.

7.3.1.3.2   Non-Maximum Suppression (NMS)

Given the large number of boxes generated during a forward pass of SSD at inference time, it is essential to prune most of the bounding box by applying a technique known as non-maximum suppression. Boxes with a confidence loss threshold less than 'ct' and IoU less than 'lt' are discarded, and only the top N predictions are kept. This ensures only the most likely predictions are retained by the network, while the noisy ones are removed.

7.3.1.4   *You Only Look Once (YOLO)*

Yolo architecture is more like FCNN (fully convolutional neural network) and passes the image (n x n) once through the FCNN and output is (m x m) prediction. Architecture will split the input image into m x m grid and for each grid, generate two bounding boxes and class probabilities for those bounding boxes.

A single convolutional network simultaneously predicts multiple bounding boxes and class probabilities for those boxes. YOLO trains on full images and directly optimizes detection performance. This unified model has several benefits over traditional methods of object detection. First, YOLO is extremely fast. Since frame detection as a regression problem, we don't need a complex pipeline. We simply run our neural network on a new image at test time to predict detections. Our base network runs at 45 frames per second with no batch processing on a Titan X GPU and a fast version runs at more than 150 fps. This means we can process streaming video in real-time with less than 25 milliseconds of latency [11]. Figure 7.5 shows the detailed architecture of YOLO.

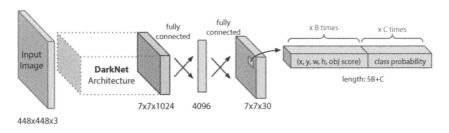

Figure 7.5 YOLO architecture.

7.3.1.4.1   Bounding Box Predictions

Each bounding box consists of 5 predictions: x, y, w, h, and confidence. As shown in Figure 7.6, the (x, y) coordinates represent the center of the box relative to the bounds of the grid cell. The width and height are predicted relative to the whole image. Finally, the confidence prediction represents the IOU between the predicted box and any ground truth box. Each grid cell also predicts C conditional class probabilities. These probabilities are conditioned on the grid cell containing an object. We only predict one set of class probabilities per grid cell, regardless of the number of boxes B.

Confidence scores of each bounding box = Pr (Classi | Object)* Pr(Object)*IOU

Where, Pr (Classi |Object) -Conditional class probability

$$IOU = \frac{\text{Area of overlap of ground truth and predicted B boxes}}{\text{Area of their Union}}$$

YOLO predicts multiple bounding boxes per grid cell. At training time, we want only one bounding box predictor to be responsible for each object. We assign one predictor to be responsible for predicting an object based on which the prediction has the highest current IOU with ground truth. This leads to specialization between the bounding box predictors. Each predictor gets better at predicting certain sizes, aspect ratios, class of an object, improving overall recall. Figure 7.7 shows the overview of bounding box and its class probability map in YOLO.

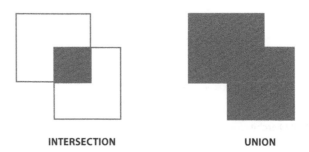

INTERSECTION   **UNION**

Figure 7.6 IOU.

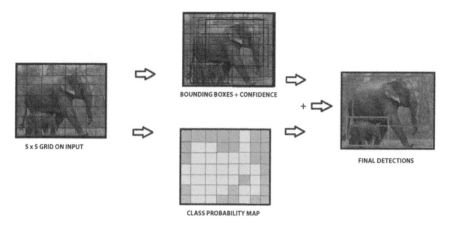

Figure 7.7 YOLO model.

7.3.2   Hardware Specifications

7.3.2.1   Raspberry-Pi 3 Model B

Image processing and Computer vision algorithms requires higher computation power, we choose Raspberry-Pi 3 as a microcontroller. Even it mounted micro SD card as a secondary memory and it is powered by high-quality 2.5A micro USB power supply. Figure 7.8 gives the specification of Raspberry-Pi3ModelB.

7.3.2.2   Night Vision OV5647 Camera Module

REES52 Raspberry Pi Night Vision OV5647 Camera module is chosen to capture video in night time also. It contains 2 Infrared LED Lights in the both side which help in night vision. Figure 7.9 gives the specification of OV5647 Camera module.

SoC	Broadcom BCM2837
CPU	4x ARM Cortex-A53, 1.2GHz
GPU	Broadcom VideoCore IV
RAM	1 GB LPDDR2 (900 MHz)
STORAGE	microSD
Ethernet	10/100 Ethernet
Wireless	2.4GHz 802.11n wireless
Video Output	HDMI
GPIO	40-pin header. populated
Ports	HDMI, 3.5mm analogue audio-video jack, 4x USB 2.0, Ethernet, Camera Serial Interface (CSI), Display Serial Interface

Figure 7.8 Specification of raspberry-Pi 3.

Sensor	1/4" Omnivision OV4647
Pixel	5 Mega Pixels
Most effective pixels	2592 × 1944
Pixel Size	1.4 um × 1.4 um
Focus type	Fixed focus
FOV	62°
Image format	VGA
Color	24-Bit True color
Lens construction	4G+IR650
Aperture	F2.4
Operating temperature	-20°C to 70°C
Dimension	25mm ×24mm
Power consumption	90Wm/30uW
Voltage	1.7V-3.0V
Pin Number	15 Pin
Output signal	YCBCR4:2:2, RGB565, RAWRGB
Frame rate	30fps

Figure 7.9 Specification of camera module.

7.3.2.3 PIR Sensor

Figure 7.10 gives the specification of PIR sensor. Since PIR detect the radiation from the living organisms in a range of 8-16 meters. It will be very useful to trigger the camera when human or animals are crossed [7].

7.3.2.4 GSM Module

Figure 7.11 shows the specification of GSM module. As there must be a communication between the checkpoints (Location of EIDS), the forest officers and local residencies. We use the GSM module to communicate between them. As the GSM module is available with the sim slot, we can use a sim to send message.

7.3.3 Proposed Work

The prototype uses a Passive Infra Red (PIR) sensor to detect the movement of the elephants. These sensors are mounted on trees in the border of the forest. PIR sensors are mounted in both high and low level from

Max Current (mA)	0.150 idle, 3.0 active
Voltage (Vdc)	3.0 - 6.0
Communication	1-wire + Enable
Range	Up to 30'
Detection Angle	180°
Operating Temp (°F)	32 to 122
Dimensions (mm)	36.0 x 36.0 x 20.2

Figure 7.10 Specification of PIR sensor.

Operating frequency	GSM 850MHz, EGSM 900MHz, DCS 1800MHz and PCS 1900MHz
Operating Voltage rating	3.2V - 4.8V dc
Output pin voltage	5V dc
Output pin current	25mA
Communication mode	UART interface, configured for full-duplex asychronous mode
Baud rate	Supports auto bauding, 9.6kb/s used.

Figure 7.11 Specification of GSM module.

ground in order to detect living beings irrespective of their size. When elephant or any other living being comes within the range of sensor, the IR radiation level received by one half of sensor increases by another half. The sensor reacts to this change and makes the output HIGH. This output is used to activate the surveillance camera that is mounted on trees or high poles. The surveillance camera captures a short video clip. A video clip is captured instead of images that have a time delay between each image, so that elephants will not escape from being captured by camera.

The video clip is the input for image processing algorithms. The need to move towards image processing is that, the PIR sensor is sensitive to radiation emitted by all living beings. So, it is mandatory to check whether, it is elephant or some other non-dangerous animals (cow, dog, deer). In this prototype, we use Raspberry-Pi 3 model B which has four ARM Cortex A53 microprocessors. The captured video is divided into the sequence of images and processed under a machine learning algorithm namely FASTER R-CNN using Tensor-Flow backend which builds a pre-trained model for the detection of elephant which is stored in the memory of the processor. In the algorithm, the sequence of images is convolved by different filters to form the feature maps with the anchor boxes on the feature maps. Then the feature maps are converted to fully connected layer where SoftMax is performed to predict the object. The neural networks detect the object by predicting the co-ordinates of the bounding boxes and the confidence scores of the presence of object, while training the model the objects in the image are assigned to a class and labeled manually.

Once the Processor processes the video and if the object is detected, the processor triggers the input of GSM module. The GSM module which works on asynchronous full-duplex mode which is used to send the messages to the forest rangers.

7.4 Experimental Results

7.4.1 Dataset Preparation

In the implementation of Faster R-CNN algorithm, we need to train the model using large number of image data. We need to train the model with large number of elephant images with elephants in different positions, different locations (background), and various illumination and lighting conditions. Classifier for accurate detection requires a minimum number of classes. So, some of non-dangerous animals that can be found in the forest boundary such as cow, deer, monkey are also considered for classification purpose. Around 300 images of elephant are collected from internet and also 200 images for other classes. Then the images are manually checked for quality as they may also contain very bad images that may affect the accuracy of the model. The poor images are the filtered out manually. Figure 7.12 shows the CSV file of data storage and the entries CSV file looks as given below.

The dataset now contains images of different resolutions. So, all the images are resized to same dimension as 200 x 200 images. Dataset contains around 500 images of different classes and of same dimensions. The images may contain the objects (animals) of different sizes. So, the area of

	A	B	C	D	E	F	G	H	I
1	filename	width	height	class	xmin	ymin	xmax	ymax	
2	cow (1).jpg	200	200	cow	29	9	152	200	
3	cow (2).jpg	200	200	cow	38	66	152	176	
4	cow (3).jpg	200	200	cow	28	32	158	175	
5	cow (4).jpg	200	200	cow	67	9	167	179	
6	cow (5).jpg	200	200	cow	40	2	177	195	
7	deer (1).jpg	200	200	deer	47	5	163	190	
8	deer (2).jpg	200	200	deer	49	14	174	187	
9	deer (3).jpg	200	200	deer	26	3	155	200	
10	deer (4).jpg	200	200	deer	29	8	181	199	
11	deer (5).jpg	200	200	deer	59	12	180	193	
12	elephant (1).jpg	200	200	elephant	24	52	115	197	
13	elephant (1).jpg	200	200	elephant	130	61	200	174	
14	elephant (10).jpg	200	200	elephant	100	11	191	200	
15	elephant (10).jpg	200	200	elephant	43	22	132	178	
16	elephant (11).jpg	200	200	elephant	66	8	138	197	
17	elephant (12).jpg	200	200	elephant	35	2	189	191	
18	elephant (13).jpg	200	200	elephant	63	15	153	189	

Figure 7.12 Sample database of CSV file.

image with the animals should be marked and labeled accordingly. To do so, a graphical annotation tool namely labeling is used. The animals in each image are manually marked by a rectangular bounding box and labeled to its class.

This is saved as XML file. The csv file is generated using these XML files. The csv file has details like filename, width, height, class, xmin, ymin, xmax, ymax. The xmin, ymin, xmax, ymax represent the coordinates of rectangular bounding box which covers the animal in that image. Figures 7.13 and 7.14 shows the identified cow and elephant image from the database.

Figure 7.13 Cow (3) image.

Figure 7.14 Elephant (11) image.

The dataset then needs to be divided into two sets – train and test dataset. The train data will be used by model for training purposes by which feature maps are created. Then the test data is used for self-validation by the model. The data is split in ratio of 4:1, test: train in a random fashion.

7.4.2   Performance Analysis of DL Algorithms

The labeled images in the train dataset is now fed to the FASTER RCNN NETWORK as input. The Conv Net generates feature map of each image. The feature map is based on the bounding box information it receives about that image. Region proposal network (RPN) is applied to the output feature maps. A sliding window convolutes over the feature map and maps lower dimensional feature maps. The bounding box regressor in another stage ensures the object to be classified is bounded as proposed. The ConvNet returns the object proposals to be classified and their object score. Then a RoI pooling layer convolves to the object proposals to produce a small feature map of fixed dimensions. The object proposals feature map is then passed onto a fully connected layer. The fully connected layer has a SoftMax layer and a linear regression layer. Here in this process, it classifies and outputs the bounding boxes for objects.

The SoftMax return class predictions based on confidence score. If the score is low, the corresponding bounding box is eliminated. The bounding box regressor returns bounding box offsets with correspondence to the object proposal RoIs. These intermediate values return by FASTER RCNN, is used to train the model. The test data is used for the self-validation. The feature vector obtained from the test data is classified and compared with the actual class. The loss is calculated based on difference between predicted output and actual output. The training process is carried out for several epochs to bring down the loss to a very minimal value and finally it generates a model.

This Classifier uses this pre trained to find the region of object and bounds it with a rectangular box. The object in the RoI is then classified to one of the classes by the classifier and precision score is also returned.

The initial trial for this work has been experimented by using the real time elephant attack video that happened at Periyanaickenpalayam in the year 2017. The video was given as input to the Elephant Detection Program. The video was sampled at a rate of 0.5 frames per sec and stored as images. Then these images are given as input to the classifier. The classifier localizes the region of elephant bounds it with a rectangular box and returns along with precision score. The following Figure 7.15 (Frame 1 to Frame 6) are some frames of the video which localizes the region where the elephant is present by bounding box and detects it as elephant.

Figure 7.15 Various frames of elephant video.

In the above experiment, the elephant in the video is spotted by convolving the frames of the video under Faster RCNN Algorithm and is classified using the SoftMax values and the accuracy percentage is found. With this accuracy percentage, the presence of elephant is confirmed. The Faster RCNN algorithm provides an efficient methodology which processes a frame of the video captured in 0.2 seconds which is much faster than previously proposed systems. In addition to that, Faster RCNN works on RPN so the accuracy is also much higher. This system uses a PIR sensor which detects the movement of elephants and then triggers the camera to capture a video, which saves the power consumption by operating camera whenever required and also confirms the movement of elephants. In case of elephant detection, our system alerts the public by messaging through mobile using GSM module, which is comparatively efficient and safe than existing systems.. Then the GSM module sends a message, "Elephant Detected" along with an image [the frame with highest matching percentage] to forest officers and nearby residents as shown in Figure 7.16.

In the above proposed method, we use the following algorithms based on their performance. The Mean average precision and the processing speed of the used algorithms are given in Table 7.1.

In the view of overall performance, faster RCNN is more efficient in predicting the elephant accurately since it has high mAP and average processing speed. It is strongly evident that the proposed system may be a great contribution to the society and the environment.

To analyze the performance of the algorithm, metrics such as mean average precision (mAP), time and frames per second (FPS) are considered which are shown in Figure 7.17.

From the Figure 7.17, we can see that Faster RCNN and SSD 300 has higher mAP than the other two models. Since mAP is very concerned in our application, we cannot prefer algorithms with lower mAP. Considering the time for response of the algorithms, Faster RCNN is the fastest among all. YOLO has is the second fastest and SSD is third. Even though YOLO has higher FPS than SSD and Faster RCNN, its mAP value is less and time

Figure 7.16 SMS indication to forest ranger.

Table 7.1 Parameter comparison of DL algorithms.

Parameters	Fast RCNN	Faster RCNN	YOLO	SSD
mAP	70.0	76.4	63.4	74.3
FPS	0.5	5	45	46

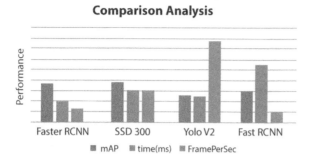

Figure 7.17 Comparison of DL algorithms.

for response is not much differing. So, YOLO V3 is not an optimal solution for our application.

But to find the most optimal algorithm for our problem, we're considering another metric namely accuracy. The accuracy of the algorithms for different size of objects is shown in Figure 7.18.

It is evident from the graph that the precision of both SSD 330 and Faster RCNN for larger objects is almost identical. But when the size of the object decreases, we can see a fall in the accuracy of the SSD 300 algorithm. Since we are detecting elephants from a far distance, we get items of smaller size as data. So, from this study, it is obvious that Faster RCNN is more optimal than SSD 300, for our application. In Figures 7.19–7.21 shows the Output of Faster RCNN, YOLO and SSD 300 networks.

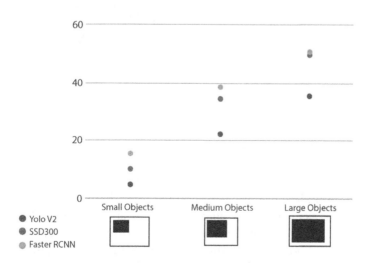

Figure 7.18 Accuracy of DL algorithms.

Figure 7.19 Output with smaller object from Faster RCNN.

Figure 7.20 Output with smaller object from YOLO.

Figure 7.21 Output with smaller object from SSD 300.

It is shown that all three were able to detect the elephants, but the localization of bounding box and precision indicates that Faster RCNN is able to detect the elephants more efficiently in our application. So, by this we infer Faster RCNN as the most optimal algorithm for detection of elephants in forest border areas. The following Figures 7.22–7.24 describe the various loss functions of faster RCNN algorithm.

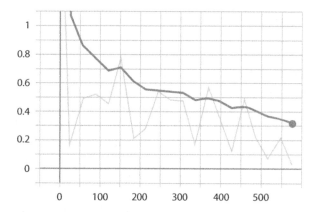

Figure 7.22 Classification loss.

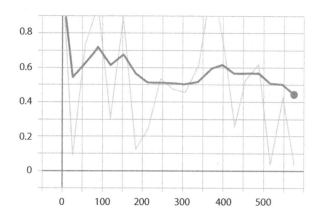

Figure 7.23 Localization loss.

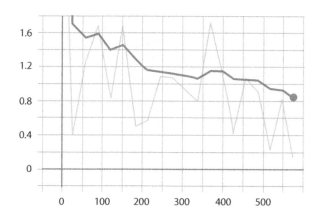

Figure 7.24 Total loss.

7.5 Conclusion

In the above concert, the suggested idea is likely to be a more sophisticated strategy where the identification of real time artifacts takes place. The elephant is correctly spotted by the Deep Learning model in the recorded footage, which is pre-trained by all available elephant images so that it is possible to reduce the possibility of false detection. In the recorded video and the accuracy percentage measurement, the Deep Learning Architectures is found to be a fantastic mechanism where the elephant is confined. The presence of the elephant is confirmed by setting a threshold value for the accuracy percentage. There are many algorithms that perform detection of objects. As the number of proposals for the completely linked layer in the algorithms used above is reduced, the model proposed is more time-efficient. After analyzing all DL architectures Faster RCNN, YOLO and SSD 300 were able to identify the elephants, but the localization of bounding box and accuracy signifies that Faster RCNN works more efficiently to detect the elephants. From this, we realized Faster RCNN as the most optimal algorithm for detection of elephants in forest border areas.

This Artificial Intelligence System functions all the more efficiently as the model is prepared on the basis of an analysis of the creatures found in the natural surroundings of the neighborhood. The approach can be used to identify the proximity of an elephant intrusion in real time. In order to achieve increasingly faster results from the various algorithms, the outputs are evaluated and find an effective way to deal with the distinction between the infringements of the animal.

References

1. Maulana, E., Nugroho, C.S., Dianisma, A.B., Animal presence detection for elephants and extruding method based on bee frequency. *Electrical Power, Electronics, Communications, Controls and Informatics Seminar (EECCIS)*, 2018.
2. Sugumar, S.J. and Jayaparvathy, R., An improved real time detection system for elephant intrusion along the forest border areas. *Sci. World J.*, Article ID 393958, 1–10, 2014.
3. Ramesh, G., Mathi, S., Pulari, S.R., Krishnamoorthy, V., An automated vision based method to detect elephants for mitigation of human-elephant conflicts. *International Conference on Advances in Computing, Communications and Informatics (ICACCI)*, 2017.

4. Suganthi, N., Rajathi, N., Farithul Inzamam, M., Elephant intrusion detection and repulsive system. *Int. J. Recent Technol. Eng.*, 07, 4, 307–310, 2018.

5. Verma, G.K. and Gupta, P., Wild animal detection from highly cluttered images using deep convolutional neural network. *Proceedings of 2nd International Conference on Computer Vision & Image Processing*, pp. 327–338.

6. Fazil, M. and Firdhous, M., IoT-enabled smart elephant detection system for combating human elephant conflict. *2018 3rd International Conference on Information Technology Research (ICITR)*.

7. Sahoo, K.C. and Pati, U.C., IoT based intrusion detection system using PIR sensor. *2017 2nd IEEE International Conference on Recent Trends in Electronics, Information & Communication Technology (RTEICT)*.

8. Shukla, P., Dua, I., Raman, B., Mittal, A., A computer vision framework for detecting and preventing human elephant collisions. *2017 IEEE International Conference on Computer Vision Workshops (ICCVW)*.

9. Ren, S., He, K., Girshick, R., Sun, J., *Faster R-CNN: Towards Real-Time Object Detection with Region Proposal Networks*, Jan. 6, 2016, arXiv: 1506.01497v3 [cs.CV].

10. Liu, W., Anguelov, D., Erhan, D., Szegedy, C., Reed, S., Fu, C.-Y., Berg, A.C., *SSD: Single Shot MultiBox Detector*, Springer International Publishing AG, 2016.

11. Maheshwari, R., Development of embedded based system to monitor elephant intrusion in forest border areas using internet of things. *Int. J. Eng. Res.*, 5, 7, 594–598, July 2016.

12. Sugumar, S.J. and Jayaparvathy, R., Design of a quadruped robot for human-conflict elephant conflict mitigation. *Artif. Life Robot.*, 18, 204–211, 2013.

13. Ashwiny, R., Mary, A., Annadurai, K., An efficient warning system for human elephant conflict. *Int. J. Sci. Res. Sci. Eng. Technol.*, 2, 2, 344–349, 2016.

14. Perera, B.M.A.O., The human-elephant conflict: A review of current status and mitigation methods. *Gajah: J. IUCN/SSC Asian Elephant Specialist Group*, 30, 41–52, 2009.

15. Santiapillai, C., Wijeyamohan, S., Bandara, G., Athurupana, R., Dissanayake, N., Read, B., An assessment of the human-elephant conflict in Sri Lanka. *Ceylon J. Sci. Biol. Sci.*, 39, 1, 21–33, 2010.

16. Sugumar, S.J. and Jayaparvathy, R., An early warning system for elephant intrusion along the forest border areas. *Curr. Sci.*, 104, 11, 1515–1526, June 10, 2013.

## 8

A Study of WSN Privacy Through AI Technique

Piyush Raja

Department of CSE, COER University, Roorkee, India

Abstract

Wireless sensor network (WSN) collects data then interpret the informations about the environment or the object they are sensing. Owing to the energy and the bandwidth limit, those sensor usually has reduced communication capability. WSN keep track of changing conditions in real time. External variables or the device designers themselves are to blame for this complex behaviour. Sensor networks often use deep learning methods to respond to certain situations, avoiding the need for wasteful overhaul. Machine learning also inspires plenty of realistic strategies for maximising resource use and extending the network's lifetime. We included a comparison guide in this paper to assist WSN designers in designing appropriate machine learning (ML) strategies for their unique implementation problems.

WSN (Wireless Sensor Network) are gaining popularity among researchers. One of the most important problems is to preserve their privacy. This region has received a significant amount of attention in recent years. Surveys and literature studies have also been conducted to provide a comprehensive overview of the various techniques. However, no previous research has focused on privacy models, or the set of assumptions utilised to construct the method. This work, in particular, focuses on this topic by reviewing 41 studies over the previous five years. We call attention to the significant variances that exist across linked studies, which might make them incompatible if used at the same time. We present a set of recommendations for developing comprehensive privacy models in order to facilitate comparison and appropriateness analysis for various circumstances.

Keywords: WSN, supervised learning, unsupervised learning, reinforcement learning

Email: piyushraja2009@gmail.com

Anamika Ahirwar, Piyush Kumar Shukla, Manish Shrivastava, Priti Maheshwary and Bhupesh Gour (eds.) Innovative Engineering with AI Applications, (155–170) © 2023 Scrivener Publishing LLC

8.1 Introduction

A wireless sensor network (WSN) is made up of a number of self-contained, small, low-cost, and low-power sensor nodes. These nodes collect information about their surroundings and work together to send it to centralised backend units known as base stations or sinks for further analysis. Sensor nodes could be fitted with thermal, acoustic, chemical, pressure, weather, and optical sensors, among others. WSNs have a lot of capacity for designing powerful applications because of their diversity. Each one has its own set of characteristics and criteria. It's a difficult challenge to create powerful algorithms that can be used in a variety of applications. WSN programmers must solve concerns such as data collection, data reliability, translation, node clustering, energy conscious routing, events scheduling, fault identification, and protection in particular. Machine learning (ML) was first used in the late 1950s as an artificial intelligence tool (AI) [1]. Its emphasis changed over time, focusing more on algorithms that are computationally feasible and stable. The extensive availability of networks in modern cultures, as well as the growth of linked gadgets that people use on a daily basis, emphasises the pervasiveness of today's information technology.

Wireless communications, such as cellular networks, rely on technology or communication equipment deployment that is planned ahead of time. However, due to present sophisticated cellular network applications, infrastructure in many locations is unreachable (i.e. earthquake hit-places, violent regions, battlefields, volcanic prone areas). Self-organization, infrastructure-free independence, flexibility, and cost savings have all grown in popularity. A Wireless Sensor Network (WSN) is the only solution to solve these problems in the example above, such as sending communications between nodes without a structure. This network also creates the possibility of a novel way for acquiring and retrieving data from the monitored area. We were inspired to work in this neighborhood by these wonderful homes.

The design and development of small wireless devices, such as sensors, capable of sensing, processing, computing, and networking, also benefited technical achievements [2]. WSNs are often made up Dozens and dozens of devices are scattered over hard terrain at irregular intervals or condition" in a defined keypoint. They are used for a number of things. During either deployment, which is a typical option, sensors are produced in an ad-hoc fashion to shape the network. Contact is formed by single-hop or multi-hop propagation, depending on the sensors. As a consequence, WSNs have piqued the scientific community's attention due to their wide range of applications, including military applications, fire detection, health and environmental protection, and habitat monitoring. Sensors are tiny computers with limited resources, such as memory, processors that are relatively slow, or resource-constrained transceivers. For certain applications, neither method is viable, particularly when sensors are widely spread or situated in remote places where human intervention is prohibited. As a consequence, one of the most difficult difficulties in WSNs is energy conservation, which is viewed as a vital component in the network's long-term sustainability. As a consequence, several algorithms and strategies have been suggested and developed from various viewpoints in order to make better use of this restricted energy budget and prolong the lifetime and operation of these devices as much as possible. In WSNs with tree topologies, data collecting is one of the most important activities. To accomplish an implementation objective, each of these sensors may detect the monitoring area and transfer data to a collecting site known as a sink or base station. After receiving the data, the sink makes an appropriate decision based on the application's requirements. The sink is a critical node that receives all data and connects the WSN to the outside world. Furthermore, WSNs establish a natural many-to-one traffic paradigm by reporting data from sensors to the sink.

This paper's purpose is somewhat different from previous ones. Rather of focusing on the methodologies used, this study focuses on the models that were explored. Models are made up of all of the assumptions that have been made about the system. Three primary sets of decisions may be recognised in a WSN situation. First, broad concerns such as objectives and dangers must be stated. After then, the network's intended operation must be defined. Finally, the capabilities and resources of the adversary must be defined. It should be emphasised that if separate contributions rely on distinct models, they may not operate well together. As a result, it's necessary to have a comprehensive picture of the models under consideration in order to determine whether two or more processes are compatible. In Figure 8.1a shows the architecture of wireless sensor networks and Figure 8.1b shows the Scheme of the Wireless sensor networks (WSNs).

The following are the key reasons why machine learning is critical in WSN applications:

1. Sensor networks are typically used to track complex conditions that change rapidly. For example, soil erosion or sea turbulence can cause a node's position to shift. Sensor

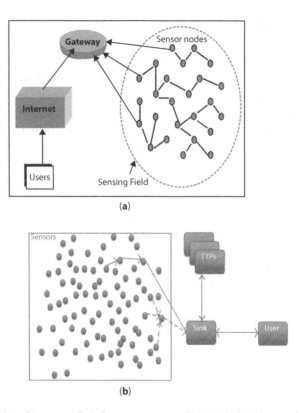

(a)

(b)

Figure 8.1 (a) Architecture of wireless sensor network (WSN). (b) Scheme of the WSNs.

networks that can adapt and run effectively in such environments are desirable [7].

2. In exploratory uses, WSNs may be used to gather new information about inaccessible, hazardous sites (e.g., volcanic eruptions and waste water monitoring). System designers may create solutions that initially do not work as intended due to the unpredictable behaviour trends that may occur in such scenarios.

3. WSNs are typically used in complex systems where researchers are unable to create precise statistical models to explain machine behaviour. And in the meantime, while some Wireless sensor tasks can be predicted using simple mathematical equations, others can necessitate the use of complex algorithms (for instance, the routing problem). Machine learning offers low-complexity predictions for the system model in related situations.

8.2   Review of Literature

The nodes switch from one x-y coordinate location to another with a separate x-y coordinate. The node's movement leaves them vulnerable to attack and it's easy to attack and vanish if they can move. Attacks are also intelligent, acting individually in various scenarios. As a result, the table above outlines the standard approaches for solving problems in WSN. The basic principles connected to WSN are introduced in this section. Following that, a brief description of the papers included in this survey is provided. They are categorised in particular based on the methodology used. This allows for the display of the variety of methodologies used, demonstrating the importance of the survey. A WSN is made up of a collection of sensors that are connected in an ad hoc manner. Sensors are commonly thought to have limited and nonremovable battery storage. Their interconnection is typically ad hoc, necessitating decentralised coordination. As a result, nodes share information and perform processing tasks in a distributed manner. A WSN generally has four entities in addition to sensors (Figure 8.2). The server, or sink, is the node that collects sensory data on the one hand. This information may reach the sink either through direct route (straight lines in Figure 8.2) or through specific sensors that collect data from nearby ones, as will be discussed later (dotted lines in Figure 8.2). The presence of a user is also assumed in order to access the network. Finally, Trusted Third Parties (TTPs) may be considered for credential management and dispute resolution, among other things [13]. These networks have been used in a variety of applications and situations with great success. Akyildiz presented a broad range of situations, ranging from military (e.g., reconnaissance) to environmental (e.g., animal tracking) to domestic (e.g., surveillance)

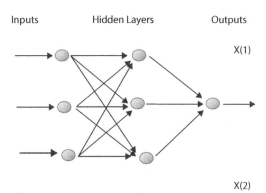

Figure 8.2 The NN architectute.

Table 8.1 Literature review.

Authors	Routing protocols	Methods	Problems formulation metrics	
Kannan *et al.*	Secure AODV routing protocol	MANET	Security problem	Accuracy
Nakayma *et al.*	Trusted AODV	MANET	Attack prevention	PDF, AT, AED, NRL.
Boukerche *et al.*	AODV	MANET	Routing problem	Accuracy
W. Wu *et al.*	AODV	MANET	Routing protocol efficiency	Accuracy
Parma Nand *et al.*	DSR	Qualnet	Routing	Number of hops per route
Samir *et al.*	DSR	MANET	Mobile pattern analysis	Accuracy
Chetna *et al.*	AODV	NS2	Black hole detection	Efficiency

(e.g., smart environments). Researchers have also looked at the security risks surrounding their use in automated manufacturing in recent years. The collection of articles under consideration is divided into sections that focus on distinct aspects of privacy protection. This section examines the methods used on each project. In Table 8.1, it shows that different authors use different methods, routing protocols, showing problem formulation matrices.

8.3 ML in WSNs

Machine learning (ML), a branch of artificial intelligence (AI), is the branch of computer science that is concerned with the analysis and interpretation of routines and procedures in technology to facilitate learning, reasoning, and decision-making without the involvement of a person. Simply defined, machine learning enables users to send massive amounts of data into computer algorithms, which then evaluate, recommend, and decide using just the supplied data. The algorithm can use the knowledge to enhance its judgement in the hereafter if any adjustments are found.

Machine learning is typically described by sensor network designers as a set of tools and algorithms that are used to construct prediction models. Machine learning researchers, on the other hand, see it as a vast space with many themes and trends. Those who want to add machine learning to WSNs should be aware of such themes. Machine learning algorithms, when used in a variety of WSNs implementations, have immense versatility. This section discusses some of the theoretical principles and techniques for implementing machine learning in WSNs. The intended structure of the model can be used to categorise existing machine learning algorithms. The three types of machine learning algorithms are supervised, unsupervised, and reinforcement learning [3].

All businesses depend on data to function. Making decisions based on data-driven insights might be the difference between staying competitive or falling farther behind. In order to harness the value of corporate and customer data and make decisions that keep a business ahead of the competition, machine learning may be the answer.

Despite the efforts of Minimal power supplies continue to be an important barrier with WSNs, especially since they are located in hostile settings or in remote locations, according to the academic researchers are widely dispersed; battery replacement or replenishment is impossible, so energy should be used efficiently to extend their life as much as possible. It's also challenging to figure out their topology [12]. Due to node failure, the topology is more likely to change after installation and topology formation. Reconstructing topology might also help you conserve electricity. Another significant challenge for WSNs is the creation of an energy-saving tour for deployed static sensors. Another important stumbling block for WSNs is poor memory. Because the sensor nodes are small computers with limited memory and operate on batteries, their data collection process must be reliable to prevent buffer overflow. The study's main goal is to develop WSNs that use a low-cost energy-saving technology. In order to do so, this research looks at two major concerns. According to the literature evaluation, there is a research gap for idle listening state and sink versatility with single-hop contact.

8.3.1 Supervised Learning

Learning by training a model on labelled data is referred to as supervised learning. It's a very common method for predicting a result. Let's say we

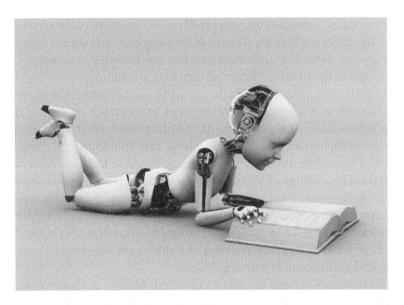

Figure 8.3 Machine learning (Source - Google).

want to know who is most likely to open an email we send. We can use the information from previous emails, as well as the "label" that indicates whether or not the recipient opened the email. We can then create a training data set with information about the recipient (such as location, demographics, and previous email engagement behaviour), as well as the label [4]. Our model learns by experimenting with a variety of methods for predicting the label based on the other data points until it discovers the best one. Now we can use that model to predict who will open our next email campaign. Figure 8.3 shows the smartness of machines due to ML.

The process of providing input data as well as correct output data to the machine learning model is known as supervised learning. A supervised learning algorithm's goal is to find a mapping function that will map the input variable(x) to the output variable(y). Supervised learning can be used in the real world for things like risk assessment, image classification, fraud detection, spam filtering, and so on.

What is the Process of Supervised Learning?
Models are trained using a labelled dataset in supervised learning, where the model learns about each type of data. The model is tested on test data (a subset of the training set) after the training process is completed, and it then predicts the output [3]. Figure 8.4 will help you understand how supervised learning works:

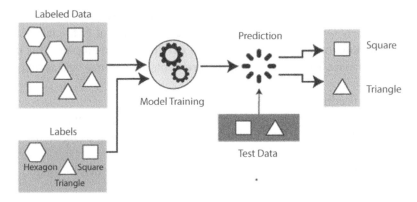

Figure 8.4 Supervised learning.

Assume we have a dataset with a variety of shapes, such as squares, rectangles, triangles, and polygons. The model must now be trained for each shape as the first step.

A labelled training set (i.e., predefined inputs and established outputs) is used to construct a machine model in supervised learning. Easy modules that operate in parallel make up neural networks. The biochemical nervous system stimulates these elements. Connections among various components, by their very existence, identify unique network functions. By changing the values of the weights (connections) among several components, a person could easily train a NN to perform a specific purpose. In certain cases, neural networks are conditioned or modified such that feedback leads to a certain target output [5]. In certain cases, neural networks are conditioned or modified such that feedback leads to a certain target output. The following diagram depicts such a situation. If the network O/P equals the real target, the network is settled upon at this stage, based on a calculation of the O/P in addition to the target. In order to train a network, certain input/target pairs are usually necessary. 'Learning' is a supervised process that occurs for any single loop or 'epoch' that is illustrated with a novel input pattern by a forward activation flow of O/Ps, in addition to backwards error propagation of weight amendments, according to this law, as it is for other types of backpropagation techniques.

In general, a neural network is illustrated for a given scheme, which allows an arbitrary 'guess' as to what it may be. These networks have been programmed to carry out complex tasks in a variety of areas, including voice, pattern recognition, vision, control systems, detection, and classification. Neural networks may also be programmed to solve problems that are difficult for traditional computers or humans to solve [14]. Despite the fact that neural networks use a variety of learning principles, this demonstration focuses solely on the delta law. The most general class of Artificial Neural Networks known as feed forward neural networks often employs this particular delta law. The NN teaching requirements are summarised as follows:

i.   Feedback neurons receive input.
ii.   The output response obtained is compared to the input data.
iii. The weights attached to neurons are managed using error data.
iv.   During the back signal, hidden units discover their mistake.
v.   Finally, the weights are changed.

8.3.2   Unsupervised Learning

Unsupervised learning does not require labelled data, unlike supervised learning. In its place, theypursue to disclose unseen outlines besides associations to theit datas. When we don't know exactly what we're looking for, this is ideal. Clustering algorithms, the most common example of unsupervised learning, take a large set of data points and find groups within them. For example, let's say we want to divide our customers into groups, but we're not sure how to do so. They can be found using clustering algorithms.

Labels are not offered to unsupervised learners (i.e., there is no output vector). Principal component analysis (PCA) is a well-known technique for compressing higher-dimensional data sets to lower-dimensional data sets for data analysis, apparition, feature extraction, or compression. After mean centering the data for each attribute, PCA requires calculating the Eigen value decomposition of a data covariance medium or singular value decay of a data matrix.

Because unlike supervised learning, we have the input data but no corresponding output data, unsupervised learning cannot be used to solve a regression or classification issue directly. Finding the underlying structure of a dataset, classifying the data into groups based on similarities, and representing the dataset in a compressed manner are the objectives of unsupervised learning.

Example: Let's say a dataset including photos of various breeds of cats and dogs is sent to the unsupervised learning algorithm. The algorithm is never trained on the provided dataset, thus it has no knowledge of its characteristics [6]. The unsupervised learning algorithm's job is to let the picture characteristics speak for themselves. This operation will be carried out using an unsupervised learning method by clustering the picture collection into the groupings based on visual similarity.

The following are a few key arguments for the significance of unsupervised learning:

a. Finding valuable insights from the data is made easier with the aid of unsupervised learning.
b. Unsupervised learning is considerably more like how humans learn to think via their own experiences, which brings it closer to actual artificial intelligence.
c. Unsupervised learning is more significant since it operates on unlabeled and unordered data.
d. Unsupervised learning is necessary to address situations where we do not always have input data and the matching output.

Unsupervised Learning Benefits
Compared to supervised learning, unsupervised learning is employed for problems that are more complicated since it lacks labelled input data.

Unsupervised learning is preferred because unlabeled data is simpler to get than labelled data.

Unsupervised Learning Drawbacks
Due to the lack of a comparable output, unsupervised learning is inherently more challenging than supervised learning.

As the input data is not labelled and the algorithms do not know the precise output in advance, the outcome of the unsupervised learning method may be less accurate. Figure 8.5 shows how that it works.

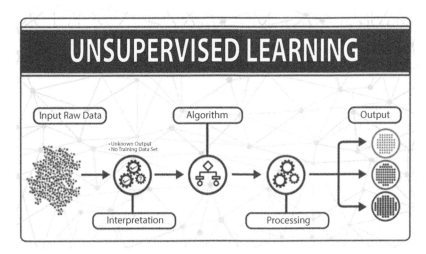

Figure 8.5 Unsupervised learning (Source - Google).

The following are the steps that are usually followed when doing PCA:

Step 1: Get data from the iris regions that has been normalised. By concatenating each row (or column) into a long vector, a 2-D iris image may be represented as a 1-D vector.

Step 2: From each image vector, subtract the mean image. The average should be calculated row by row.

Step 3: Compute the covariance matrix to get the eigen vectors and eigen values.

Step 4: Examine the covariance matrix's eigenvectors and Eigen values.

Step 5: The eigenvectors are sorted according to their Eigen values, from high to low. Forming a function vector by selecting elements.

Step 6: Build a new data set We basically take the transpose of the vector and increase it on the left of the initial data set, transposed, until we've selected the components.

Final Dataset = RowFeatureVector * RowMeanAdjust

Where RowFeatureVector is the matrix with the eigenvectors from the columns transposed to the rows, with the most significant eigenvector at the top, and RowMeanAdjust is the mean used to transpose the results. Each editorial contains data elements, with each row containing a split axis [7]. Principal components analysis is mostly used to reduce the amount of variables in a dataset while preserving the data's contradictions, as well as to find unexplained phenomena in the data and label them according to how much of the data's knowledge they report for.

8.3.3 Reinforcement Learning

Developers provide a way of rewarding desired actions and penalising undesirable behaviours in reinforcement learning. In order to motivate the agent, this technique provides positive values to desired acts and negative values to undesirable behaviours [8]. This trains the agent to seek maximal overall reward over the long run in order to arrive at the best possible outcome [11].

The agent is prevented from stagnating on smaller tasks by these long-term objectives. The agent eventually learns to steer clear of the bad and look for the good. Artificial intelligence (AI) has embraced this learning strategy as a technique to control unsupervised machine learning using incentives and punishments.

Although reinforcement learning has attracted a lot of attention in the field of artificial intelligence, there are still several limitations to its acceptance and use in the actual world.

A feedback loop is involved in reinforcement learning. The algorithm decides on an action first, then monitors data from the outside world to see how it affects the outcome. As this occurs repeatedly, the model learns the best course of action. This is akin to how we learn through trial and error. When learning to walk, for example, we might begin by moving our legs while receiving feedback from the environment and adapting our actions to maximise the reward (walking). Picking which ads to display on a website is an example of reinforcement learning in action. We want to maximise engagement in this case [5]. However, we have a lot of ads to choose from, and the payout is unknown, so how do we decide. The reinforcement learning solution is similar to A/B testing, but in this case, we let the reinforcement learning algorithm choose the variant that is most likely to win based on feedback and adjust to different conditions.

Although it has great promise, reinforcement learning can be challenging to implement and has only a limited number of applications. This form of machine learning's need on environment exploration is one of the obstacles to its widespread use.

For instance, if you were to use a robot that relied on reinforcement learning to manoeuvre around a challenging physical environment, it would search for new states and adopt new behaviours. However, given how rapidly the environment changes in the actual world, it is challenging to consistently make the right decisions.

This method's efficacy may be limited by the amount of time and computational resources needed and Figure 8.6 shows its working system.

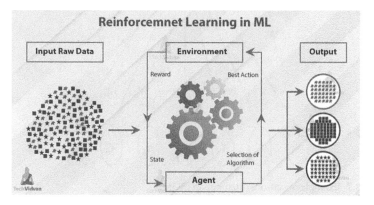

Figure 8.6 Reinforcement learning (Source – Google).

Reinforcement learning allows a sensor node (for example) to learn from communicating with its surroundings. One of the most often used network models is the Self-Organizing Map. It is a member of the learning networks. The Self-Organizing Map is a form of unsupervised study. When a Self-Organizing Map is used to remove features, it is referred to as a Self-Organizing Function Map. There are 5 cluster units Yi and 7 input units Xi in Figure 8.7. The clusters are grouped in a line [9].

Kohonen created the Self-Organizing Map. The SOM has proven to be effective in a variety of situations. It preserves mapping by mapping high-dimensional space to map units. Neuron units often arranged themselves in a lattice on a plane [10]. The term "preserving land" refers to the act of reserving the space between two points. Furthermore, the Self-Organizing Map has the potential to generalise. It entails identifying patterns that have never been seen before. The following is a representation of the Self-Organizing Map I 2-D:

$$Y = \{x.........................., X_{acw}\}$$

A connection connects the neurons to the neurons next to them. The neurons are often connected as can be seen in Figure 8.7.

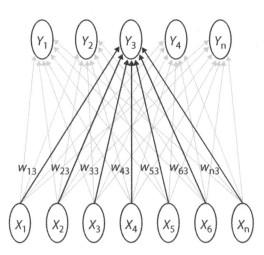

Figure 8.7 Example of self-organizing map (SOM).

8.4   Conclusion

Since wireless sensor networks vary from conventional networks in a variety of ways, protocols and tools that overcome specific problems and limitations are needed. As a result, creative technologies for energy-aware and real-time routing, protection, scheduling, localization, node clustering, data aggregation, fault detection, and data integrity are needed for wireless sensor networks. Machine learning is a collection of strategies for improving a wireless sensor network's ability to respond to the complex behaviour of its surroundings. However, the concept of area establishes the parameters for how such a relationship can be carried out.

References

1. Ayodele, T.O., Introduction to computer learning, in: *New Advances in Machine Learning*, InTech, 17–26, 2010.
2. Duffy, A.H., The "what" and "how" in design learning. *IEEE Expert*, 12, 3, 71–76, 1997.
3. Langley, P. and Simon, H.A., Applications of machine learning and rule induction. *Commun. ACM*, 38, 11, 54–64, 1995.
4. Paradis, L. and Han, Q., A study of fault control in wireless sensor networks. *J. Netw. Syst. Manage.*, 15, 2, 171–190, 2007.
5. Krishnamachari, B., Estrin, D., Wicker, S., The effects of data aggregation in wireless sensor networks. *22nd International Conference on Distributed Computing Systems Workshops*, pp. 575–578, 2002.
6. Al-Karaki, J. and Kamal, A., Routing techniques in wireless sensor networks: A survey. *IEEE Wirel. Commun.*, 11, 6, 6–28, 2004.
7. Das, S., Abraham, A., Panigrahi, B.K., *Computational intelligence: Foundations, insights, and recent trends*, pp. 27–37, John Wiley & Sons, Inc, 2010.
8. Conte, R., Gilbert, N., Sichman, J.S., MAS and social simulation: A suitable commitment, in: *Multi-Agent Systems and Agent-Based Simulation*. MABS 1998. Lecture Notes in Computer Science, vol. 1534. Springer, Berlin, Heidelberg, 1998, https://doi.org/10.1007/10692956_1.
9. Nand, P. and Sharma, S.C., Comparison of MANET routing protocols and performance analysis of the DSR protocol, in: *Advances in Computing, Communication and Control*, vol. 125, 2011.
10. Das, S.R., Castaeda, R., Yan, J., Simulation-based performance assessment of routing protocols for mobile ad hoc networks. *Mobile Netw. App.*, 1, 5–11, 2000.

11. Khetmal, C., Kelkar, S., Bhosale, N., MANET: Black hole node detection in AODV. *Int. J. Comput. Eng. Res.*, 03–09, 2013.
12. Abbasi, A.A. and Younis, M., A study on clustering algorithms for wireless sensor networks, 07–12, 2019.
13. Yun, S., Lee, J., Chung, W., Kim, E., Kim, S., A soft computing approach to localization in wireless sensor networks. *Expert Syst. Appl.*, 36, 4, 7552–7561, 2009.
14. Kannan, S. *et al.*, Secure data transmission in MANETs using AODV. *IJCCER*, 02–09, 2014.

## 9

Introduction to AI Technique and Analysis of Time Series Data Using Facebook Prophet Model

S. Sivaramakrishnan[1]*, C.R. Rathish[2], S. Premalatha[3] and Niranjana C.[4]

[1]Department of Information Science and Engineering, New Horizon College of Engineering, Bangalore, India
[2]Department of CE, New Horizon College of Engineering, Bangalore, India
[3]Department of Electronics and Communication, K S R Institute for Engineering and Technology, Tiruchengode, India
[4]Sri Venkateshwara College of Engineering, Bangalore, India

Abstract

Artificial Intelligence (AI) builds machines to work as human beings by communicating the intelligence to the machines. AI highlights the creation of intelligent machines that accept the desired input data, work on it, operate, and respond like human beings. It is also used for making decisions by reading the real-time data, recognizing the given scenario, and finally responding to the structured set of data fed to interpret the conclusion. To build intelligent machines it is vital to understand the function of the human brain. The machines can only act, operate and react according to the information available about the scenario under which it works. Thus the AI must contain sufficient information which is a tedious task. Hence, to make a machine into a computer-controlled robot or designing software that performs and responds exactly the way a human being does, began the development of AI. The set of inputs will have many classifications and hence requires supervision that is mathematically analyzed by Machine Learning technology. This technology has higher challenges where the information required for the intelligent system will be of higher volume and each time the information must be updated. The set of software programs has no proper guidelines which makes it inefficient in some cases. These challenges can be controlled by some techniques that rectify the error, alter the data depending on scenarios and boost the speed of

*Corresponding author: sivaramkrish.s@gmail.com

Anamika Ahirwar, Piyush Kumar Shukla, Manish Shrivastava, Priti Maheshwary and Bhupesh Gour (eds.) Innovative Engineering with AI Applications, (171–188) © 2023 Scrivener Publishing LLC

execution by optimizing the efficiency. Some frameworks come up with the implementation of various intelligent systems. Feature extraction framework identifies a minimal set of informative attributes from the provided dataset assuring zero correlation. A deep learning framework drastically reduces the learning time of models with the usage of parallel-computing GPUs. A Neural Network framework consists of interconnections where each node calculates the weighted sum of values passed on to its input and after a series of epochs the other network parameters merge to optimal values ending up with the appropriate model. AI plays a major role in many sectors. With the enhancement, it improves the quality of our lives or it may show the negative effects of it.

Keywords: Artificial intelligence, machine learning, neural networks

9.1 Introduction

The field of artificial intelligence (AI) strives to build intelligent entities as well as understand them. These built intelligent entities are fascinating and beneficial in their own right. AI during the early stage of development has produced many significant products. AI currently embodies a huge variety of subfields, from general-purpose areas to specific tasks. In 1950 Turing discussed that an intelligent system has the capability to achieve human-level performance in all cognitive tasks [1–4]. The test he proposed is that the computer must be questioned by a human and passes the test if the investigator cannot tell whether it is a computer or a human at the other end. If the computer passes, then it is said to be intelligent.

9.2 What is AI?

The definitions can be designed in two main dimensions as shown in Figure 9.1

- The top of the box is concerned with the processes of thoughts and the bottom labels the reflection of thoughts.
- The definitions on the left measure success in connection with human performance, and the right measure against an ideal concept of intelligence (i.e.) rationality.

System that think like Humans	System that think rationally
System that act like Humans	System that act rationally

Figure 9.1 The four categorized definitions of AI.

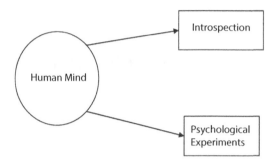

Figure 9.2 Cognitive model.

9.2.1 Process of Thoughts – Human Approach

When we need to know about the human way of thinking a given program then one needs to know about how the human mind works. This approach is called the cognitive model and the same is represented as shown in Figure 9.2 [5, 6].

The model can be developed by introspecting the inputs/outputs in the human mind through experiments such that if the program's input/output and timing matches human behavior it builds up a computer model from AI and experimental techniques from psychology to develop many testing theories of how a human mind works.

Thus the process of converting a computer into a computer-controlled robot with software that thinks and reflects back exactly the way a human mind thinks is what AI is all about. And based on this AI can be classified as weak AI and Strong AI as mentioned in Figure 9.3 [7, 8]. The lateral is designed to carry out a particular task and the former to carry out complex task.

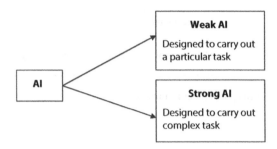

Figure 9.3 Classification of AI.

9.3 Main Frameworks of Artificial Intelligence

The three frameworks that contribute to the accomplishment of various intelligent systems are Feature Engineering, Artificial Neural Networks, Deep Learning.

9.3.1 Feature Engineering

The description of each individual data object in Machine Learning is represented by a variable called Feature [9–11]. Informative features are useful for differentiating and characterizing various groups of objects. They produce accurate and predictive models yielding good results in different data analytic tasks. The various stages of feature engineering are shown in Figure 9.4.

This feature engineering helps in constructing new features from existing one, generating new sets of features and extracting the minimal set of data and selecting a set of features to improve the quality of dataset.

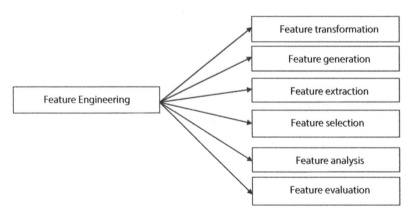

Figure 9.4 Stages of features engineering.

Table 9.1 Similarity between brain and neural network.

Brain	Neural network
Neuron	Node
Connection of neurons	Connection weight

9.3.2   Artificial Neural Networks

Neural networks are a small part of AI. Humans use the brain to store knowledge and the computer uses memory to store a set of information. The neural network emulates the process of the brain. The neural network is developed by connecting a number of nodes, which are elements corresponding to the neurons of the brain [12–14]. The Table 9.1 encapsulates the similarity between the brain and neural network.

Here each node computes the weighted sum of values generated to its input and forms an appropriate model after feedforward and back propagation stages. In supervised machine learning algorithms, the neural network provides the framework. Most commonly used neural networks are Recurrent Neural Networks (RNN) and Convolutional Neural Networks (CNN).

9.3.3   Deep Learning

Deep Learning is formulated with algorithms to learn numerous levels of representation in order to design complex relationships between data [15–17]. The feature that defines higher level concepts from lower level one and vice is called deep architecture. The basic layout representing Architecture of Deep learning is shown in Figure 9.5. It plays a vital role in

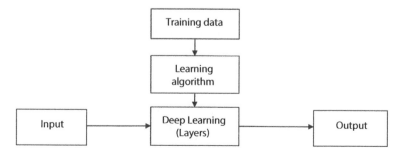

Figure 9.5 Architecture of deep learning.

pattern recognition, speech recognition, optimization etc. The main reasons for the development of deep learning are:

- Increased chip processing abilities
- Increased size of data used for training
- Advancement in machine learning

For example, in image processing model the computer cannot identify the raw input data (image). Hence it can be represented in the form of pixels. With this value of pixels, it is difficult to predict an image. This difficulty can be broken down by deep learning techniques. First the image is loaded in the visible layer, where the layer contains variables that we are able to observe. There are several hidden layers that extract the set of images that is observed from the other layer. With the help of pixel corners the image is revealed one by one thus making sense to the fed input. Figure 9.6 describes the various stages in processing the image.

Stage 1. Detection of corners and contours

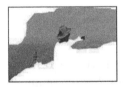

Stage 2. 1st layer of hidden layer

Stage 3. 2nd layer of hidden layer

Stage 4: Final Model

Figure 9.6 Various stages in processing image.

Thus with each hierarchy of concepts it defines the entire relationship between the input and output forming a flexible and high power model.

9.4   Techniques of AI

9.4.1   Machine Learning

Any form of technology that is embedded with some intelligent feature is called AI. Machine Learning is in fact a branch of AI but it pinpoints to a specific field [18, 19]. Some technological groups of AI are identified by Machine Learning. Machine Learning is an approach where the model is formed with a set of data. The data can be audio, document, image etc. It trains the machine to recognize the correct data and make intelligent decisions with the data or patterns thus forming an end product called a model as shown in Figure 9.7.

Now can this training data be survived in the actual working field?

No. Then how come machine learning plays a vital role in AI. The training data may develop a model in applications like speech recognition and image processing. But when dealing with mathematical equations or physical laws there is an inexorable challenge. The data applied for modeling and the data used in field application are different as mentioned in Figure 9.8.

Machine learning gives over a structural challenge due to the difference between training and input data. The accurate model cannot be achieved with the wrong training data. The outcome of machine learning heavily depends on generalization where the performance of the final model maintains its stability regardless of what data it is. Good generalization yields a good output model.

Example 1: To convert an analog signal to digital signal

There are various analog signals in the real world. Here let us have a look at the microphone. The input (training data) fed to the microphone is analyzed by the intelligent machine and provides us with a good output model. Machine learning does know that the output from the microphone consists of various noise that is to be filtered. So the output model developed will have lower generalizability which is called as overfitting.

Figure 9.7 Machine learning model.

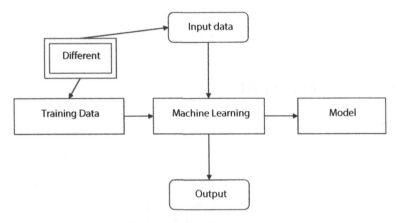

Figure 9.8 Machine learning model with distinct data.

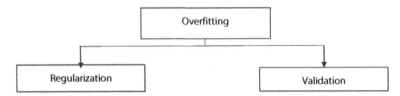

Figure 9.9 Process of avoiding overfitting.

The two methods regularization and validation as shown in Figure 9.9 are used to overcome the challenge. Regularization builds a simple model which is cost effective. Although it fails to produce an accurate model it specifies the overall characteristics of the output. Validation is used to monitor the performance of training data.

Based on the training method the machine learning technique has been divided as supervised, unsupervised and reinforcement learning as shown in Figure 9.10 [20, 21].

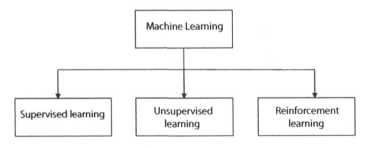

Figure 9.10 Types of machine learning.

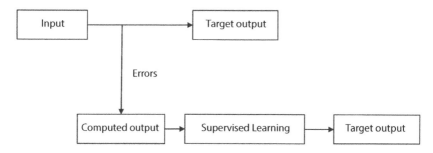

Figure 9.11 Supervised learning model.

9.4.1.1 Supervised Learning

The aim of supervised learning is the learning standard where the datasets are optimized to shrink the difference between the target output and the computed output as represented in Figure 9.11.

Here the model has a set of correct input and output data. The output that a model needs from each training input is called target output, the one that is computed by the learning algorithm is called computed output. In supervised learning, each training input data should consist of target output and that is what the model is expect to produce for the given input. In some cases, the machine learning may fail to produce the targeted output causing an error between the computed and target output. So the Supervised learning minimizes the error with a revision of model producing set of input and correct output pairs.

9.4.1.2 Unsupervised Learning

The Unsupervised learning maximizes the similarities between the target and computing output. This algorithm does not work with data that is not trained properly forming clusters of unknown data outputs. The clusters of unknown output are iterated until it produces a good performance output model.

9.4.1.3 Reinforcement Learning

Let's consider the input is received from the external environment and the output is achieved as per the action. The environment offers reward or the penalty to the received output. If the reward is given, the current output forms the final model or the output is again updated with new inputs. The evaluator gives the feedback about the penalty or reward. These types of

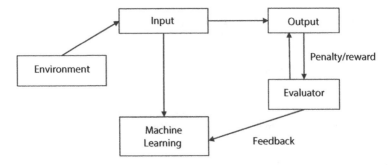

Figure 9.12 Unsupervised learning model.

algorithms are mainly used in games. If one wins a stage it will be declared as winner or one should start the game from the beginning to reach the desired level as represented in Figure 9.12.

9.4.2   Natural Language Processing (NLP)

Natural language processing (NLP) represents the function of software and hardware components in a computer system that explores the spoken and written language [22]. It converts the human language to computer language like C, C++, Java. NLP uses two approaches to analyses the type of input:

- Linguistic analyses
- Statistical analysis

The language can be processed in different approaches:

- Machine Translation approach
- Lingual approach
- Transfer approach
- Empirical approach

The source language is directly converted into the target language is called as Machine language approach. The lingual approach converts source language into an inter lingual transition language then to target language. The transfer approach converts source language into a representation that a machine can recognize then it is converted to target language. At last the final text is generated. Empirical approach is used when there is a memory based translation (Large amount of raw data). Figure 9.13 represents the NLP pyramid.

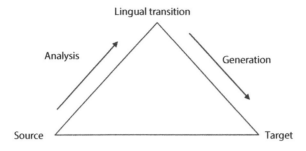

Figure 9.13 NLP pyramid.

9.4.3   Automation and Robotics

The best example for intelligent robots is humans. A robot is an intelligent system that connects a human action. Humans can cope up with any uncertain situations thinking what needs to be done at what time. We think of obstacles in many sorts of objects and recover from errors. The industrial robots that were developed at first were not flexible and did repetitive tasks in a sequence. Of course practical robots need not resemble humans exactly like humans. After the introduction of AI technology in robots the picture started changing. All industries started to take a bold move with intense development efforts underway.

9.4.4   Machine Vision

Machine vision has developed building tools that empower the understanding of visual information that will never be accompanied with illustrative text information [23]. The text data needs nothing to interpret what it is and it is easy for the machine to understand the given text whereas image inspection needs a combination of high-level concepts to process and interpret inherent visual characteristics. The interaction between humans and machines has influenced the evolution of machine vision systems. The development of flexible and rugged vision algorithms has come to play from machine learning technology therefore improving the power of vision systems.

Machine vision combines one or more sensing methods and computer technologies. For example, a camera receives a light from an image, it converts the light energy to a format that the computer can recognize as represented in Figure 9.14. The computer extracts the data from the image and processes the data, compares the data with other standards and provides the results in the form of a response to the machine.

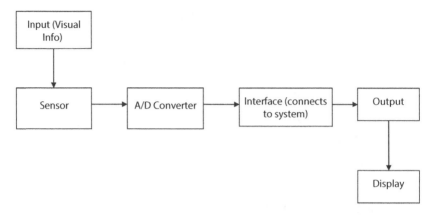

Figure 9.14 Machine vision standards.

9.5 Application of AI in Various Fields

AI has significant demand in several fields and few are listed below.

1. Marketing: With advancement in AI, more real time applications will be possible in this field [24]. The products needed for daily basis was once purchased from the shop but now there are many platforms that deliver products to the doorstep showing us the results just by reading our mind

2. Optimization: The particle swarm optimization (PSO) is used to find the effective path from the various paths available and this algorithm was inspired from the flock of birds searching for a food in a specific region of interest [25, 26].

3. Banking sector: The development of AI protects us from online frauds [27]. It provides solutions for all our queries through an online chatbot application.

4. Finance sector: AI plays a major role in prediction of future profit margin with past data.

5. Healthcare: Using AI technique there is a lot of equipment to predict the health condition. Many clinical support systems have been developed in recent times [28].

6. Time series analysis: The time series analysis helps in understanding the pattern of the data and analysis of the data will help in predicting future forecast [29]. The time series analysis also will be greatly helpful in marketing and finance sectors. There are many model used for time series analysis

like Moving average model (MA), Auto Regression Moving average model (ARMA), Auto Regression Integrated Moving Average Model (ARIMA) etc. Recently Facebook launched a Facebook Prophet model for forecasting that involves the time series data [30]. The next session elaborates the time series analysis with the help of Facebook prophet model using the Google trend data.

9.6   Time Series Analysis Using Facebook Prophet Model

Facebook has launched prophet model for analyzing the time series data and the significance of this method is it can automatically recognize the weekly, monthly, and yearly trend. This model studies the data and could predict the forecast more accurately. This model can even handle the effect of holiday in predicting the future sales, profit etc. The programming language supported by this model includes R and Python. For analyzing a data, necessary cleaning of the data has to be carried out, in the sense to remove the missing data or to replace missing data with overall average value, median value etc. And as the size of data increases the complexity in cleaning the data also increases and the advantage of the Facebook prophet model is it takes care of the missing data and there is no need of manual effort to clean up the data and it take care of outliers in the data.

The Google trend data for vitamin D is used as a source data for the prophet model. The Google trend is normalized between 0 and 100 and the maximum 100 indicates that it was trending heavily in that period of time. The data collected over past five years from 2016 for vitamin D is used in this prophet model and the model will predict analysis for the next one year.

The description of the vitamin D data collected over the past five years is shown in Figure 9.15.

The above figure indicates that there are total of 260 data available from the Google trend data and as mentioned the data are normalized and will have a maximum value of 100.

This data is used by the prophet model and the model analysis the data and with this it can able to forecast the feature values. The prediction is carried out for the next one year and the resultant visualization is represented as shown in Figure 9.16.

In the above figure the dark circles represents the actual value and the blue color line indicates the forecasted value using the prophet model. The x axis

	y
count	260.000000
mean	45.573077
std	13.349708
min	29.000000
25%	37.000000
50%	41.000000
75%	50.000000
max	100.000000

Figure 9.15 Data description.

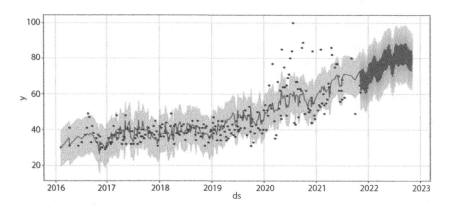

Figure 9.16 Visualization of predicted value.

indicates the year and the y axis indicates the normalized value of the search of vitamin D which varies from 0 to 100. From the figure it can be noted clearly that the model trains from the past five year of data from 2016 to 2021 and predicts the data for the year 2022 to 2023. It could be clearly seen that the model follows the trends in the past and predicts the feature trend.

The important significance of this model is forecasting the overall trend, weekly and yearly trend as represented in Figures 9.17 to 9.19.

From the above figure understanding the pattern becomes easier. Looking at the early trend as represented in Figure 9.19 it could be clearly noted that the search of vitamin D peaks in June and gradually reduces by the end of December. Figure 9.18 represents the weekly trend of the vitamin D. The above Figure 9.19 will be very useful for vitamin D manufacturing company and based on the above data they can plan the production of the vitamin D capsule. Thus the AI helps in forecasting the data which can be used to increase or decrease the production. One more interesting fact to note in

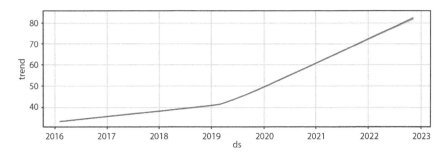

Figure 9.17 Overall trend of the vitamin D.

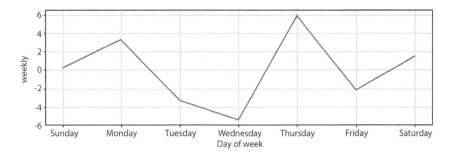

Figure 9.18 Weekly trend of vitamin D.

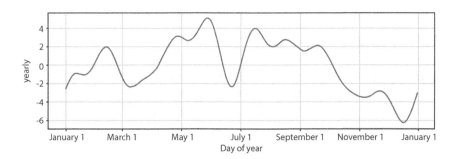

Figure 9.19 Yearly trend of vitamin D.

Figure 9.17 is after the COVID-19 break out the search for the vitamin D has increased sharply and the forecast suggestion that the trend will follow.

Figure 9.20 and 9.21 represented below shows the forecasted value. The column ds represented in Figure 9.20 indicates the year of prediction and the column yhat represented in Figure 9.21 is the predicted values of the trend for the corresponding year.

	ds	trend	yhat_lower	yhat_upper	trend_lower	trend_upper
620	2022-11-03	81.868840	74.522685	94.343770	81.188842	82.554736
621	2022-11-04	81.900209	66.463506	86.439597	81.217368	82.588989
622	2022-11-05	81.931579	69.786802	90.365965	81.246652	82.621511
623	2022-11-06	81.962949	68.887080	87.790486	81.275937	82.656834
624	2022-11-07	81.994319	71.528895	91.754656	81.305221	82.692157

Figure 9.20 Prediction (ds column indicates the year).

yearly	yearly_lower	yearly_upper	multiplicative_terms	multiplicative_terms_lower	multiplicative_terms_upper	yhat
-3.465617	-3.465617	-3.465617	0.0	0.0	0.0	84.336727
-3.488903	-3.488903	-3.488903	0.0	0.0	0.0	76.219486
-3.503819	-3.503819	-3.503819	0.0	0.0	0.0	79.914623
-3.509712	-3.509712	-3.509712	0.0	0.0	0.0	78.704692
-3.506089	-3.506089	-3.506089	0.0	0.0	0.0	81.781565

Figure 9.21 Predicted trend (yhat column indicates predicted trend).

9.7 Feature Scope of AI

Today the technological field is said to be weak AI because of its limitations. But the future of AI will be stronger. AI accomplishes many specific tasks that are predetermined but it is expected to overcome humans in all cognitive tasks in future. The world's education will have many transformations, inculcating classical ways of education. Moreover, the industries will have robots and automation replacing labours. AI will protect our nation developing military robots which will perform the task of soldiers.

9.8 Conclusion

Artificially intelligent systems will have a greater impact on our lives. It is a boon to the world. It sets milestones to all industries like biotechnology, medicines, telecommunication, gaming etc. It provides noticeable results and it has a long way to prove its true power. Modern technologies cannot be dreamt without computers, algorithms, hardware and software that simplify every task. With AI most of the process will be managed without human force. The main theory is that intelligence can be represented in terms of structured data that is programmed to a digital computer. AI has a high challenge in finding ways to program the machine that cuts down the complexity of human thoughts.

References

1. Turing, A.M. and Jack Copeland, B., *The Essential Turing: Seminal Writings in Computing, Logic, Philosophy, Artificial Intelligence, and Artificial Life, Plus the Secrets of Enigma*, Clarendon Press, New York, Oxford University Press, 2004.

2. Nirenburg, S., Cognitive systems: Toward human-level functionality. *AI Mag.*, 38, 4, 5–12, 2017.

3. Jackson, P.C., *Toward Human-Level Artificial Intelligence: Representation and Computation of Meaning in Natural Language*, Dover Publications, Mineola, New York, 2019.

4. Goertzel, B., Artificial general intelligence: Concept, state of the art, and future prospects. *J. Artif. Gen. Intell.*, 5, 1, 1–4, 2014.

5. Ackerman, R., Gal, A., Sagi, T., Shraga, R., A cognitive model of human bias in matching, in: *Pacific Rim International Conference on Artificial Intelligence*, Springer, Cham, pp. 632–646, August 2019.

6. Bourgin, D.D., Peterson, J.C., Reichman, D., Russell, S.J., Griffiths, T.L., Cognitive model priors for predicting human decisions, in: *International Conference on Machine Learning*, PMLR, pp. 5133–5141, May 2019.

7. Coppin, B., *Artificial Intelligence Illuminated*, Jones & Bartlett Learning, London, UK, 2004.

8. Wei, L., Legal risk and criminal imputation of weak artificial intelligence. *IOP Conf. Ser. Mater. Sci. Eng. IOP Publishing*, 490, 6, 062085, April 2019.

9. Zheng, A. and Casari, A., *Feature Engineering for Machine Learning: Principles and Techniques for Data Scientists*, O'Reilly Media, Inc, USA, 2018.

10. Heaton, J., An empirical analysis of feature engineering for predictive modeling, in: *SoutheastCon 2016*, IEEE, pp. 1–6, March 2016.

11. Harika, V.R. and Sivaramakrishnan, S., Image overlays on a video frame using HOG algorithm. *2020 IEEE International Conference on Advances and Developments in Electrical and Electronics Engineering (ICADEE)*, pp. 1–5, 2020.

12. Yegnanarayana, B., *Artificial Neural Networks*, PHI Learning Pvt. Ltd, New Delhi, India, 2009.

13. Gurney, K., *An Introduction to Neural Networks*, CRC Press, London, UK, 2018.

14. Yu, J., Yang, L., Xu, N., Yang, J., Huang, T., *Slimmable Neural Networks*, 2018, arXiv preprint arXiv:1812.08928.
15. Sivaramakrishnan, S. and Vasupradha, Centroid and path determination ofplanets for deep space autonomous optical navigation. *IJARESM*, 8, 11, 42–48, 2020.
16. Yan, L.C., Yoshua, B., Geoffrey, H., Deep learning. *Nature*, 521, 7553, 436–444, 2015.
17. Xin, Y., Kong, L., Liu, Z., Chen, Y., Li, Y., Zhu, H., Gao, M., Hou, H., Wang, C., Machine learning and deep learning methods for cybersecurity. *IEEE Access*, 6, 35365–35381, 2018.
18. Jordan, M.I. and Mitchell, T.M., Machine learning: Trends, perspectives, and prospects. *Science*, 349, 6245, 255–260, 2015.
19. Mohri, M., Rostamizadeh, A., Talwalkar, A., *Foundations of Machine Learning*, MIT Press, London, UK, 2018.
20. Kotsiantis, S.B., Zaharakis, I., Pintelas, P., Supervised machine learning: A review of classification techniques, in: *Emerging Artificial Intelligence Applications in Computer Engineering*, vol. 160, pp. 3–24, 2007.
21. Kotsiantis, S.B., Zaharakis, I.D., Pintelas, P.E., Machine learning: A review of classification and combining techniques. *Artif. Intell. Rev.*, 26, 3, 159–190, 2006.
22. Indurkhya, N. and Damerau, F.J. (Eds.), *Handbook of Natural Language Processing (Vol. 2)*, CRC Press, New York, USA, 2010.
23. Forsyth, D. and Ponce, J., *Computer Vision: A Modern Approach*, p. 792, Prentice Hall, Essex, England, 2011.
24. Overgoor, G., Chica, M., Rand, W., Weishampel, A., Letting the computers take over: Using AI to solve marketing problems. *Calif. Manage. Rev.*, 61, 4, 156–185, 2019.
25. Shi, Y., Particle swarm optimization. *IEEE Connections*, 2, 1, 8–13, 2004.
26. Babukarthik, R.G., Sivaramakrishnan, S., Rashmi, S., Roopashree, S., An expert system for solving multi-objective decision making problems: MPSO. *Kala Sarovar*, 23, 48–58, 2020.
27. Singh, K., Banks banking on ai. *Int. J. Adv. Res. Manage. Soc. Sci.*, 9, 9, 1–11, 2020.
28. Babukarthik, R.G., Fernandez, T.F., Sivaramakrishnan, S., Milan, A., 15 lethal vulnerability of robotics in industrial sectors, in: *Big Data Management in Sensing: Applications in AI and IoT*, pp. 227–238, River Publishers, New York, USA, 2021.
29. Sivaramakrishnan, S., Fernandez, T.F., Babukarthik, R.G., Premalatha, S., 4 forecasting time series data using ARIMA and facebook prophet models, in: *Big Data Management in Sensing: Applications in AI and IoT*, pp. 47–60, River Publishers, New York, USA, 2021.
30. Khayyat, M., Laabidi, K., Almalki, N., Al-zahrani, M., Time series facebook prophet model and python for COVID-19 outbreak prediction. *CMC-Comput. Mater. Con.*, 67, 3, 3781–3793, 2021.

## 10

A Comparative Intelligent Environmental Analysis of Air-Pollution in COVID: Application of IoT and AI Using ML in a Study Conducted at the North Indian Zone

Rohit Rastogi[1]*, Abhishek Goyal[2], Akshit Rajan Rastogi[1] and Neha Gupta[1]

[1]Dept. of CSE, ABES Engineering College, Ghaziabad, U.P., India
[2]Dept. of CSE, KIET Engineering College, Ghaziabad, U.P., India

Abstract

In the populated and developing countries, governments consider the regulation and protection of environment as a major task and should take into consideration the concept of Smart Environment Monitoring. The main motive of these systems is to enhance the environment with various technology including sensors, processors, data sets and other devices connected across the globe through a network. This system can basically help in monitoring air quality which is necessary in the field of meteorological studies and movement factors. Also, these factors contribute a lot in air pollution. So, forecasting air quality index using an Intelligent Environment system includes a machine learning model in order to predict air quality index for NCR (National Capital Region). The values of major pollutants like SO_2, PM2.5, CO, PM10, NO_2, and O_3. In recent years, machine learning in most emerging technology for predicting on historical data with 99.99% of accuracy.

The authors' team has implemented different machine learning algorithms of classification and regression techniques like Linear Regression, multiple linear regression, KNN, Random Forest Regression, Decision Tree Regression, Support Vector Regression, and Artificial Neural Networks. To make our prediction more accurate, mean square error, mean absolute error and R square errors have been considered. To prognosticating air quality index of NCR, India in different aspects like stubble farming, motor vehicle emission, and open construction practices which result in polluting the air quality of NCR.

*Corresponding author: rohit.rastogi@abes.ac.in

Anamika Ahirwar, Piyush Kumar Shukla, Manish Shrivastava, Priti Maheshwary and Bhupesh Gour (eds.) Innovative Engineering with AI Applications, (189–208) © 2023 Scrivener Publishing LLC

The manuscript is helping to frame a structured view of air quality prediction methods in reader's mind and also gives suggestions for other prediction methods as well. The real challenge is to decide which method will be applied in predicting the air quality. Hence, it is important to test and use all these methods.

Keywords: Machine learning, air pollution prediction, linear regression, artificial neural network, KNN, SO_2, PM2.5

10. 1　Introduction

This chapter discusses the different parameters of air quality and environment using various machine learning algorithms. This paper also introduces us with the reason behind the contamination of air. Pollution can cause harm to not only air but to water bodies as well. It can take the form of noise, heat, and even light. The substances which are responsible for pollution can be either foreign substance or they may have been naturally occurred in the nature. Pollution is mostly classified as to be caused by any one single source rather than many.

10.1.1　Intelligent Environment Systems

In this era of globalization, every country in the world is facing problems related to environment. In order to control these problems, it has become a primary concern of thinking for the various organizations and governments. This emerging problem produces a need of monitoring of environment and finding more environment nourishing solutions. And, this need brings smart monitoring techniques into the picture [5].

Intelligent Environment Systems plays an important role in approximately all sectors. This field is becoming a must have for cities with increased industrialization, high population and massive transportation, as these sectors are the main reason behind increasing pollution [18].

10.1.2　Types of Pollution

Pollution is mainly of four types: water pollution, soil pollution, noise pollution and air pollution. We here elaborate detail about air pollution. A factor which induces air pollution is stubble farming, motor vehicle emission, topological factor, and open construction work. The ordinance of environmental contamination has drawn public examination. NCR (National Capital Region) is one of the most contaminated territories in the world [17].

10.1.3   Components in Pollution Particles

Different researches have carried out several experiments and have come to a conclusion that the concentration of pollutants in NCR is alarmingly higher as compared to any other region [16].

This has made the lives of all the residents less for up to 6 years. While some researchers have [1] concluded that pollution has affected human fitness. Hence, we enhancing the air quality forecasting is one of the best objectives for civilization. Sulphur dioxide, PM2.5 and NO are major pollutants found in the air. Sulphur dioxide is a gas, present in air [6].

This combines easily with different substances to form harmful substances like sulphur acid, sulfurous acid etc. Sulfur dioxide affects social fitness when it is inhaled in. It causes a burning feeling in the nose, throat, and airways to result into coughing, wheezing, the brevity of breath, or a tense feeling around the chest. The concentration of Sulphur dioxide in the environment affects the places we can live in [3]. PM2.5 is also known as fine particulate matter (2.5 micrometers is one 400th of a millimeter). Fine particulate matter (PM2.5) is important among the pollutant index because it is a big concern to people's health when its level in the air becomes high [11]. So, it has been categorized according to Air quality index table.

10.1.4   Research Problem Introduction and Motivation

- With an average of 98.6 Particulate Matter (PM 2.5) concentration, Delhi was the most polluted city in the world. 21 cities out of 30, which were the most polluted, were from India.
- India leads the charts for the most polluted cities in the world. All those cities in India, who were to be monitored as per WHO, didn't report for the annual pollution exposure 2019.

10.2   Related Previous Work

Numerous other models exist to check the concentration of pollutants in cities like Delhi. Traditionally analytical models and statistical models include synthetic variation models and atmospheric dispersal models, which were applied for prognostication. Recently it was seen that machine learning methods give a more accurate result in cases of prognostication models.

10.2.1   Machine Learning Models

We know that machine learning has made our lives easier because of their accurate predictions. But when these algorithms are combined with that of AI's, the results become clearer. A machine learning approach takes various different factors into account unlike the statistical approach. Artificial Neural Networks (ANNs) have emerged to be one of the several broadly accepted methods for the prognostication of air quality [2]. Many researchers have built their models based on regression. Artificial intelligence algorithms such as fuzzy logic, generative algorithm, Principal component analysis (PCA) along with ANNs have been applied to create such models like Adaptive Neuro Fuzzy Interface System (ANFIS) model [13] etc. Another machine learning models that have been recognized add Support Vector Machine (SVM) situated model, PCA-SVM and several also. A modified Lasso and Ridge regression technique model [15] is where K-nearest neighbor algorithm has also been implemented to determine concentrations of PM2.5, SO2 and PM10. Another study conducted in Quito, Ecuador [14], worked on six meteorological constituents for predicting AQI concentrations. K. Hu *et al.* [2], planned a machine training model HazeEst for prognosticating the air index. Here, first, the method was evaluated using seven distinctive regression technique, and finally, SVR (Support vector regressor) was chosen as the ultimate prognostication model. The main goal is to prognosticate an air contamination level in an urban area with the ground data set [15].

10.2.2   Regression Techniques Applications

This method has used the linear regression and Support vector regression for the forecast of the contamination of the next month, the next day, and any date of future. The method improves to prognosticate any date contamination details within one period based on independent parameters and examining pollution parts and determine future pollution. Time Series Analysis was also used for the identification of future data points which have seasonality and trends in air pollution prediction [3].

This designed method performs two significant tasks. (i) Identifies the levels of pollutants (S02, PM2.5, CO, benzene) based upon provided meteorological values. (ii) Prognosticates the level of pollutants for a special date [10]. Logistic regression is used to identify a data sample is either contaminated or not contaminated. Auto regression is used to prognosticate projected values of pollutants based upon the early pollutants' interpretations.

The prime aim is to prognosticate the air pollution level within a particular area with the raw data set [11].

- Air quality prediction using machine learning model by Tripathi, C.B. [17].
- Nandigala Venkat Anurag, Yagnavalk Burra, S. Sharanya they carried out case study on Air Quality Index Prediction with Meteorological Data Using Feature Based Weighted Xgboost by analyzing trend in air quality with year wise the explore key factor that responsible for Air Quality Index predication [4].
- Chavi Srivastava, Shyamli Singh, and Amit Prakash Singh they also carried out case study on Estimation of Air Pollution in Delhi Using Machine Learning Techniques by estimate the value of AQI by train machine learning model on various regression model like linear regression and etc. [12].
- Shivangi Nigam, B.P.S. Rao, N. Kumar, V. A. Mhaisalkar evaluate the Air Quality Index – A Comparative Study for Assessing the Status of Air Quality they evaluate dataset to find specific trends in season related to previous years data with present year and find some pattern in dataset which is use full to find different factor which is best fit for estimate value of AQI and trends according season and lot of factor having correlation between them [8].

10.3 Methodology Adopted in Research

10.3.1 Data Source

To prognosticate the air quality of The NCR area, authors' team wanted the pollutant concentration of all the elements available in the air, which will be available in the cpcb.nic.in the website, which holds all the data that contaminates the area every year. Research Team used data from several stations which measures many elements present in the atmosphere. Data is taken from 10 different stations in NCR. These data are stored in the form of a table which consists of a total of 3469 rows and having eight columns in each row. The AQI formulae will be applied in order to calculate the AQI by using the various regression algorithm for a particular year.

The first step, to build such a model is to collect the raw dataset. The air pollutant dataset was collected from government website cpcb.com which place all record of air pollutant of every year in day wise format, of various formats. The snapshot for the same is shown in Table 10.1.

Duration: 1 January, 2017 – 1 January, 2020

Various Station: Anand Vihar, Delhi – DPCC, Indirapuram, Ghaziabad – UPPCB, AshokVihar, Delhi – DPCC, Bawana, Delhi – DPCC, etc.

Daily Time Span: 0:00 to 23:59 h (24 h)

1. Number of tuples recorded per day: 1
2. Total number of tuples in wanted duration: 3469 after cleaning

NOTE: The data is collected from different station

Table 10.1 Sample dataset of air pollutant.

	From date	PM2.5	PM10	NO2	Ozone	CO	AQI
0	26-09-2017-00:00	75.77	104.98	24.72	45.75	104.98	75.73758
1	27-09-2017-00:00	103.23	149.3	25.07	55.18	149.3	97.67374
2	28-09-2017-00:00	34.32	116.97	25.37	54.59	116.97	81.67202
3	29-09-2017-00:00	80.18	112.76	25.89	55.45	112.76	79.58828
4	30-09-2017-00:00	36.15	112.9	25.33	51.86	112.9	79.65758
5	01-10-2017-00:00	67.24	109.68	25.04	48.03	109.68	78.06384
6	02-10-2017-00:00	38.83	55.34	24.88	43.57	55.34	51.16828
7	03-10-2017-00:00	51.2	72.22	25.68	53.17	72.22	59.52303
8	04-10-2017-00:00	78.04	112.26	26.3	56.01	112.26	79.34081
9	05-10-2017-00:00	77.16	101.28	27.79	58.34	101.28	73.90626
10	06-10-2017-00:00	62.62	86.48	27.36	59.36	86.48	66.58101
11	07-10-2017-00:00	17.91	24.48	26.31	54.66	24.48	22.66667
12	08-10-2017-00:00	37.63	108.94	25.92	59.16	108.94	77.69758
13	09-10-2017-00:00	128.1	153.99	24.42	48.71	153.99	99.99505
14	10-10-2017-00:00	30.39	139.72	24.62	51.28	139.72	92.93212
15	11-10-2017-00:00	74.4	119.73	25.11	50.32	119.73	83.03808
16	12-10-2017-00:00	29.88	166.77	28.46	69.42	116.77	106.8256
17	13-10-2017-00:00	92.2	151.41	28.1	63.01	151.41	98.71808

10.3.2   Data Pre-Processing

Removing Rows with Missing Values

- The easiest way to take care of such missing values is to remove the whole row. But, these information should be contained in different rows so that there is no loss of data. Deleting the whole row has not been proved to be so beneficial.

Fixing Errors in the Structure
Typographical or grammatical errors should be always avoided. But, if any how these error are present in dataset, we need to remove it so that they do not cause a problem with the machine learning model. Such errors create confusion in the code.

10.3.3   Calculating AQI

An air quality index (AQI) is used by the government to tell the people how much the cities are polluted. Public health risks increase with the increase in AQI. Different countries have their own AQI. Here, we had focused on the AQI used in India.

10.3.4   Computing AQI

The air quality index is a linear function of the pollutant concentration. At the boundary between AQI categories, there is a discontinuous jump of one AQI unit. To convert from concentration to AQI this equation is used:
(As per given Figure 10.1, the formula to calculate AQI)
Table 10.2 is showing AQI Category, pollutants and Health Breakpoints.

$$I = \frac{I_{high} - I_{low}}{C_{high} - C_{low}} (C - C_{low}) + I_{low}$$

Where:

C_{low} = the concentration breakpoint that is $\leq C$,
C_{high} = the concentration breakpoint that is $\geq C$,
I_{low} = the index breakpoint corresponding to C_{low},
I_{high} = the index breakpoint corresponding to C_{high}.

Figure 10.1 The equation to calculate AQI.

Table 10.2 EPA table.

AQI Category, Pollutants and Health Breakpoints

AQI Category (Range)	$PM_{1.0}$(24hr)	$PM_{2.5}$(24hr)	NO_2(24hr)	O_3(8hr)	CO(8hr)	SO_2(24hr)	NH_3(24hr)	Pb(24hr)
Good (0-50)	0-50	0-30	0-40	0-50	0-1.0	0-40	0-200	0-0.5
Satisfactory (51-100)	51-100	31-60	41-80	51-100	1.1-2.0	41-80	201-400	0.5-1.0
Moderately polluted (101-200)	101-250	61-90	81-180	101-168	2.1-10	81-380	401-800	1.1-2.0
Poor (201-300)	251-350	91-120	181-280	169-208	10-17	381-800	801-1200	2.1-3.0
Very poor (301-400)	351-430	121-250	281-400	209-748	17-34	801-1600	1200-1800	3.1-3.5
Severe (401-500)	430+	250+	400+	748+	34+	1600+	1800+	3.5+

10.3.5 Data Pre-Processing

Following Steps were performed for data preprocessing and collection.

Data Refinement

The data to be analyzed by first cleaned, by removing all the unfavorable values. The missing values in case of the target object, i.e., the pollutants are estimated using an imputer function to perform the interpolation. The strategy used here for estimation is the mean value. Data pre-processing projection of the null values by heat map is shown in Figure 10.2 and Figure 10.3.

Removing null rows having maximum number of null values as show in Figure 10.6.

Fill Null Values

Values are shown in Figure 10.4 and correlation of data is shown in Figure 10.5.

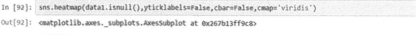

```
In [92]:  sns.heatmap(data1.isnull(),yticklabels=False,cbar=False,cmap='viridis')
Out[92]:  <matplotlib.axes._subplots.AxesSubplot at 0x267b13ff9c8>
```

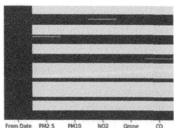

Figure 10.2 Heat map of our dataset.

In [93]:
```
#In this data there have lot of missing values
#we need to drop that rows
```

In [94]:
```
mis=["None","0"]
data1=pd.read_csv(r'C:\Users\ravi\Desktop\project AQI\raw dataset1\AQIDATA.csv',na_values=mis)
```

In [95]:
```
sns.heatmap(data1.isnull(),yticklabels=False,cbar=False,cmap='viridis')
```

Out[95]: <matplotlib.axes._subplots.AxesSubplot at 0x267b2b49988>

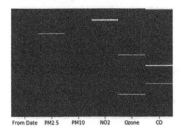

Figure 10.3 Heat map after removing null rows.

In [166]:
```
a=data1['PM2.5']
a.fillna(np.mean(a),inplace=True)
data1['PM2.5']=a
a=data1['NO2']
a.fillna(np.mean(a),inplace=True)
data1['NO2']=a
a=data1['CO']
a.fillna(np.mean(a),inplace=True)
data1['CO']=a
a=data1['PM10']
a.fillna(np.mean(a),inplace=True)
data1['CO']=a
```

In [167]:
```
sns.heatmap(data1.isnull(),yticklabels=False,cbar=False,cmap='viridis')
```

Out[167]: <matplotlib.axes._subplots.AxesSubplot at 0x267b3098e08>

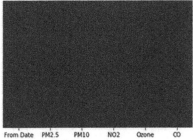

Figure 10.4 Filling missing values by mean.

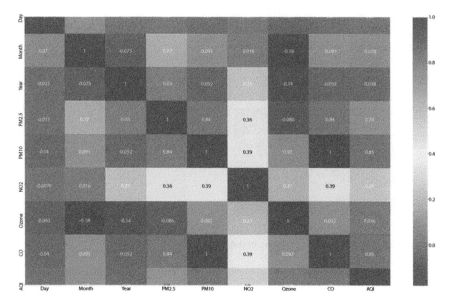

Figure 10.5 Correlation in dataset.

Now, visualize the dataset. We'd try to find the correlation between attributes using 'heat map' as shown in Figure 10.5.

10.3.6 Feature Selection

Feature selection is the method of choosing a subset from the features that contain important data. In the case of unnecessary data, feature extraction implies used. Feature extraction includes the choice of best input parameters of the chosen input dataset. The unified dataset which was gathered is used for further analysis. The maximum amount of inputs available for review is seven, hence all the inputs are selected for the computations (as per Figure 10.6).

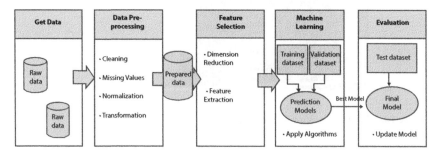

Figure 10.6 Model for training the dataset.

Training the Model
Data splitting was done as 80% for training and 20% for testing.

10.4   Results and Discussion

10.4.1   Collective Analysis

The machine learning model to predict air pollution was one the most important objective of the research paper. We here predict air pollution on particular data i.e. 1 January 2020. We take data of previous years the data from www.cpcb.nic.in. By using linear regression, Lasso-Ridge regression, KNN and support vector machine. We actually compare actual value and predicted values. Self-explanatory Data Visualization as shown in Figure 10.7 to Figure 10.9 as per order of Year, Month and their averages.

After evaluation of different type of regression model, it was found that the best fit model for predict AQI is K-nearest neighbor model which having accuracy of 97.5 percentage. This model is best fit.

Here, we show that the almost all values is equal some particular values show anomalous behavior. If we see average of AQI in month wise Figures 10.8 and 10.9, we easily say that AQI not only depends on concentration of particle it also show that AQI also depends on temperature, humidity, etc. It concludes that we need more data and Add more column in dataset of other factor like temperature and etc.

We clearly see that, if we particularly show average July and august month in 2017 it is far more differ than other years same month.

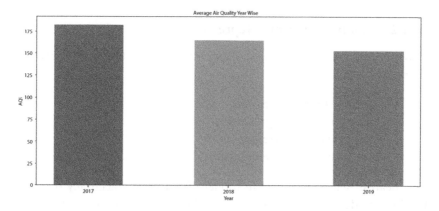

Figure 10.7 Average of AQI year wise.

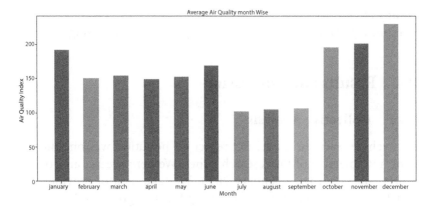

Figure 10.8 Average of AQI monthwise.

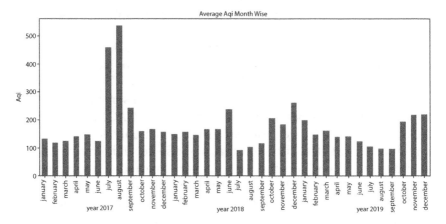

Figure 10.9 Average of AQI according to month.

10.4.2 Applying Various Repressors

Here we used various regression algorithm for predicting dependent variable such that

- Multiple linear regression
- Lasso and Ridge regression
- Support vector regressor
- k-nearest neighbors regression

K nearest neighbor is best fit model which having accuracy of 97.5%. It is best model of predicting air quality index prediction on independent variable (PM2.5, PM10 and etc.) as shown in Figure 10.10 and Figure 10.11.

```
from sklearn import metrics
print('Mean Absolute Error',metrics.mean_absolute_error(y_test,y_pred))
print('Mean Squared Error',metrics.mean_squared_error(y_test,y_pred))
print('Root Mean Squared Error',np.sqrt(metrics.mean_squared_error(y_test,y_pred)))
```

```
Mean Absolute Error 3.2368965287207674
Mean Squared Error 403.8241207128776
Root Mean Squared Error 20.0953756051704
```

```
from sklearn.metrics import r2_score
score=r2_score(y_test,y_pred)
score
```

```
0.9749835186889328
```

Figure 10.10 Accuracy of k-nearest neighbor.

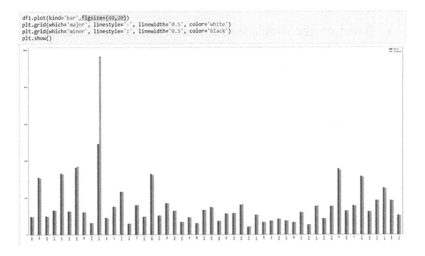

Figure 10.11 Comparison between actual values and predicted values.

As shown Figure 10.11 comparing actual values with predicted values.

Figure 10.11 shows comparison between actual values and predicted values here we show that actual values are almost equal to predicted values except some values.

10.4.3   Comparison with Existing State-of-the-Art Technologies

This project has used several factors like temperature, occasion and weather conditions in order to improve the results.

Table 10.3 Model evaluation.

Models	Mean absolute error	Root mean squared error
Multiple Linear Regression	38.386647	65.075391
Lasso Regression	38.344869	65.059393
Ridge Regression	38.385283	65.075104
Support Vector Regressor	0.099856	0.387394
K-Nearest Neighbors	3.236896	20.095375

Performance Evaluation

- Based on the comparison of out-of-sample RMSE among the models, along with taking into account the interpretability of the model, we have decided that k nearest neighbor is the best model. For reference, following is the performance of the models and comparison of their in-sample and out-of-sample RMSE values (as per Table 10.3).

Evaluation

- After implementing different types of algorithm, we need to evaluate which algorithm is best for predict AQI of NCR. Table 10.3 show root mean and r squared values of algorithm which mention in above paragraph.

10.5   Novelties in the Work

This research used various algorithms of regression and classification like LR, SDGR, RFR, DTR, SVM, and ANN. To make the predictions more accurate the research team has used MSE and MAE with R square. For predicting air quality index of NCR (National Capital Region) in different aspects of like stubble farming, Motor vehicle emission, and open construction practice which impact of air quality of NCR.

10.6   Future Research Directions

There is a lot of scope in future regarding this topic as various aspects can be covered regarding this field. Also, air pollution and environment analysis can also be done with the help of Advanced Machine Learning Algorithms or Deep Neural Networks. In order to build a good predicting model, we can find the air quality index by taking various parameters into consideration like temperature, humidity, etc. Also, models implemented in this paper can be applied to a greater number of stations for increase the training input [2]. It is also observed that the approach can also help to identify the predictor(s) for which the variance is not properly captured (reason for heteroscedasticity). This will also help to solve the problem for normality as well. We can still search for other avenues in order to look for quality controlled data. The next research seekers can also train their model for next year data and also, solve the problem of auto-correlations [7].

10.7   Limitations

Various limitations were faced in writing this challenging paper and carrying out such a difficult task. The experiment needs further more tiny constraints for future predicting AQI. In this paper, instruments applied for finding readings were limited to some range and generated the limited results [9]. So, to get more refined results, one needs more refined instruments. Due to the limitation of the data, some aspects are still left to be covered which can be interesting research area. Also, this experiment was confined to a small place, so in order to view the environmental situation from different perspectives, one may need to extend future research to different parts of the country or continent [7].

10.8   Conclusions

In the populated and developing countries, governments consider the regulation of air as a major task. Monitoring air quality using Intelligent and Smart Environment Solutions is a necessity due to various pollution causing activities including stubble burning and open construction practices contributing a lot in the air pollution. So, we can forecast air quality index using machine learning algorithms working as a part of Smart Environment systems in order to predict air quality index for NCR zone at India.

For making an advanced training and predicting model, any researcher seeker and interested can take various parameters into examination like temperature, concentration of each gas in the atmosphere, pressure, etc. Place of experiment is also a major parameter to take into consideration as each and every place has its own environment related problems.

Air quality indexes of major pollutants like PM2.5, PM10, CO, NO_2, SO_2, and O_3. In recent years machine learning in most emerging technology for predicting on historical data with 99.99% of accuracy. Advanced fields including Artificial Intelligence, Data Analytics, Deep Learning Algorithms, etc. can be very helpful in saving the environment from pollution.

Acknowledgements

The authors want to extend sincere thanks to management and officials of ABES Engineering College, Ghaziabad who gave all facilities, permissions and support to conduct the experiment and we also want to extend thanks to professors and guides from reputed universities, Dr. D.K. Chaturvedi of DEI, Dr. Santosh Satya of IIT Delhi and Dr. Navneet Arora of IIT Roorkee for their motivation and encouragement. We also extend sincere thanks to the Almighty and all direct and in direct supporters and well-wishers.

Key Terms and Definitions

Multiple Linear Regression
Multiple Linear Regression (MLR) is a statistical technique for finding the linear relation between the independent variables (predictors) and the dependent or response variable. The general MLR model is built from N observations of the multiple predictor variables xk (k = 1, 2,.., m) and the observed target data y.

Lasso and Ridge Regression
Ridge regression and Lasso regression are very similar in working to Linear Regression. The only difference is the addition of the l1 penalty in Lasso Regression and the l2 penalty in Ridge Regression. The primary reason why these penalty terms are added is two ensure there is regularization, shrinking the weights of the model to zero or close to zero to ensure that the model does not overfit the data.

Support Vector Regressor
Support Vector Machine can also be used as a regression method, maintaining all the main features that characterize the algorithm (maximal margin). The Support Vector Regression (SVR) uses the same principles as the SVM for classification, with only a few minor differences. First of all, because output is a real number it becomes very difficult to predict the information at hand, which has infinite possibilities.

k-Nearest Neighbor Regression
K nearest neighbor is a simple algorithm that stores all available cases and predicts the numerical target based on a similarity measure (e.g., distance functions). KNN has been used in statistical estimation and pattern recognition already in the beginning of 1970's as a non-parametric technique.

Data Visualization
Data visualization is used to represent dataset and understand it through various plots and graphs. In air quality, we have used heat map, correlation matrix, and boxplot to visualize the data. Through, Data visualization, we get to know the relation between various attributes of the dataset. Python offers multiple libraries for data visualization and analysis.

Few popular plotting libraries:

- Matplotlib: low level, provides lots of freedom.
- Pandas Visualization: easy to use interface, built on Matplotlib.
- Seaborn: high-level interface, great default styles.
- ggplot: based on R's ggplot2, uses grammar of graphics..
- Plotly: can create interactive plots.

Additional Readings

World's Air Pollution: Real-time Air Quality Index
https://waqi.info/

National Air Quality Index
https://app.cpcbccr.com/AQI_India/

New Delhi Real-time Air Quality Index (AQI) & Pollution Report ...

https://air-quality.com/place/india/new-delhi/dd4464ff?lang=en&standard=aqi_us

AQI India: Real-Time Air Quality Index | Air Pollution Level
https://www.aqi.in/

New Delhi, Delhi Air Pollution Level, Real-Time Air Quality Index (AQI)
https://www.aqi.in/dashboard/india/delhi/new-delhi

Annex:
Code for Auto Correlation

```
In [26]: import seaborn as sns
         #get correlation of each features in dataset
         corrmat=dataset.corr()
         top_corr_features=corrmat.index
         plt.figure(figsize=(30,20))
         #plot the heat map
         g=sns.heatmap(dataset[top_corr_features].corr(),annot=True,cmap='RdYlGn')
```

References

1. Aggarwal, P. and Jain, S., Impact of air pollutants from surface transport sources on human health: A modelling and epidemiological approach. *Environ. Int.*, 83, 146–157, 2015.
2. Baawain, M., Systematic approach for the prediction of ground level air pollution (around an industrial port) using an artificial neural network. *Aerosol Air Qual. Res.*, 14, 1, 2014.
3. Bhalgat, P., Pitale, S., Bhoite, S., Air quality prediction using machine learning algorithms. *IJCATR*, 8, 09, 367–370, 2019.
4. Bhalla, N. and O'Boyle, J., Who is responsible for Delhi air pollution? Indian newspapers' framing of causes and solutions. *Int. J. Commun.*, 12, 41–64, 2018.
5. Dipanda, A., Damiani, E., Yetongnon, K., Special issue on intelligent systems and applications in vision, image and information computing. *J. Reliab. Intell. Environ.*, 2, 117–118, 2016. https://doi.org/10.1007/s40860-016-0032-8.
6. Gallardo, M., Lavado, L., Panizo, L. *et al.*, A constraint-based language for modelling intelligent environments. *J. Reliab. Intell. Environ.*, 3, 55–79, 2017. https://doi.org/10.1007/s40860-017-0040-3.
7. Hornos, M.J., Application of software engineering techniques to improve the reliability of intelligent environments. *J. Reliab. Intell. Environ.*, 3, 1–3, 2017. https://doi.org/10.1007/s40860-017-0043-0.
8. Hornos, M.J. and Rodríguez-Domínguez, C., Increasing user confidence in intelligent environments. *J. Reliab. Intell. Environ.*, 4, 71–73, 2018. https://doi.org/10.1007/s40860-018-0063-4.

9. Jalan, I. and Dholakia, H., *Issue Brief, What is Polluting Delhi's Air? Understanding Uncertainties in Emissions Inventories*, Council on Energy, Environment and Water, New Delhi, India, March 2019, www.ceew.in.

10. Kumar, S., Air pollution and climate change: Case study National Capital Territory of Delhi. *Int. J. Sci. Eng. Res.*, 9, 6, 844–848, 2018.

11. Pandey, G., Zhang, B., Jian, L., Predicting sub-micron air pollution indicators: A machine learning approach. *Environ. Sci. Process. Impacts*, 15, 5, 996–1005, 2013.

12. Rizwan, S.A., Nonengkynrith, B., Gupta, S.K., Center for Community Medicine, All India Institute of Medical Sciences, New Delhi, India, 2007.

13. Sharma, A.K. and Baliyan, P., Air pollution and public health: The challenges for Delhi, India. *Rev. Environ. Health*, 33, 1, 77–86, Mar. 2018.

14. Singh, S. and Singh, A.P., Estimation of air pollution in Delhi using machine learning techniques. *International Conference on Computing, Power and Communication Technologies*, 2018, https://www.researchgate.net/publication/332430367.

15. Siris, V.A., Fotiou, N., Mertzianis, A. *et al.*, Smart Application-aware IoT data Collection. *J. Reliab. Intell. Environ.*, 5, 17–28, 2019, https://doi.org/10.1007/s40860-019-00077-y.

16. Srivastava, C., Singh, A.P., Singh, S., *Estimation of Air Pollution in Delhi Using Machine Learning Techniques*, 2018, https://www.researchgate.net/publication/332430367.

17. Tripathi, C.B., Baredar, P., Tripathi, L., Air pollution in Delhi: biomass energy and suitable environment policies are sustainable pathways for health safety. *Curr. Sci.*, 117, 7, 1153–1160, Oct. 10, 2019.

18. Wilson, T., Legay, A., Sedwards, S. *et al.*, Group abstraction for assisted navigation of social activities in intelligent environments. *J. Reliab. Intell. Environ.*, 4, 107–120, 2018, https://doi.org/10.1007/s40860-018-0058-1.

## 11

Eye-Based Cursor Control and Eye Coding Using Hog Algorithm and Neural Network

S. Sivaramakrishnan[1]*, Vasuprada G.[2], V. R. Harika[2], Vishnupriya P.[2] and Supriya Castelino[2]

[1]Department of Information Science and Engineering, New Horizon College of Engineering, Bangalore, India
[2]Department of Electronics and Communication, Dayananda Sagar University, Bangalore, India

Abstract

For the physically challenged people cursor control using the eye movement plays a major role in helping them to perform the necessary task. Non-intrusive gaze estimation technique can help in the communication between humans and computers. The eye-gaze will be handy for the communication between physical challenged person and the computer. The pupil movement patterns also called as Eye Accessing Cues (EAC) is related to human brain's cognitive processes. This method in particular will be beneficial to the physical challenged people with disabilities such as Amyotrophic Lateral Sclerosis (ALS). In this chapter, a technique is proposed to control the mouse cursor in real time using the pupil movements. With the application of the image processing and graphic user interfacing technique (GUI) the cursor control can be rolled into reality using blink detection and gaze estimation. Hog algorithm helps in identifying the eye blink and pupil movements. Based on the detection the cursor control is carried out either directly tracking the pupil movement or tracking the same with the help of camera connected to the system. In this chapter the gaze direction is performed using Hog algorithm and machine learning algorithm. Finally, the cursor control is implemented by GUI automation. The same technique can be expanded to help the physically challenged person to write content and also to do python coding.

Keywords: Eye gaze detection, hog algorithm, cursor control, GUI automation

---

*Corresponding author: sivaramkrish.s@gmail.com

Anamika Ahirwar, Piyush Kumar Shukla, Manish Shrivastava, Priti Maheshwary and Bhupesh Gour (eds.) Innovative Engineering with AI Applications, (209–226) © 2023 Scrivener Publishing LLC

11.1 Introduction

To meet the challenges of the modern world the technology keeps on updating and certainly the technology has helped human begins to greater extend. This chapter proposes the use of the latest technology to help the people with severe disabilities to communicate to the real world with the help of the computer by tracking the eye movement. The proposed technique tracks the pupil movement with the help of the web camera. The proposed technique is efficient and simple. The technique used to communicate with the help of eye movement is called as eye writing and this technique help the physical challenged people especially with ALS (amyotrophic lateral sclerosis) there by then can express and convey message to other people. The coding is done using python programming for the hog algorithm to implement this technique and it an effective method to help people communication with eye detection and eye gazing and more importantly they can achieve it without the help of others.

The hog algorithm in the image processing technique is used to extract the features of human being and find its application in face detection. The region of interest for this application is around eye and the pupil movement can be obtained using the facial landmarks and with help of the geometric relationship. The data gathered in the area of interest can be used further to detect eye blink and other location of pupil help in the movement of the cursor which is explained in the subsequent session. The pupil can move left, right, top and bottom and based on the movement the necessary control action can be carried out. The control action result in the movement of the cursor. So the cursor control is due to two factors namely blink detection and gaze determination. This technique also helps the physically challenged people to write a coding in python language and compile the same. The eye based control technique can also be used with the emerging technology like augmented reality (AR) as the tacking technique used in eye gazing will add weightage to AR. The two technique used for classifying the direction of the eye movement are Hog Based technique and Machine learning technique which are elaborated in details in the following sessions.

11.2 Related Work

In the article "Hand free Control PC control "a simple matching technique is proposed [1]. Support vector machine (SVM) learning algorithm is used for appropriate window positioning. This technique offers a real time cursor control as it could offer high speed and accuracy. The programming is done in JAVA language as the computational cost is less and has an advantage of platform independence.

In the article "Enhanced Cursor Control Using Eye Mouse" the face detection is carried out using viola-jones algorithm [2]. Here Spherical Eyeball Model and Houghman circle detection algorithm are used for locating the iris. With the help of the calibration points the gaze position is determined. This method provides better performance and accurate tracking of the eye movement.

In the article "A face as a Mouse for disabled person" the detection of the facial features like eyes, nose, and the distance between two eyes is detected using the clustering algorithm [3]. The cursor movement in this method is directly proportional to the eye movements. The method offers an advantage of precise eye tracking also it is cost effective.

In the article "Sleepiness Detection System Bases on Facial Expression" Dlib tool is used along with the camera for identifying the mouth and the eye movements [4]. This method could detect the blink detection with an accuracy of around 90% and drowsiness detection with an accuracy of about 91.7%.

In the article "Communication through real-time video oculography using face landmark detection" the technique used, plays a major role in assisting the person to communication to the real world [5]. The combination of expression used in face is used to convey different information. The image processing tools such as opencv and dlib tool is used for building the model. The dlib tool detects the eye blink using the facial landmarks. The various eye pattern helps to provide corresponding visual or audio communication. This method also provides better efficiency in differentiating the voluntary and involuntary blinks.

In the article "Eye blink detection using the facial landmarks" an algorithm is proposed to operate in real time for the identification of blink in the video sequence [5]. The model is trained with various landmarks in the face using the data and this helps in identifying the eye blink detection. This technique also helps in finding the level of eye opening and calculates the eye aspect ratio effectively. The Markov model is used to measures the eye closure so as to determine blink detection. For accurate classification, machine learning algorithm SVM was used in the model.

In the article "Eye-Gaze determination using Convolutional Neural network" for the detection of eye gaze direction and Eye Accessing Cues (EAC) the real time framework is used [6]. The viola-jones algorithm is used for detection of face features. For the estimation of the gaze direction Convolution neural network (CNN) is used. The advantage of this method is it offers computational time of 42 ms and also works well with rotation of the face. With the CNN this method provides better human to computer interaction.

In the article "Precise Eye-Gaze Detection and tracking system" the authors have used real time system which provides contact free eye tracking [7]. The technique detects the center for pupil accurately and thereby can follow the movement of head. PupilGlint vector is used to determine the line of gaze and the validation of the glints is done using iris outline. This method process 25 frames per second and provides the advantage of less tracking error caused due movement of head and slow blinking.

In the article "Facial and eye Gaze Detection" SVM algorithm is used and the computer vision technology help in locating the facial features [8]. The system is trained with 3D data and thereby the neural network helps in accurate gaze position. One disadvantage of this method is high processing time for determining the gaze movement involving the 3D rotations. Also the mean square error does not offer satisfactory result.

In the article "Eye writer" a technique is proposed to determine the dark and the bright pupils of the eyes which felicitates in the eye tracking [9]. PS3 camera is used along with computer vision technology for capturing the high quality image. IR illumination is used to improve the quality of the image and MOSFET included in the model is used to vary the resistance. This model has an advantage of low cost as the technique uses the open source tools.

11.3   Methodology

The eye based cursor control is achieved by the combination of action such as gaze detection, GUI automation and blink detection. Figure 11.1 represented below shown the eye based cursor control. Through the webcam the

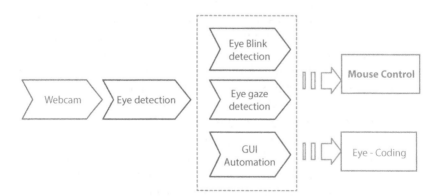

Figure 11.1 Eye-based cursor and coding control.

region of interest is captured followed by that the eye blink detection, eye gaze detection and GUI Automation is performed using the Hog Algorithm and finally the mouse control and program coding is carried out.

11.3.1   Eye Blink Detection

As mention the HOG algorithm is used to detect the blink of the eye in the region of interest. OpenCV and dlib tool are used to detect the face of a person and thereby in the region of interest the blink detection is carried out [10, 11]. The next step is to detect the position of left and the right eye which can be accomplished with the help of the facing landmarks. Then the distance between horizontal as well as vertical direction is calculated. The measured parameter helps in estimating ratio of horizontal to vertical length. The above mentioned calculation is carried out for both the eyes. A threshold length is then fixed and if the measured distance is less than the threshold length then the blink is said to be detected. On the occurrence of the blink detection the necessary control action like mouse clicking such as right click or left click and scrolling events can be carried out. Figure 11.2 shows represents the identifying of the facial features with the help of

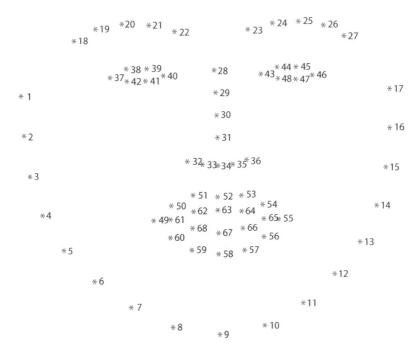

Figure 11.2 Facial landmarks.

the facial points. The figure is obtained by using the HOG algorithm and various points represents the facial landmarks.

11.3.2   Hog Algorithm

Histogram of Oriented Gradients in short called as HOG algorithm is a simple, efficient and powerful feature descriptor which detects the object using local intensity gradient distribution. HOG algorithm find its application not only in face detection but also in detecting the object. The HOG is a two stage process algorithm. In the stage one, the histogram of small part of the image is found and later all the histogram is combined to form a single one. Figure 11.3 clearly shows how HOG algorithm process an input image.

As shown in the above figure in the stage one histogram is obtained for small parts of the image and in stage two overall histograms are obtained. Hence this algorithm has high accuracy in locating the facial features. Also for each input images a unique feature vector is obtained.

Figure 11.4 represented below shows the landmark points made over a human eye using the HOG algorithm.

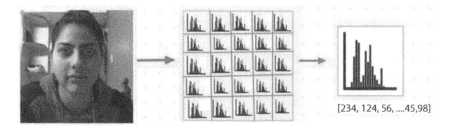

Figure 11.3 Two-stage processing of HOG algorithm.

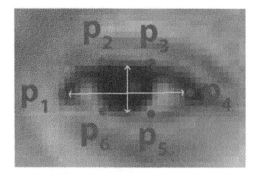

Figure 11.4 Landmark on human eye.

11.3.3   Eye Gaze Detection

Eye gaze detection can be implemented using either of these two techniques:

1. Deep learning and CNN
2. Gaze determination using HOG algorithm

11.3.3.1   Deep Learning and CNN

Deep learning is a subset of Artificial intelligence which is concerned with emulating the learning approach similar to human begins to overcome certain task. CNN is a special type of neural network model which works with 2D images. The model is first trained with a good number of images and with the knowledge gain it can predict the category of a new image. Like now human brain is connected with neuron, the CNN also have neuron which is designed mathematically which tries to replicate what human neuron does. CNN consists of multiple layers and each layer consists of neurons and each neuron in one layer is connected to all the neuron in the next layer. The fully connected network some time vulnerable to overfitting and to overcome the same, the regularization technique such as varying the weight of neuron is performed. The CNN hold the advantage of less processing time compared to other algorithm used for image. So the CNN quickly learn with the trained data and can accurately predict the classification of image of unknown data. Our objective here is to detect the gaze direction using CNN and there are totally five categories namely

- Right
- Left
- Centre
- Up
- Down

For each of the above category, the CNN is trained with a set of data called as training data set and some set of data are used for validation to check the efficiency of the model. Since the model deal with classification of the image into five categories, the category method is used while coding in python for the gaze determination. The necessary libraries to be import during coding are opencv, numpy, matplotlib, and the framework used is tensorflow. The root mean square error is monitored and it is optimized so as to adjust the learning rate automatically [12]. The labeling of the data can be done with the help of the Image Data Generator method available in python. In the CNN max pooling followed by dense layer are used to build the model and for the final layer ReLu activation function is used. ReLu stands for rectified linear unit which provides two outputs one is the direct input if the input is positive else the output is zero. Most of the CNN and Artificial Neural networks (ANN) uses ReLu as the default activation function [13]. The other activation function which are used is softmax activation function, which return the maximum value in the list [14, 15]. It is also better to start with ReLu activation function first before trying with the other activation function. To determine the loss while training the data, categorical cross entropy is used in multi class classification.

11.3.3.2 Hog Algorithm for Gaze Determination

Histogram of Oriented Gradients (HOG) is applied over the region of interest, for eye gazing the region of interest is human face. It is a descriptive algorithm which performs the necessary computation along the grid of cells in the identified region of interest. The facial landmarks obtained is mention in the Figure 11.4 and these identified points are useful in determining the gaze ratio for all the five categories namely up, down, left, right and center. And the gaze ratio is defined as the ratio of number of pixels extending in the white region in the left side to the right side of eye. And the gaze ratio is used to determine the eye gaze in all the four direction.

11.3.4 GUI Automation

The library used to obtain the Graphical User Interface is 'pyautogui' which is available in python programming. The keyboard and the mouse can be controlled by user with the help of the 'puautogui' library and thereby the automatic interaction can happen. Thus the automatic mouse clicks, keystrokes from a keyboard, cursor navigation, cursor positioning and display of message is achieved. With the help of the detection of eye blink and the eye gaze detection the GUI automation is performed. For example, if left eye blink is detected then left click in the mouse is automated and on the detection of right blink, right click is automated. One important thing to be considered is the eye blink period is to be defined in advance so any involuntary blink will not be taken into the account. By closing the eye for certain duration the person can able to select the key to be pressed for eye based coding. The code compiling is carried out using hotkey feature which is available in the 'pyautogui' library. The keyset used consists of the keyboard keys and frequently used keywords thereby it makes the easy for the person to easily perform eye based control.

11.4   Experimental Analysis

As mentioned earlier two types of operation can be performed namely eye based cursor control and eye coding. The hardware and the software requirement are as follows. The in-built web in the laptop or an external web with a minimum resolution of 0.922 mega pixel is required. But the algorithm used in this chapter namely HOG algorithm or the deep learning model can perform well even if the resolution is around 0.6 megapixels. The python programming is used which has the advantage of many libraries as mention early in the chapter which can support image processing techniques.

11.4.1   Eye-Based Cursor Control

The combined action of gaze detection and the eye blink detection felicities the cursor control. So whenever a gaze is detected, the cursor is programmed to move in a certain direction and for the number of pixel distance mentioned. Figure 11.5 represented below shown the image used for the HOG algorithm. This input image is monitored for the blink and the gaze detection. And based on the detection the left click, right click, scroll can be performed.

11.4.2   Eye Coding

The technique used to write the content with the movement of the eye is called as eye detection [16–18]. This can be achieved with opencv and coding in python, where the keyboard is controlled with gaze movement. For this process a virtual keypad is created as shown in the Figure 11.6 below. The virtual keypad is divided into rows and columns. Each cell has a unique value and when the cell is highlighted the desired key is pressed by closing the eye for a duration of 2 seconds. The time duration of 2 seconds is provided so as to eliminate any action because of involuntary blink.

Figure 11.5 Image captured for processing.

(0,0)	(100,0)	(200,0)
(0,100)	(100,100)	(200,100)
(0,200)	(100,200)	(200,200)

Figure 11.6 Virtual keypad.

Figure 11.7 shown below is the virtual keyboard, Figures 11.8, 11.9, and 11.10 represents the gaze detected for left, right and bottom respectively. Figure 11.7 will be the image which will appear once the python program is run. The three gaze direction are used to access the keypad. For user friendly approach the frequently used words are represented in the keypads, which help the user to avoid so much time in typing letter by letter. To correct the mistyped back the user can even use backspace to delete the letter.

Figures 11.8, 11.9, and 11.10 are the keypads which is created by dividing the numpy image into group of cell. The letter represented in each cell is the letter to type out for the communication.

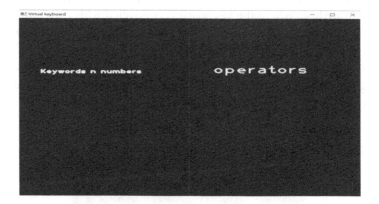

Figure 11.7 Virtual keyboard.

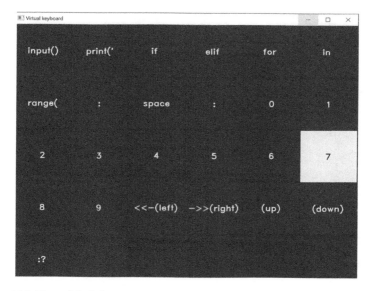

Figure 11.8 Keypad for left gaze.

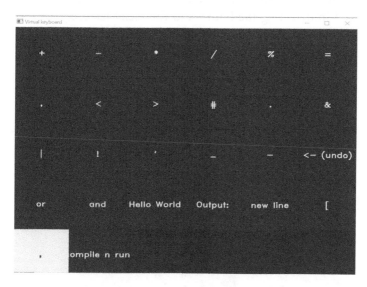

Figure 11.9 Keypad for the right gaze.

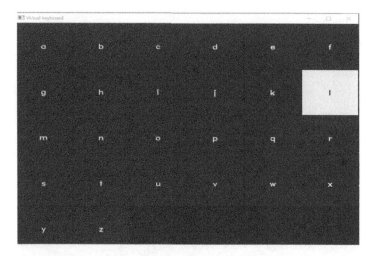

Figure 11.10 Keypad for the bottom gaze.

11.5   Observation and Results

Figures 11.11, 11.12, and 11.13 represents the left eye blink, right eye blink and both eye blink and as the output indicates the HOG algorithm performs well in detecting the blinks and the facial features. Also it can be observed that the distance between the face and the camera is not sensitive

Figure 11.11 Left eye blink.

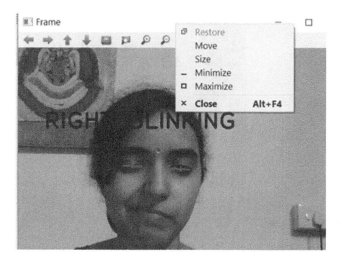

Figure 11.12 Right eye blink.

Figure 11.13 Both eye blink detection.

to the result achieved. The possibility of the error might be only due to poor illuminance.

The cursor control is automated with the combination of blink and the gaze detection. Figures 11.14 to 11.17 represents the various gaze detected.

Figure 11.18 shows the simulation of the eye coding.

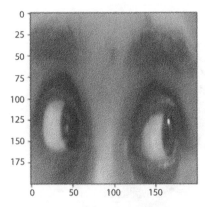

Figure 11.14 Right gaze.

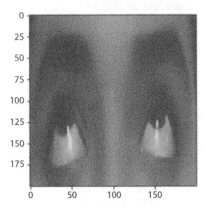

Figure 11.15 Up gaze.

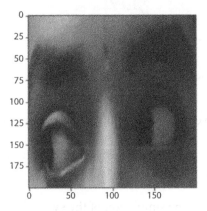

Figure 11.16 Left gaze.

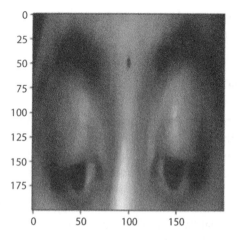

Figure 11.17 Down gaze.

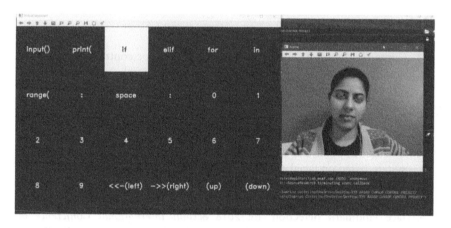

Figure 11.18 Simulation of eye coding.

11.6   Conclusion

This chapter discussed the solution for people with severe disabilities by using their laptop, personal computer, or smart phones to communication to the real world. Usage of the HOG or machine learning model helps them to achieve typing or even perform coding with the help of low cost system. With the real time detection of the movement of the eye the cursor moves over and helps them to convey the information to the closed ones. Since there is no need of any special hardware and as mention a normal laptop or even smart phone is sufficient the overall cost of the system is very less and the software platform used is also open source. Thus the system apart from normal communication can also be used to code and compile programs.

11.7 Future Scope

The eye gaze control can also be implemented with the detection of head movements and the facial expressions. The content in chapter concentrates on four directions which can be further extended to diagonal direction as well. Eye control from communication to other person can also be extended to control other devices. The eye gaze and cursor control technique can further be used in the latest technologies for various application such as Augment reality, Virtual reality, navigation, smart homes, smart farming, smart wearables etc.

References

1. Gupta, A., Rathi, A., Radhika, D.Y., "Hands-free pc control" controlling of mouse cursor using eye movement. *Int. J. Sci. Res. Publ.*, 2, 4, 1–5, 2012.
2. Narayan, M.S. and Raghoji, W.P., Enhanced cursor control using eye mouse. *IJAECS*, 3, 31–35, 2016.
3. Dongre, S. and Patil, S., A face as a mouse for disabled person. *A Monthly Journal of Computer Science and Information Technology*, pp. 156–160, 2015.
4. Tsuzuki, Y., Mizusako, M., Yasushi, M., Hashimoto, H., Sleepiness detection system based on facial expressions. *IECON 2019-45th Annual Conference of the IEEE Industrial Electronics Society*, vol. 1, pp. 6934–6939, 2019.
5. Rakshita, R., Communication through real-time video oculography using face landmark detection, in: *2018 Second International Conference on Inventive Communication and Computational Technologies (ICICCT)*, pp. 1094–1098, 2018.
6. Soukupova, T. and Cech, J., Eye blink detection using facial landmarks, in: *21st Computer Vision Winter Workshop*, Rimske Toplice, Slovenia, 2016.
7. George, A. and Routray, A., Real-time eye gaze direction classification using convolutional neural network, in: *2016 International Conference on Signal Processing and Communications (SPCOM)*, IEEE, pp. 1–5, 2016.
8. Perez, A., Cordoba, M.L., Garcia, A., Mendez, R., Munoz, M.L., Pedraza, J.L., Sanchez, F., A precise eyegaze detection and tracking system, in *International Conference in Central Europe on Computer Graphics, Visualization and Computer Vision 2003*, vol. 3, February, Plzen, pp. 105–108, 2003.

9. Park, K.R., Lee, J.J., Kim, J., Facial and eye gaze detection, in: *International Workshop on Biologically Motivated Computer Vision*, Springer, pp. 368–376, 2002.

10. Valsalan, A., Anoop, T., Harikumar, T., Shan, N., Eye writer. *IOSR-JECE*, 1, 20–22, 2016.

11. Harika, V.R. and Sivaramakrishnan, S., Image overlays on a video frame using HOG algorithm. *2020 IEEE International Conference on Advances and Developments in Electrical and Electronics Engineering (ICADEE)*, pp. 1–5, 2020.

12. Sivaramakrishnan, S. and Vasupradha, Centroid and path determination of planets for deep space autonomous optical navigation. *IJARESM*, 8, 11, 42–48, 2020.

13. Gandhi, R., A look at gradient descent and rms prop optimizers. *Towards Data Science*, 1, 19–24, Jun 2018.

14. Brownlee, J., A gentle introduction to the rectified linear unit (ReLU), *Machine learning mastery*, 1, 6–12, 2019.

15. Goodfelow, I., Bengio, Y., Courville, A., Deep learning (adaptive computation and machine learning series), 2016.

16. Cano, S., Write using your eyes-gaze controlled keyboard with python and opencv. *ICADACC*, 2, 12–16, 2019.

17. Khare, V., Krishna, S.G., Sanisetty, S.K., Cursor control using eye ball movement, in: *2019 Fifth International Conference on Science Technology Engineering and Mathematics (ICONSTEM)*, vol. 1, IEEE, pp. 232–235, 2019.

18. Murata, A., Eye-gaze input versus mouse: Cursor control as a function of age. *Int. J. Hum. Comput. Interact.*, 21, 1, 1–14, 2006.

## 12

Role of Artificial Intelligence in the Agricultural System

Nilesh Kunhare[1], Rajeev Kumar Gupta[2]* and Yatendra Sahu[3]

[1]Vellore Institute of Technology (VIT) University, Bhopal, India
[2]Pandit Deendayal Petroleum University, Gujarat, India
[3]Indian Institute of Information Technology (IIIT), Bhopal, India

Abstract

In the economic sector, agriculture plays an important role. The biggest and emerging issue in the world is automation in agriculture. The population is increasingly rising, and the demand for food and jobs is also growing. These criteria were not fulfilled by the conventional methods used by farmers sufficient to satisfy them. New automated approaches have also been incorporated. These modern approaches have fulfilled food needs and have also provided billions of people with jobs. Artificial intelligence agriculture has brought about a revolution in agriculture. This technology has protected crop yield against many factors, such as climate change, population development, jobs, and food security issues. This chapter aims to explore various artificial intelligence applications, such as irrigation, weaving, sensor sprinkling, and other means in robots and drones, in agriculture. These technologies save excess water, pesticides, herbicides, preserve soil fertility, even lead to the efficient application of human resources and increase productivity and efficiency. This segment looks at several scientists' work to quickly overview the latest automation of agriculture, robotic weeding, and drone systems. The different soil water sensing methods and two automated weeding techniques are discussed. This chapter will also address drones' application and the various techniques used to spray drones and track crops.

Keywords: Crops, UAVs, machine learning, IoT, forecasting, machine learning, deep learning

*Corresponding author: rajeevmanit12276@gmail.com

Anamika Ahirwar, Piyush Kumar Shukla, Manish Shrivastava, Priti Maheshwary and Bhupesh Gour (eds.) Innovative Engineering with AI Applications, (227–242) © 2023 Scrivener Publishing LLC

12.1 Introduction

With the introduction of technology, many sectors worldwide have undergone a rapid transition. Surprisingly, though the least digitized, agriculture has seen traction in agricultural technology growth and commercialization. Artificial Intelligence (AI) is now playing an essential role in our everyday lives, broadening our perspectives and transforming the world [1]. Plessen [2] gave a method for preparing harvests based on the combination of crop distribution and vehicle routing. This new technology now helps many industries of employees who have been limited to just a minimal market. The AI department draws on the vast fields of Genetics, Psychology, Engineering and agricultural automation implementation. Jha et al. [3]. The article also explores a method for recognizing and irrigating flowers and leaves using IoT for botanical farming [4]. This technology is developed by studying how humans think, how humans learn and make decisions, and how they function while solving problems. On this ground, intelligent software and systems are developed. The basic concept of AI is to create a technology that works like the human brain. These softwares are supplied with training data and, like the human brain, these intelligent devices provide us with the optimal output for any valid input. AI's main areas include machine learning (ML) [5] and deep learning (DL) [6]. ML will learn anything without being precisely programmed, and DL is learning from deep neural networks, while AI is the science of creating intelligent devices and programs [7]. The principal subjective of AI is to promote ANN problems.

Numerous environmental parameters that affect farming must be established at various locations to automate agricultural operations. Temperature, humidity, and water level are significant ecological parameters. Multiple types of sensors are mounted on the ground to track specific agricultural and micro-controller-related environmental parameters. In environmental conditions, the microcontroller controls various actuators or agricultural machinery (pumps, fans, etc.) without any human interference. Without human intervention, these sensed data can be saved in the cloud also. The wireless microcontroller sends sensed parameters to the cloud. GSM or CDMA/GPRS technologies are used for the majority of wireless environmental monitoring [8]. However, they have many drawbacks, including high network construction costs, low access rates, etc. The objects have a unique identity as part of the internet. Version 6 of the Internet Protocol (IPv6) [9], version 4 of the Internet Protocol (IPv4) is commonly used as the special entity recognition.

12.2   Artificial Intelligence Effect on Farming

Artificial information system encourages effectiveness and competitiveness in various fields. Solutions from AI help to solve the difficulties of tradition in all fields. Equally AI helps farmers in agriculture to enhance their effectiveness and to reduce negative impacts on the environment. In order to change the ultimate result, AI was firmly and openly adopted by the agriculture industry. AI moves the production of our food where emissions from the agriculture sector have decreased by 20%. The adaptation of AI technology helps monitor and handle any environmental circumstances that are uninvited.

The majority of start-ups now adapt AI-enabled approaches to boost agricultural production efficiencies in agriculture. The market survey report notes that global AI is projected to hit $1.550 million by the end of 2025 in agriculture [10]. Implementing IA-intensive approaches may quickly detect and respond intelligently to diseases or climate changes. Agriculture companies with the help of AI process farm data in order to minimize adverse effects. The world's population will reach over nine billion by 2050, which will increase 70% to meet demand. If the world's population increases, the supply chain of demand is not supplied by groundwater and services. Therefore, we need a better strategy, and how we farm and be most productive must be more successful.

In this chapter, the challenges that farmers face were based on using conventional agriculture methods and how artificial intelligence revolutionizes agriculture by replacing traditional methods with better methods and allowing the world to become a better place.

12.2.1   Agriculture Lifecycle

We may break the agricultural process into various parts as shown in Figure 12.1.

Soil preparation: This is the first step of agriculture in which farmers prepare the soil for seed. It includes breaking down large clusters of soil and extracting scraps like rocks, roots, and sticks. Add fertilizers and organic matter to create an optimal situation for crops, according to the crop type.

Seeding: The gap between two seeds, the depth for planting seeds, needs to be taken into account at this point. Climate conditions, including temperature, humidity, and precipitation play an essential role at this stage.

Adding fertilizers: Preserving fertility in soils is crucial in enabling farmers to continue cultivating nutritious and safe crops. Since these

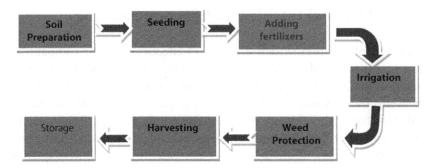

Figure 12.1 Lifecycle of agriculture.

substances contain plant nutrients, including nitrogen, phosphorus, and potassium, farmers turn to fertilizers. To complement the necessary elements present naturally in the soils, fertilizers plant nutrients in agricultural fields. This process also decides the crop quality.

Irrigation: The soil is kept moist and kept humid at this level. Under watering or watering can hinder crop growth, leading to damaged crops if not done correctly. Unintended plants that grow near crops or on farms are weeds protection.

Weed protection: Weed protection is essential as weed yield decreases, production costs increase, harvest interferes, and crop quality decreases.

Harvesting: It is the harvesting process from the fields of mature plants. For this operation, it needs a lot of employees, and it is labor-intensive. This process involves harvest treatment, such as washing, sorting, packing, and cooling.

Storage: The post-harvest process in which goods are stored to safeguard food protection other than during farming. The packaging and transport of crops are also included.

Storage: the post-harvest process in which goods are stored to safeguard food protection other than during farming times. The packaging and transport of crops is also included.

12.2.2   Problems with Traditional Methods of Farming

- In the lifecycle of agriculture, climate factors, including precipitation, temperature, and humidity, plays an essential role. Climate changes result in rising deforestation and emissions, so it is hard for farmers to decide on land preparation, sow seed, and harvesting.
- Each crop needs unique soil nutrition. The soil needs to contain three principal nutrients nitrogen (N), phosphorous (P),

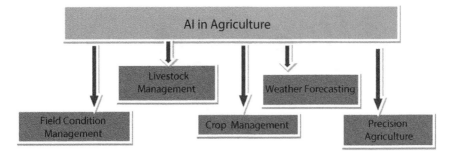

Figure 12.2 AI in agriculture system diagram [10].

and potassium (K). Nutrient deficiency can result in low crop quality.
- As can be seen from the farm life cycle, weeds' defense has a critical role to play. Unless regulated, production costs can increase, and nutrients absorbed from the soil may cause the soil's nutritional deficiency. Application of AI is shown in Figure 12.2.

12.3 Applications of Artificial Intelligence in Agriculture

12.3.1 Forecasting Weather Details

AI enables the farmer to maintain advanced weather knowledge up-to-date. Because of the predictable outcome, farmers' returns and revenues without risking crops. The analysis of the data produced enables farmers to use AI to learn and understand precautions. A wise decision can be taken in time by using this practice. Figure 12.3 shows how the data is communicated between the IoT devices.

12.3.2 Crop and Soil Quality Surveillance

Using AI is an important way in which potential soil defects and nutrient shortages can be detected or monitored. AI detects potential flaws with the camera-captured images with the image recognition method. Using AI deep learning framework, flora trends in agriculture can be analyzed. Applications with this form of AI promote the understanding of soil defects, plant pests, and diseases. Figure 12.4 shows crop and soil quality surveillance process.

Figure 12.3 Forecasting weather details [11].

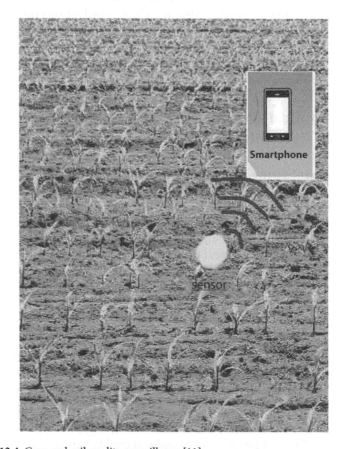

Figure 12.4 Crop and soil quality surveillance [11].

12.3.3   Pesticide Use Reduction

Farmers use AI to control weeds through computer vision, robotics, and machine learning. Data are collected with the AI's aid to track the weed, which only sprays chemical substances when the weeds are found in farmers. This decreased the use of the chemical by spreading a whole field directly. As a result, AI reduces the number of chemical sprays commonly used by herbicides in the area.

12.3.4   AI Farming Bots

Farmers are helped by AI-enabling agriculture to find efficient ways of protecting their plants against weeds. It also helps to resolve the difficulty of work. AI bots can harvest crops at a higher volume and speed than human workers in the agricultural sector. Using computer vision, weed control, and spraying will helps farmers to find more successful ways to protect their plants from weeds.

12.3.5   AI-Based Monitoring Systems

1. Monitoring of Microclimates
   - Use environmental sensors for monitoring such aspects as temperature, relative humidity, sunlight, carbon dioxide, wind velocity, and generate crop growth mages.
   - Send warnings via SMS/e-mail when the incident occurs to maintain optimum conditions.
   - Display historical data and create trend graphs.
2. Monitoring of Soil, Medium, Water
   - PH, conductivity, temperature, humidity, soil/media track, etc. the best conditions for the development
   - Track consistency of water, including pH, conductivity, temperature, oxygen dissolved, etc.
   - Send warnings via SMS/e-mail when the incident occurs to maintain optimum conditions
   - View historically stored data and create patterns in graphs
3. Monitor Station for the Climate
   - Use sensors for monitoring conditions of the atmosphere: temperature, moisture relative to the wind, direction of the wind, rain, snow, and sunlight.
   - Maximize greenhouse production by studying the interplay and external temperature differential.

- Use historical analyses to forecast short-term temperature changes to increase indoor climate stability

4. Power Monitoring and Analysis
   - To see and monitor the electrical status of greenhouses, use sensors [11]
   - To measure and evaluate the costs of individual devices, use documented power data
   - Using shading networks automatically to minimize sunlight intensity and power consumption [12]
   - Assess and change independent energy sources, according to the needs.
   - Measure the overall cost of producing and using electricity

12.3.6   AI-Based Irrigation System

1. Drip Method of Irrigation
   To control the conductivity of soil moisture, pH levels, etc., use drip irrigation sensors.
   - To monitor conditions and quality, use soil moisture sensors
   - Permeability ensures pipeline water is used
   - Drip devices attached to a PE pipe control the flow automatically.
   - Weeds cannot grow without water between crops
   - Drip irrigation systems: running, water, energy, and yield enhancement systems
   - The crop roots retain ideal conditions to improve productivity when irrigated and fertilized directly to the ground.

Sprinkle Method
The method used for the Sprinkle Method is shown in Figure 12.5.

- Sprinkler device monitor soil moisture sensors
- Signals from analog to analog sensors are converted
- Transform signals to a linear value of the soil humidity meter
- Track conductivity of soil moisture, pH, and other sprinkler data for best usage.
- Include monitoring strategies, timetable, and quantity
- Automatic salinity correction while freezing.
- Small construction costs and quick foliar absorption increase greenhouse moisture and decrease the temperature
- Control framework for low cost and manufacturing irrigation

Figure 12.5 Sprinkle method [11].

12.4   Robots in Agriculture

Robot production by AI companies can easily accomplish several tasks in agriculture. This robot is trained to manage weeds and crops faster than humans with higher volumes. These types of robots are equipped to check crop quality and simultaneously detect weeds while planting and packaging. The robots are also capable of confronting the difficulties of farm work.

Agricultural robots automate sluggish, repetitive, and uncomfortable activities for farmers so that they can concentrate more on raising overall yields. For some of agriculture's most famous robots:

- Harvesting and picking [13]
- Regulation of weeds [14]
- Autonomous mowing, pruning, seeding, spraying, and thinning [4]
- Phenotyping
- Sorting and packing
- Utility platforms

The precise use and speed of robots in agriculture are among the most common robot applications because of their ability to increase yields and

Figure 12.6 Robot in agriculture [17].

minimize crop waste. However, it can be hard to automate these programs. For instance, there are several obstacles to a robotic system designed to collect sweet peppers. The location and maturity of pepper must be assessed by visual systems under harsh conditions, including dust, changing light intensity, temperature changes, and wind movement. But more than advanced vision systems are still required to choose a pepper. A robotic arm has as many challenges to traverse environments to grab and position a pepper gently. This method varies significantly from the selecting and placing of a metal component on a link line. In a complex environment, the agricultural robotic arm must be versatile and precise enough not to damage the harvested pepper [15].

Farmers have become increasingly familiar with harvesting or picking robots, but hundreds of other creative ways in which the agricultural sector uses robotic automation to increase their production. Food demand is beyond the available agricultural lands, and farmers must resolve this void. Farming robots are just helping them [16]. Figure 12.6 shows how robot is used in agriculture.

12.5   Drones for Agriculture

SkySqurrel technologies brought drone-based Ariel imaging solutions for crop health monitoring. The drone gathers data from fields and transfers

Figure 12.7 Drone for agriculture [17].

data from the drone to a device through a USB drive and is analyzed by experts [17]. Using the drones, which are also known as UAVs, farmers may collect data from the comfort of a single take-off zone over the entire field. With more models offering longer flight times, higher payload capacities, and the possibility to flight under variable conditions. Drones are more available to farmers, farm insurers, and researchers. Drones are used for agricultural operations of all sizes to reduce the time and costs involved in collecting crop data [18]. Figure 12.7 illustrates how drone is used in agriculture.

12.6   Advantage of AI Implementation in Farming

The use of artificial intelligence products in agriculture helps farmers understand temperature, precipitation, wind speed, and solar radiation. The study of historical values provides a more transparent comparison of the desired effects. The best aspect of AI introduced in agriculture is that human farmers' jobs are not abolished, but their processes are enhanced.

- AI offers better ways in which essential crops are processed, harvested, and sold.

- Implementation of the AI emphasizes the monitoring of defective crops and enhancement of crop production potentials.
- The development of technology for artificial intelligence has improved the productivity of agribusinesses.
- AI is used in automated weather forecasting machine adaptations or the detection of diseases or pests.
- Artificial intelligence can also boost crop management practices, making more technology companies invest in agriculture algorithms.
- AI solutions can address farmers' problems, such as climatic changes, pests, and weeds infestations that reduce yields.
- Agricultural influence of artificial intelligence.

AI technology quickly corrects the problems and advises concrete steps to fix the issue. To find solutions rapidly, AI is efficient in tracking the details. See how AI is used to boost performance with minimal environmental costs in agriculture. AI can identify a disease with 98% precision. Therefore, AI allows farmers to track fruit and vegetables by adapting the luminaire to speed up production.

12.6.1   Intelligent Agriculture Cloud Platform

12.6.1.1   Remote Control and Administration in Real Time

Real-time testing and next line control via computers, tablets, cell phones, and other devices remotely. Manage systems spread across multiples greenhouses, nutrients, temperatures, etc. Provide various degrees of authority for employees. Obtain information in real-time via SMS and email notifications History data and charts analysis—integrated research charts for improved crop cultivation. For potential review and queries, sensor data are automatically uploaded to the cloud. Provides public and private cloud.

12.6.1.2   Consultation of Remote Experts

Share the experience of greenhouses and other greenhouses with guidance. Enhance the training of farmers by supplying them with the most recent green technologies. Information about the production system documents, for example. Place, farmers, quality of soil, growth, harvest time, use of fertilizer, etc. We have automated record output for an accurate quality record regulation, residues of pesticides, etc.

12.7   Research, Challenges, and Scope for the Future

Artificial intelligence in agriculture has developed applications and devices that support inaccurate and regulated farming by providing farmers with proper guidance in water management, crop rotation, and early harvesting. With the application of machine-learning algorithms connected with satellite and Drone imagery, AI-enabled technology predicts weather, analyses crop sustainability, and evaluates farms with low temperature, precipitation, wind speed, and solar radiation for the presence of diseases, pests, and insufficient plant nutrition in farms.

AI profit can be obtained from farmers without connectivity with simple tools like an SMS and the sewing app. Meanwhile, Wi-Fi farmers may use AI applications to receive a continually tailored AI plan for their countries. Farmers will meet the world's needs for increasing food production and income without reducing valuable natural resources through IoT and AI-driven solutions. AI will enable farmers to grow into farm technologists in the future, using data to maximize yields in individual plant rows. Pareek et al. [19] have proposed an artificial neural network (NNN) model to predict the cell fill of a sloped plate seed measuring unit. The PSO algorithm has been used to obtain optimum operating parameter values that are equal to 100% cell fill. Tewari et al. [20] have built a system consisting of image acquisition web cameras, image processing portable computers, system operations microcontrollers, and spray nozzles with the solenoid valve's help. The chromatic aberrating (CA) image segmentation method was used to detect the diseased zone of paddy plants. The device further determined the severity level from paddy plants' disease, which was based on a fixed time-length of the solenoid valves to spray the required agrochemical quantities on the diseased paddy plants. New automated methods have been implemented by Talaviya et al. [4] These modern approaches met food demands and also gave billions of people a chance to work. This technology has protected crop yields against different factors such as changing climate conditions, population growth, jobs, and food security issues. This paper focuses on the audit of various applications in agriculture of artificial intelligence: irrigation, weeding, spraying with sensors and other devices integrated with robots and drones.

Anami et al. [21] developed the deep-convolutional neural network (DCNN) System to automatically identify and distinguish various biotic and abiotic crop stresses. The work has adopted the VGG-16 CNN model pre-trained to automatically identify stressed paddy cropping images collected during the boot growth process. The qualified models achieve an average data set accuracy of 92.89%, showing the technological feasibilities for depth learning with 30.000 pictures of five different paddy crops with 12 different stress categories (including normal/healthy).

12.8   Conclusion

Artificial agricultural intelligence not only aids farmers to automate their agriculture and transforms them into accurate crop production for greater crop yield and better quality by using fewer resources. Companies that contribute to the development of machine learning or goods or services based on artificial intelligence, such as farm data training, drones, and automated machine processing, can provide the industry with a better technological advance, enabling the whole world to tackle food-producing problems for the increasing population.

References

1. Vinuesa, R. *et al.*, The role of artificial intelligence in achieving the sustainable development goals. *Nat. Commun.*, 11, 1–10, 2020.
2. Plessen, M.G., Coupling of crop assignment and vehicle routing for harvest planning in agriculture. *arXiv*, 2, 99–109, 2017.
3. Jha, K., Doshi, A., Patel, P., Shah, M., A comprehensive review on automation in agriculture using artificial intelligence. *Artif. Intell. Agric.*, 2, 1–11, 2019.
4. Talaviya, T., Shah, D., Patel, N., Yagnik, H., Shah, M., Implementation of artificial intelligence in agriculture for optimisation of irrigation and application of pesticides and herbicides. *Artif. Intell. Agric.*, 4, 58–73, 2020.
5. Liakos, K.G., Busato, P., Moshou, D., Pearson, S., Bochtis, D., Machine learning in agriculture: A review. *Sensors (Switzerland)*, 18, 1–15, 2018.
6. Kamilaris, A. and Prenafeta-Boldú, F.X., Deep learning in agriculture: A survey. *Comput. Electron. Agric.*, 147, 70–90, 2018.
7. Kodali, R.K. and Sahu, A., An IoT based soil moisture monitoring on Losant platform, in: *Proceedings of the 2016 2nd International Conference on Contemporary Computing and Informatics, IC3I 2016*, 2016.
8. Gupta, R. and Jain, K., Competition effect of a new mobile technology on an incumbent technology: An Indian case study. *Telecomm. Policy*, l. 40, 332–342 2016.
9. Melorose, J., Perroy, R., Careas, S., Compression format for IPv6 datagrams over IEEE 802.15.4-based networks. *Statew. Agric. L. Use Baseline 2015*, 2015.
10. Misra, N.N., Dixit, Y., Al-Mallahi, A., Bhullar, M.S., Upadhyay, R., Martynenko, A., IoT, big data and artificial intelligence in agriculture and food industry. *IEEE Internet Things J.*, 1–19, 2020.

11. https://www.proxis.ua/files/documents/Advantech%20Intelligent%20 Agricultural%20Solutions%2008181118.pdf

12. Murugesh, R., Hanumanthaiah, A., Ramanadhan, U., Vasudevan, N., Designing a wireless solar power monitor for wireless sensor network applications, in: *Proceedings of the 8th International Advance Computing Conference, IACC 2018*, 2018.

13. Zhao, Y., Gong, L., Huang, Y., Liu, C., A review of key techniques of vision-based control for harvesting robot. *Comput. Electron. Agric.*, 127, 311–323 2016.

14. Newswire, P.R., *Agricultural Robots and Drones 2017-2027: Technologies, Markets, Players*, PR Newswire, Dublin, US, 2017.

15. Tran, T.H. *et al.*, The study on extraction process and analysis of components in essential oils of black pepper (Piper nigrum L.) seeds harvested in Gia Lai Province, Vietnam. *Processes*, 7, 1–18, 2019.

16. Xiong, Y., Ge, Y., Grimstad, L., From, P.J., An autonomous strawberry-harvesting robot: Design, development, integration, and field evaluation. *J. Field Robot.*, 37, 202–219, 2020.

17. https://www.proxis.ua/files/documents/Advantech%20Intelligent%20 Agricultural%20Solutions%2008181118.pdf

18. Hufkens, K. *et al.*, Monitoring crop phenology using a smartphone based near-surface remote sensing approach. *Agric. For. Meteorol.*, 265, 327–337, 2019.

19. Pareek, C.M., Tewari, V.K., Machavaram, R., Nare, B., Optimizing the seed-cell filling performance of an inclined plate seed metering device using integrated ANN-PSO algorithm. *Artif. Intell. Agric.*, 5, 1–12, 2020.

20. Tewari, V.K., Pareek, C.M., Lal, G., Dhruw, L.K., Singh, N., Image processing based real-time variable-rate chemical spraying system for disease control in paddy crop. *Artif. Intell. Agric.*, 4, 21–30, 2020.

21. Anami, B.S., Malvade, N.N., Palaiah, S., Deep learning approach for recognition and classification of yield affecting paddy crop stresses using field images. *Artif. Intell. Agric.*, 1–13, 2020.

13

Improving Wireless Sensor Networks Effectiveness with Artificial Intelligence

Piyush Raja[1]*, Santosh Kumar[2], Digvijay Singh[1] and Taresh Singh[3]

[1]Department of CSE, COER University, Roorkee, India
[2]PSIT College of Higher Education, Kanpur, India
[3]GRD IMT, Dehradun, Uttarakhand, India

Abstract

Although Artificial Intelligence's key goal is to create systems that mimic a person's intellectual and social ability, Distributed Artificial Intelligence follows similar objective then with an emphasis scheduled social principles. A concept of multi-agent networks is a new model designed for improvement of Distributed Artificial Intelligence. Multi-agent structures are composed of several interconnected intelligent systems called agents that can be deployed as software, a dedicated computer, or a robot. In a multi-agent environment, intelligent Agent exchange information with one another in order to coordinate their organisation, delegate assignments, and share information. Multi-agent systems, artificial societies, and simulated organizations are all part of a new computing paradigm that includes issues like cooperation and competition, coordination, collaboration, communication and language protocols, negotiation, consensus creation, conflict detection and resolution, and collective intelligence activities carried out by mediators (e.g. problem solving, preparation, knowledge, decision constructing in distributed method), cognitive multiple intellect actions, social then active constructing, distributed management and switch, security, consistency, and robustnes. Circulated intellectual sensor network may be situated viewed as a structure made up of numerous mediators (The sensor node), with sensors cooperating to form a collective system whose aim would be to collect data from physical sources variables of systems. Sensor networks may thus be viewed as multi-agent structures or artificially ordered communities that use sensors to sense their surroundings. However, how can Artificial Intelligence mechanisms be implemented inside WSNs? The dilemma can be approached in two ways: the first solution has programmers consider the

---

*Corresponding author: piyushraja2009@gmail.com

Anamika Ahirwar, Piyush Kumar Shukla, Manish Shrivastava, Priti Maheshwary and Bhupesh Gour (eds.) *Innovative Engineering with AI Applications*, (243–256) © 2023 Scrivener Publishing LLC

overall goal to be achieved and develop together agents and multi-agent system's interaction process. In the second strategy, the author imagines and builds a group of self-interested agents, which then use evolutionary learning methods to adapt and communicate in a secure manner.

Keywords: WSN, AI, multi-agent systems, simulation models

13.1   Introduction

Although the prime intention of Artificial Intelligence (AI) is to build devices that replicate a person's intellectual and social abilities, Distributed Artificial Intelligence focuses on human cultures. The concept of multi-agent networks is a novel model for Distributed Artificial Intelligence advancement. A multi-agent structure consists of several integrated artificial structures known as agent, which could remain implemented as software, a dedicated device, otherwise as the robot. Intelligent agents cooperate to each other with a multi-agent environment to organise their organisation, delegate tasks, and exchange knowledge [13]. The problem can be solved by these ways: the first is for programmers to think about

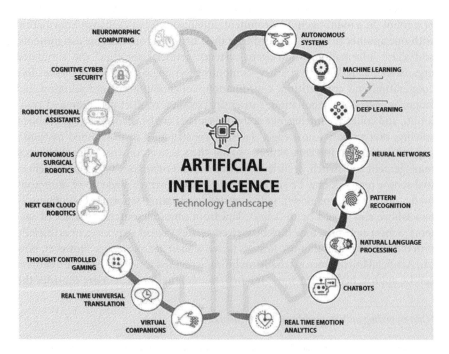

Figure 13.1 Artificial intelligence (Sources: aitimejournal.com).

the end objective and improve each other agent and multi-agents system's interaction mechanism. Figure 13.1 shows the life cycle of AI.

13.2   Wireless Sensor Network (WSNs)

Sensor Networks (SNs) are the devices made up of thousands of tiny stations known as sensor nodes. The main purpose of sensor nodes is to track, log, and inform other stations of a certain condition to changed location. The SN is often the collection of sophisticated transducers connected by a network to track and record conditions in a variety of locations (Figure 13.2).

Temperature, humidity, heat, wind direction and speed, light rate, vibration intensity, sound intensity, power-line voltage, chemical concentrations, pollutant levels, and critical body function are about the most often monitored parameters.

Sensor nodes can be thought of as miniature computers with incredibly simple interfaces and materials. While these instruments have limited computing capacities on their own, when combined, they have significant processing power. The radio transceivers unit, the slight microcontrollers, then vitality source, normally a battery, are generally included in each sensor network node [1]. Sensor nodes can range in size from the size of a shoebox to mass off the grain of dust (Romer and Mattern, 2004). In most cases, a sensor network is the wireless ad hoc network, in which each sensor boosts the multi-hop routing algorithms. They are necessary to remind the sensor nodes to face more extreme power limitations than PDAs, cell phones, or laptop computers [3]. One controller is normally in charge of

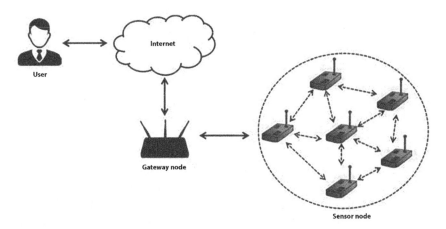

Figure 13.2 Sensor nodes are connected.

the whole network: the base location. The prime characteristics of a base station is to serve like the gateway to another network while still acting as an efficient data processor and storage centre. WSNs have been the presumptive panacea for tackling a variety of large-scale decision and information retrieval challenges thanks to advancements in microelectronics and wireless communications. WSNs have a wide range of uses, but most of them include surveillance, tracking or regulating, habitat surveillance, entity tracking, nuclear reactor control, fire detection, and road traffic observations. The WSN is dispersed across an area, collecting data through its sensor nodes. For environmental surveillance, the multiplicity of the WSN ought to exist [4]. Owing to the prototype design of the programmes, all of them have been short-lived. Since they offer important price funds in addition allow new functionalities, WSN is built for machinery Condition-Based Maintenance (CBM).

Despite the development of a range of innovative WSN programmes and solutions, a number of new issues or difficulties remain to be solved or changed. Optimal routing methods, the length of the WSN (the lifetime of the nodes is always very limited), reconfigurability without redeployment, and so on are examples of such issues.

Finally, as the popularity of WSNs has grown, there is no shared forum. Some symbolic designs, such as Berkeley Motes, the first commercial motes platform, have a larger consumer and developer community. However, since a sensor node is a processing unit with simple components, exploration test center also in businesses tend to design and manufacture their own sensors. Mica Mote, Tmote Sky, BTnode, Waspmote, Sun Spot, G-Node, and TIP sequence mote are some of the platforms available.

13.3 AI and Multi-Agent Systems

Classical Artificial Intelligence sought to replicate a human's analytical and social skills in machineries. Rational agents are at the heart for present approach to Artificial Intelligence (AI). "An agent is something who could intellect their environments through the sensor and acts on them using actuators [14]." A rational agent is one that seeks to maximize an optimal output metric at all times. A logical agent can be described in a variety of ways, including human agents (with eyes as sensors and hands as actuators), robotic agents (with cameras as sensors and the wheel as actuator), and software agent (having the GUI as sensor and as an actuator). AI could be defined as analysis also of their ideas and design of artificial rational

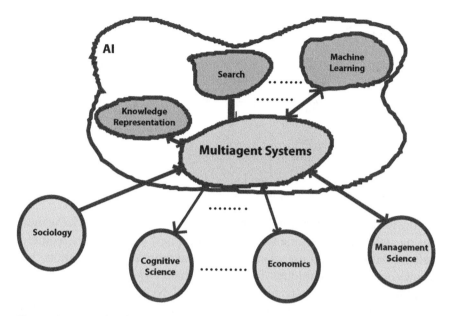

Figure 13.3 AI and multi-agent systems.

agents from this viewpoint. Figure 13.3 shows AI with its different multi agent systems.

Except this, the agents remains rarely standalone programs. They coexist and communicate with other agents in a variety of ways in certain contexts. Intelligent Web tech agents, soccer-playing machines, e-commerce negotiation agents, and machine vision committed agents. Multi-Agent Systems (MAS) locate the system that contains a set of agents that can theoretically communicate with one another, and Distributed AI is the subfield of AI that transacts with ideas then architecture of multi-agent systems (DAI).

13.4 WSN and AI

An intelligent sensor changes its internal behavior to improve its ability toward data collection through physical atmosphere besides transmit it to a base station or a host device with great manner. Self-calibration, self-validation, and reward are all features of intelligent sensors. Figure 13.4 shows AI and WSNs how effecting our daily lifes and how efficient.

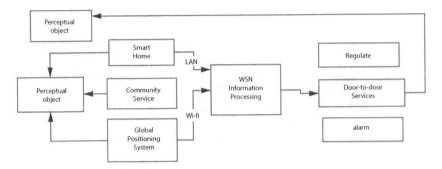

Figure 13.4 AI and WSN in daily life of the elderly.

The term "self-calibration" refers to the sensor's ability to track the measuring state and determine whether or not a new calibration is required. Self-validation makes use of statistical simulation, error separation, and knowledge-based techniques. To achieve high precision, self-compensation employs compensation techniques. Artificial Neural Networks (ANN), Fuzzy Logic, and Neuro-Fuzzy are examples of artificial intelligence approaches commonly used in industry [4]. Wireless intelligent sensors are created by embedding intelligent sensor systems in Wireless Sensor Networks. Building intelligent sensor systems necessitates the use of artificial intelligence techniques. WSNs' primary analysis concerns are coverage, connectivity network lifespan, and data fidelity. In recent years, there has been a surge in interest in Artificial Intelligence and DAI, and whom methods for overcoming WSN constraints, developing new algorithms, and developing new WSN implementations. Initial sensor collection and task assignment, as well as runtime adaptation of assigned tasks/resources, are all part of resource management. Power, bandwidth, and network lifespan are among the parameters to be configured. The use of mutual intelligence in resource management within WSNs was advocated in this case by Distributed Independent Reinforcement Learning (Shah *et al.*, 2008). Finally, intelligent network-working and collaboration applications are proposed as optimization elements for WSNs.

13.5   Multi-Agent Constructed Simulation

The simulation MABS that aims to simulate the behaviour of agents with the aim of study their associations and their belongings of their decisions. As a result, the experiences of the agents have a huge impact to final result. Figure 13.5 shows the overview of the multi-agent simulation system. How the journey of UI agents to different models.

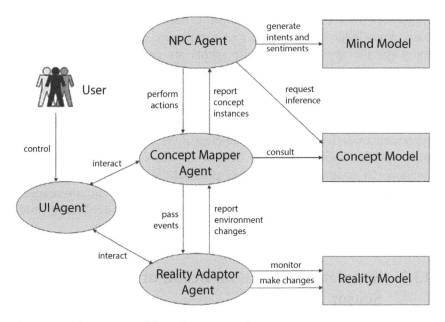

Figure 13.5 The overview of the multi-agent simulation system.

MABS models are also utilized on investigation to reflect and under-stand social structures, along with measure emerging approaches to change and politics on various systems. Since MABS is a relatively new field, also some approaches besides resources for its production. In reality, machine modelling, software engineering, and agent-oriented software engineering all make contributions (AOSE) [5]. The methodology permits the repre-sentation of core facets of distributed systems, such as organisation, logic, collaboration, and teamwork mechanisms, among other things. Instead of offering implementation techniques, the main feature of WSN simulators is to replicate a WSN process and simulate all hardware characteristics for each node in the simulated WSN [2]. The basic concept is to suggest a paradigm that permits the extremely dispersed sensor network to function like multi-agents framework. Agents work together in this situation to save and boost services within the WSN. Finally, MABS will make a significant contribution to the development of implementation plans and operations.

13.6 Multi-Agent Model Plan

Model proposal is a multi-agent hybrid model that simulates the deploy-ment of software agents over each WSN. This is accomplished by a layered framework that combines deterministic hardware models with agent-based knowledge to analyse various techniques, such as multiple agents for a specific application. Mobile agents are used to manage network infrastructure and provide information. Main deterministic models for WSN performance are used to do this, such as the protocol model, which includes totally infusion protocols; also its operation is typically dependent on the state of the physical platform of nodes, the physical model, which represents underlying hardware and measurement devices, and the media model, which connects node to "real world" via a radio channel and one or more. In addition, topology and physical variables are used depends upon their characteristics they would be simulated. The programme agents are then used to complete all of the tasks needed by the application study scenario.

13.7   Simulation Models on Behalf of Wireless Sensor Network

Current modelling models attempt to depict how a WSN operates. For example, in Egea-Lopez *et al.* (2006), Egea-Lopez *et al.* introduced a general simulations model that proceeds existing WSN simulator components into account. As a result, deterministic models exist to describe hardware, the environment, electricity, and radio channels, among other things. This model is also valuable to learning how a WSN works in real life, but those that never permit to the evaluation of various implementation methods. Furthermore, the number of simulation nodes is much less than that of a real network, since scalability is limited by the computing needed to simulate full hardware [3]. Cheong later presents a new proposal in Cheong [1]. The use of various simulation methods also designed in order to WSN, and the ability to guide execution from simulation, are some of the work's strengths [11]. Cheong, on the other hand, suggests a programming model dependent on characters, which are a hybrid of objects and agents. Actors are contact objects of data flow, but they are unaware of their surroundings and unable to make choices. Wang and Jiang propose another solution in Wang, in which they present a technique for controlling and optimizing capital in a WSN using mobile agents. Control, encoding, and memory optimization are all examples of resource optimization.

13.8   Model Plan

A layered architecture that uses deterministic hardware models of agent-based intelligence is proposed to simulate the deployment of software agents over each WSN. This is achieved in order to compare various techniques, such as different agents for a specific application.

To monitor network capabilities and promote intelligence, we intend to use mobile agents. The main deterministic models are used to do this; these models define features such as node platform, power usage, radio station, and media [6]. In addition, topology and physical variables are applied based on the application that would be simulated. And then, virtual agents are used to complete all of the tasks needed by the application research scenario. Three separate layers are provided below that allow intelligence to be performed through agents over a WSN.

13.8.1   Hardware Layer

One of the most important layers is hardware, which takes charge of specifying all modules that are relevant to hardware requirements and the context in which the network will be implemented. Maximum model of the layer remains defined through current WSN(Wireless Sensor Network) simulator. Any models that define these components are presented below [7] and shown in Figure 13.6 (a, b and c).

- Node Model: Egea-Lopez *et al.* (2006) described this model, in which a node is divided into protocols, hardware, and media. The operation of protocols is dependent on hardware specifications and includes all of a node's communication protocols.
- Environment Model: It holds essential variables of the physical region where networks will be implemented. A node's sensor should capable for identify to these variables; otherwise, higher-layer agents would not be executed [8]. In addition, this model specifies topologies, otherwise arrangement of how the nodes are organized; they have several topologies for a WSN, including square, star, ad hoc, and irregular topologies (Piedrahita and colleagues, 2010).

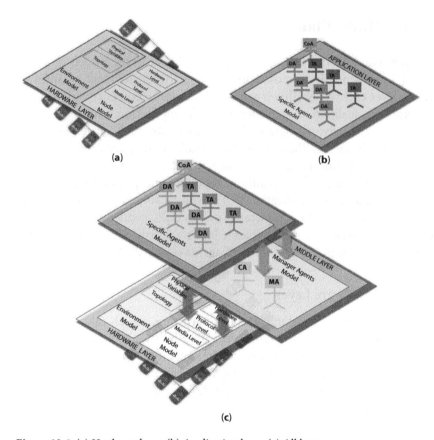

Figure 13.6 (a) Hardware layer. (b) Application layer. (c) All layers.

13.8.2   Middle Layer

Another important layer is middle, which takes charge of connecting with WSN and agent needed for a specific presentation. Consequently, this layer has two agents that screen also the tackle capital.

- Agent of Manager Capital (MA): It is a sophisticated mobile agent that makes choices on memory and power management. It is aware of the requisite fee of the agent to complete a mission, and it either refuses or confirms the execution of an agent [10]. This is a decision-making agent dependent on Georgeff *et al.*'s BDI model (1998). It also indicates whether the bunch of jobs could also do using the specified hardware.

- CA stands for Capturing Agent of physical variables, and it is a mobile agent that is knowledgeable of physical variables when they relate to a specific function. It makes decisions on whether the reason is propagated and transmitted.

13.8.3 Application Layer

The implementation layer reflects the WSN's deployment for a specific research case or application. As a result, this layer contains agents that execute the functions that the program requires.

The Coordinator Agent (CoA) is an agent that is aware of jobs demanded by a study case and maintains a queue of implementation tasks. As a result, it plans, organises, and negotiates them in order for them to be properly executed by a TA [9]. It also uses a BDI model to make choices.

- Tasks Agent (TA): A reactive agent that completes tasks delegated by a CoA for as long as the CoA specifies.
- Deliberative Agent (DA): This is a mobile agent that also makes judgments using the BDI model. A CoA should not have to manage, coordinate, or discuss its activities. As an outcome, they finish the series of tasks in order to accomplish its own target, fixed by an MAS to which it belongs.

Since not all SN platforms can execute a rational agent, there is a specific treatment for device multi-agent systems [12]. For a basic application, the collection for TAs with a CoA that controls and directs the whole system, and for a complex application, there is a group of DAs that collaborate to accomplish a general objective.

13.9 Conclusion

To refine a network of Distributed Wireless Sensors (DWS), DAI principles, algorithms, and applications can be used. WSN optimization using logical agents is possible with the Multi-Agent System approach.

Since the suggested model uses multi-agent systems in conjunction with layered architecture to promote intelligence and mimic any WSN, it is feasible to incorporate a solution that allows a sensor network to act like an intelligent multi-agent system. All that is required is knowledge of last request wherever WSN would be deployed. A layered architecture may also provide a WSN framework modularity and structure. Furthermore, the suggested model focuses on how a WSN functions and how to make it intelligent. A distributed sensor network could be installed in an effective way and accomplish the stated goals of taking physical parameter extents through its own various types of rational agents that could be reconfigured to fit some kind of application and measures, as well as to fit the most appropriate strategy to achieve the proposed objectives from the perspective of multi-agents, artificial swarm intelligence, and artificial intelligence. Checking the model with a real WSN is something else that needs to be done. To complete the testing, some research cases of multi-agent systems for specific applications are expected. The Solarium SunSPOT simulator is a good method to use. This simulator provides a practical environment for developing and analysing SunSPOT devices except hardware platforms. Following the completion of this research, the model could be run on a real WSN of SunSPOT devices.

References

1. Cheong, E., in (2k7). Aimed at WSN, performer-in favor of programming is used, Actor-oriented programming for wireless sensor networks. 7–15, 2007.
2. Conte, R., Gilbert, N., Sichman, J., MAS and social simulation: A suitable commitment, *Multi-agent systems and agent-based simulation*, pp. 1–9, Springer, 1998.
3. Cruller, D., Estrin, D., Srivastava, M., Overview of sensor networks. *Computer*, 37, 8, 41–49, 2004.
4. Davoudani, D., Hart, E., Paechter, B., *Artificial Immune Systems*, pp. 288–299, 2007.
5. Georgeff, M., Pell, B., Pollack, M., Tambe, M., Wooldridge, M., Wooldridge, M., The belief-desire-intention model of agency, Intelligent agents V. agent theories, architectures, and languages: *5th International Workshop, ATAL'98, Proceedings*, Springer, Paris, France, July 1998, pp. 630–630, 1998.
6. The belief-desire intention model of agency. *5th International Workshop, ATAL'98, Paris, France, Intelligent Agents V. Agent Theories, Architectures, and Languages*, July 1998.
7. *5th International Workshop, ATAL'98, Proceedings*, Paris, France, Springer, pp. 630–630, July 1998.
8. Levis, P., Lee, N., Welsh, M., Culler, D., TOSSIM: Accurate and scalable simulation of whole TinyOS implementations. *Proceedings of the 1st International Conference on Embedded Networked Sensor Systems*, ACM, p. 137, 2003.
9. Moreno, J., Velásquez, J., Ovalle, D., A methodological approach to the construction of simulation models based on the multi-agent paradigm, in: *Advances in Systems and Informatics*, vol. 4, 2009.

10. www.mdpi.com/1424-8220/20/15/4143

11. www.semanticscholar.org/paper/Multi-Agent-Distributed-Artificial-Intelligent-and-GenzaN/77075b348c2a8aeaa86af7c4df8efa3fade83c0b

12. www.researchgate.net/figure/The-overview-of-the-multi-agent-simulation system_fig2_221320334

13. www.aitimejournal.com/@nisha.arya.ahmed/what-is-artificial-intelligence-ai

14. Russell, S.J. and Norving, P., *Artificial intelligence: A modern approach.* 111–114, 2003 .

Index

Printed and bound by CPI Group (UK) Ltd, Croydon, CR0 4YY

27/10/2024

14580126-0001